D1715070

HOW THE GOSPELS
BECAME HISTORY

SYNKRISIS

*Comparative Approaches to Early Christianity
in Greco-Roman Culture*

SERIES EDITORS

Dale B. Martin (Yale University)
L. L. Welborn (Fordham University)

Synkrisis is a project that invites scholars of early Christianity and the Greco-Roman world to collaborate toward the goal of rigorous comparison. Each volume in the series provides immersion in an aspect of Greco-Roman culture, so as to make possible a comparison of the controlling logics that emerge from the discourses of Greco-Roman and early Christian writers. In contrast to older "history of religions" approaches, which looked for similarities between religions in order to posit relations of influence and dependency, Synkrisis embraces a fuller conception of the complexities of culture, viewing Greco-Roman religions and early Christianity as members of a comparative class. The differential comparisons promoted by Synkrisis may serve to refine and correct the theoretical and historical models employed by scholars who seek to understand and interpret the Greco-Roman world. With its allusion to the rhetorical exercises of the Greco-Roman world, the series title recognizes that the comparative enterprise is a construction of the scholar's mind and serves the scholar's theoretical interests.

HOW THE GOSPELS BECAME HISTORY

JESUS AND
MEDITERRANEAN MYTHS

M. David Litwa

Yale
UNIVERSITY PRESS

New Haven & London

Yale University Press books may be purchased in
quantity for educational, business, or promotional use.
For information, please e-mail sales.press@yale.edu
(U.S. office) or sales@yaleup.co.uk (U.K. office).

Set in Baskerville type by Newgen North America.
Printed in the United States of America.

Library of Congress Control Number: 2018964308
ISBN 978-0-300-24263-8 (hardcover : alk. paper)

A catalogue record for this book is available from the British Library.

This paper meets the requirements of
ANSI /NISO Z39.48-1992 (Permanence of Paper).

10 9 8 7 6 5 4 3 2 1

For Elham دلم,
Love and inspiration

ὦ φίλοι οἶδα μὲν οὕνεκ' ἀληθείη πάρα μύθοις

οὓς ἐγὼ ἐξερέω· μάλα δ' ἀργαλέη γε τέτυκται

ἀνδράσι καὶ δύσζηλος ἐπὶ φρένα πίστιος ὁρμή.

—*Empedocles DK 31 B114*

CONTENTS

CONTENTS

CONTENTS

HOW THE GOSPELS
BECAME HISTORY

INTRODUCTION
THE GOSPELS, MYTHOGRAPHY,
AND HISTORIOGRAPHY

A mythic belief is the acceptance of things that are not the case and are
made up . . . and in which many people place credence.
—*Sextus Empiricus*[1]

This book compares stories in the canonical gospels with stories often
classified as Greek and Roman "myths."[2] It is tempting to level the playing field and call both the Greco-Roman and Christian stories myths, but
such a classification would involve subtle distortions in how these ancient
stories were originally perceived.[3] "Myths" in popular jargon are false stories. Both the gospel authors (evangelists) and the Greco-Roman writers
studied here considered much of their sacred lore to relate what had actually happened and in this sense to be true.

To be sure, the stories compared here include fantastic or seemingly
impossible elements that many modern persons would find difficult to believe. But to classify all these stories as myths due to these elements would
concede too much to modern sensibilities. In this work I am mostly concerned with ancient conceptualities and structures of plausibility.[4] Thus I
will not attempt to define a modern concept of myth and apply it to the

1

gospels.[5] With the exception of my concluding chapter, I am solely concerned with ancient concepts of myth. To remind readers of this fact, I will commonly employ the Greek term *mythos* (plural *mythoi*).

In the late first century CE, many young children would have learned the meaning of *mythos* in the ancient equivalent of primary school.[6] We can reconstruct something of what they learned from surviving handbooks of grammar. The grammarian Asclepiades of Myrlea (first century BCE), for instance, defined three kinds of stories: history (*historia*), fiction (*plasma*), and *mythos*. History, he said, is "an exposition of true things that actually happened"; fiction is an exposition of things that did not happen but could have; *mythos* is an exposition of things that could not have happened, such as the winged horse Pegasus's springing from the severed head of the gorgon Medusa.[7] A *mythos*, in this rendition, was a story relating events generally considered to be fantastical or impossible.

Asclepiades's threefold categorization was rehearsed in a handbook that the orator Quintilian wrote around the same time the gospels were written (the late first century CE). He said, "We accept three kinds of narrative . . . : fable, found in tragedies and poems and remote not only from the truth but also from the appearance of truth; fiction, made up by comedians as false but like the truth; and history, which contains the exposition of events that happened."[8]

In this account, *mythos* is translated as "fable" (*fabula*) and is considered to be untrue. By untrue, Quintilian evidently meant that the events recounted in fable did not actually happen. Not only did they not happen, they did not even resemble events that happen. Quintilian did not give examples, but one can again think of Pegasus born from the gorgon.

After reading these definitions, one might have the impression that *mythoi* or *fabulae* were thought to be stories that were by definition untrue. Yet the relation between *mythoi* and truth was more complex. Plato famously created an *eikos mythos*—a plausible myth that he intended, in some fashion, to speak the undercurrent of truth.[9] Truth could also be found in *mythoi*, for the ancients hid their wisdom even in strange and fantastical stories. Aelius Theon, a first-century CE author of a manual on preliminary rhetorical exercises, gave the following definition of *mythos*: "*Mythos*," he wrote, "is a false story [*logos*] offering an image [*eikonizōn*] of truth."[10]

Plutarch, a Greek contemporary of the evangelists (46–120 CE), expounded on a similar definition. "*Mythos*," he opined, "means a false story [*logos*] resembling the truth [*eoikōs alēthinōi*]. Accordingly, it is far removed from actual events [*ergōn*]."[11] Plutarch posited an ontological hierarchy based in part on his Platonic philosophy. The actual events (*erga*) are considered most real, while the historical narrative (*logos*) relating those events is a second-order representation. Even less real is *mythos*, a third-order simulation of the second-order account (*logos*).

For a Platonist such as Plutarch, a simulation always involved some degree of distortion. A *mythos* in some fashion distorted the *logos* of actual events. A *mythos* therefore needed to be "cleansed" in order to restore it to the level of historical narrative (*logos*). In Plutarch's own words, "Let me therefore purify the mythical [*to mythōdes*] by making her submit to reason and take on the appearance of history [*historias opsin*]."[12]

This quote, in particular the final phrase, is crucial for this study, and it is appropriate here to provide a preliminary statement of my central claim. The gospel writers—insofar as their social and educational situation allowed—wrote their stories so that they took on the appearance of *historia*. Whether or not the evangelists *did* report actual events is a separate question and is not my concern. Evidently they *thought* they did. At any rate, my focus is on how the evangelists used historical tropes to convince readers that they spoke of real—and thus "true"—events.

It is important to understand what the evangelists were doing in terms of the literary theory of their time. According to both Theon and Plutarch, the definition of *mythos* included what Asclepiades and Quintilian called *plasma*—"fiction," or more literally "a made-up story." *Plasma* designated a story that did not happen but could have happened and in many cases seemed to have happened.[13] For Plutarch specifically, there is nothing necessarily impossible about a *mythos*. In fact, a *mythos* can resemble an account of what occurred, even if the resemblance implies a failure to accurately represent the events.[14] As a result, there was no absolute division between *mythos* and *historia*.[15] A *mythos*, just like *historia*, could be believed, especially if the *mythos* was embedded in historiography or history-like literature.[16]

Whether or not one follows the Asclepiadean or the Plutarchan concept of *mythos*, however, one can agree that there was a basic conceptual division between *mythos* (an account of what did *not* happen) and *historia* (an account of what did happen). Pure *historia* related an account of real events, whereas pure *mythos* reported mythical (meaning *fantastical*) events that either could not or did not happen. Admittedly, pure *mythos* and pure *historia* are only ideal types. In actual literature they mixed and blended without apology or sense of contradiction.[17]

Gospels and *Mythoi*

Rhetorically, at least, ancient Christians took the stance that their gospel stories were anything but *mythoi*. In the remark of the Christian theologian Origen (around 250 CE): "We certainly do not consider the stories in our Bible to be myths [*mythous*]."[18] He vociferously denied that Christian stories are "fictions" (*plasmata*), *mythoi*, or fantastical tales (*terateia*).[19]

On this point, Origen was following the lead of earlier Christian writers. A writer claiming to be the apostle Peter denied that he and his fellow apostles promoted "cleverly devised *mythoi*" (2 Pet. 1:16). In turn, an author claiming to be Paul associated *mythos* with Jewish lore (2 Tim. 4:4; Titus 1:14) and "old wives' tales" (1 Tim. 1:4; 4:7).[20]

These slights against elderly female and Jewish storytellers indicate some of the background for the polemic. By the time these documents were written (probably in the early second century CE), Christians were in the process of defining themselves over and against culturally demeaned "others." They were trying to say that *their* stories were true and thus respectable to the rational, male, educated elite in the Mediterranean world. Among the socially privileged of that time, a polemic against *mythoi* was conventional.[21]

The main point is this: for early Christians, virtually nothing the evangelists related about Jesus was considered to be overly fantastical or impossible. In fact, the miraculous tales they recounted about Jesus were entirely appropriate for a being considered to be divine. In short, gospel stories were originally written and received by Christians as *historia,* as stories relating actual events.[22]

Critical Responses

To be sure, later skeptics of Christianity, such as Celsus (around 180 CE), considered the Christian gospels to include fantastical and impossible elements. Thus he classified gospel stories as *mythoi*. In general, Celsus referred to "scriptural myths" (*tōn graphōn mythōn*).[23] He mentioned specifically Jesus's resurrection as a story comparable to other *mythoi* about Orpheus,

Zalmoxis, Pythagoras, Protesilaus, and Heracles going in and out of Hades.[24] When treating Ophite Christians, Celsus called the "resurrection of the flesh by the tree [that is, the cross]" a *mythos* too outrageous to be spoken to children.[25] Origen rightly suspected that Celsus would have considered the transfiguration and other miracles (*paradoxa*) of Jesus to be "fictions no different from myths" (*plasmata kai mythōn ouden diapheronta*).[26]

At the same time, a critic such as Celsus cannot be considered a representative reader of the gospels. It may have been that the kinds of things the evangelists related about Jesus would not have been generally considered impossible or overly fantastical by a wider Greco-Roman readership. Of course we cannot know their responses for certain (and individual readers varied in what they were willing to believe). Nevertheless, we can obtain an idea about what educated readers would have thought of as historiography by their descriptions of it.

Historiography and Truth

The main characteristic of ancient historiography (*historia*) was that it related, or was thought to relate, events that actually occurred. Aristotle defined *historia* as the genre of literature that related "what happened" (*ta genomena*).[27] His understanding was followed by the previously mentioned Asclepiades: "History is the presentation of true things that have happened" (*alēthōn tinōn esti kai gegonotōn*).[28] Likewise the Roman orator Cicero (first century BCE) wrote, "history denotes events that have happened" (*historia est gesta res*).[29]

Since ancient historiography was thought to relate past reality, and since reality was often equated with truth, historiography in the ancient world was generally valued as a discourse that aimed at or represented the truth. We just observed how closely Asclepiades equated what is "true" with "what happened." True things are assumed to be things that have happened. In the words of Andreas Mehl, ancient historians made "a *claim to truth* that rested on the investigation of facts, thus raising the expectation that the narrator was reliably able to recognize and describe past actions and situations."[30]

That historians strove to record truth (at least ideally) is abundantly supported in ancient literature. There are two principles of historiography,

Cicero wrote, which are "known to all people." The first is to say nothing false. The second is to speak the whole truth.[31] Other historians related similar claims: history ever aims at truth (Polybius);[32] history is the "light of truth" (Cicero),[33] the prophetess of truth (Diodorus of Sicily),[34] and truth's very foundation (Dionysius of Halicarnassus).[35] For Pliny the Younger (about 61–113 CE), "history ought never to step outside of truth."[36] Lucian of Samosata—author of the only fully surviving manual on how to write history—urged that history (*historia*) could not admit the tiniest lie just as the windpipe cannot allow even the tiniest morsel of food to enter.[37] Lucian may have been mocking by exaggeration, but his vivid image nonetheless plays on a commonly assumed ideal: historians were supposed to record (in the modern phrase) "the truth and nothing but the truth."

One must understand, however, that "truth" in these contexts often had a pragmatic meaning. It often amounted to impartiality, or the absence of "bias" (*studium*).[38] An impartial account not controlled by malice or flattery was generally considered to be "true."[39] And in many cases truth was only an ideal. Cicero argued that an orator could on occasion falsify *historia* to speak more keenly or cleverly (*argutius*).[40] He also advised a friend to transgress the canons of historiography whenever it added to his (Cicero's) glory.[41]

The point here is about perception. Historiography could still be the discourse of truth even if it did not always relate what happened. In this study I am not concerned whether a particular report actually represents what happened. It is only the persistent *rhetoric* of truth telling that is important for my purposes. This rhetoric is enough to show that the ancients generally wanted historiography to function in their culture as a discourse coded as "true." Thus those who wanted to tap into the social capital of this discourse would be keen to use historiography as a means to communicate their identity-forming events.

The Forms of Historiography

Some New Testament scholars give the impression that ancient historiography had very high standards of rationality and documentation. Richard C. Miller, for instance, excludes the gospels from ancient historiography because the evangelists did not, he claims, weigh sources, apologize for including "the supernatural," and endeavor to distinguish their accounts from "analogous fictive narratives in classical literature."[42] Yet simply by writing in sober, nonpoetic forms, the evangelists distinguished their accounts from the dominant *mythoi* found, for instance, in Homer and Euripides. They did not, moreover, need to apologize for describing miraculous events since these events were a regular feature of ancient historiography. Finally, the evangelists weighed their sources in the sense that they strongly valued eyewitnesses over hearsay (Luke 1:2) and were careful selectors of material to include and exclude from previous texts.[43]

At a deeper level, Miller's comments reveal a misunderstanding about how most ancient historiographies were written. Ancient historiography did not have a single form with a single set of lofty standards. There were at least two basic models for historiography, as represented by the classical historians Herodotus (about 484–425 BCE) and Thucydides (460–395 BCE). Cicero called Herodotus "the father of history" but also the author of "innumerable fables" (that is, *mythoi*).[44] Herodotus modeled a kind of mythic historiography that included fantastical and entertaining stories, some of which could be believed and some of which proved incredible.

Thucydides, on the other hand, was known for explicitly rejecting "the mythical" (*to mythōdes*), by which he meant fantastical and entertaining stories.[45] Thucydides thus set a rhetorical high bar for historiography characterized by unadorned facticity.[46] In the second century CE, for instance, Lucian called Thucydides "the lawgiver of historical writing."[47]

Yet hardly any later historian lived up to—or even aimed to live up to—the standards of Thucydides. Many of them followed the tradition of Herodotus by weaving in fantastic and entertaining tales. The philosopher Seneca (4 BCE–65 CE), for instance, complained against the Greek historian Ephorus (about 400–330 BCE),

> It is no great effort to destroy the authority of Ephorus: he is a historian. Some historians get praise by relating unbelievable stories [*incredibilium*]. By means of the wondrous [*miraculo*] they arouse a reader who would likely go and do something else if he were led through run-of-the-mill stories. Some historians are credulous; others are negligent. On some, falsehood creeps unawares; some enjoy lying. The former do not avoid falsehood, the latter seek it out. . . . They do not think that their work can be approved and become popular unless they sprinkle it with lies.[48]

This is a hostile account that twists the truth by exaggeration; but there is much one can learn from it. In general, ancient historians—including Ephorus—proudly distinguished historiography (ancient writing about events thought to have happened) from mythography (ancient writing about ancient events whose historicity was questionable).[49] This conceptual distinction, however, did not mean that ancient historians completely excluded the miraculous from their texts. As a genre, historiography was sometimes different from mythography more in its rhetorical conventions than in its content.[50]

Mythoi in the ancient world were widely viewed as entertaining. According to Seneca, historians tapped into the entertainment value of *mythoi* to spice up their writing. At the same time, historiographers strove to maintain high standards of plausibility. They could pass off a fantastical story as something they heard of and did not subscribe to, or they could give two different versions of a story: one miraculous, the other rationalizing. An overdose of the miraculous would backfire. Critics such as Seneca would accuse miracle-mongering historians of being naive or liars. In spite of this criticism, historians who skillfully blended *mythoi* into their work were often quite successful—a fact that Lucian lamented in the mid-second century CE.[51]

During Lucian's time, historiography was common among the literati, and producing a historical document gave these writers considerable authority. Biography was an important subgenre of historiography that focused on a single (often heroic) person from birth to death (see chapter 2).

To speak of Jesus, the evangelists could have used drama, lyric, hymn, dialogue, fable, or epic. Yet they chose a genre closest to biography. They made the various stories of Jesus into a "life of Jesus," a type of literature the ancients called *bios*. They did this, I propose, because historiography was the form of discourse invested with important symbolic capital by both religious insiders (Christians) and outsiders (potential converts). Of all the forms of discourse, historiography was one that functioned as "true" in the sense of relating "what actually occurred."

An epic, too, could relate what was thought to have happened. Vergil's *Aeneid,* for instance, recounts the story of Aeneas, Rome's most ancient founder.[52] Yet by writing poetry, Vergil chose a genre known for including egregious fictions for the sake of hooking an audience: monsters, ghosts, harpies, and the like.[53] Generally speaking, the discourse of historiography was different. It deliberately hid its inventions and emplotments in order to present itself as a transparent medium referring to external events that common sense could agree to have happened. Since "what happened" was culturally assumed to be "real," and the "real" was taken to be "true," then historical discourse was perceived to relate truth.[54]

If a narrative was to be believed, then, it was important that it conform to historiographical discourse. This point is important, because even if one is not prepared to accept the gospels as histories, one can still admit that they are history-*like* or *designed,* at least in a limited sense, to look like historiography. This is the main argument of this book. It is not that the gospels are historical (in the sense of relating what happened); it is not even that the gospels are in every way historiographical. What is argued is that the gospels *look enough* like historiography to be read as records of real, and thus true, events.

This argument does not imply that the evangelists were of the same intellectual and literary caliber as Cicero or Plutarch. Plutarch and Cicero belonged to an elite culture to which the evangelists by and large did not attain. Nonetheless, the evangelists were still edging toward this dominant culture and felt its pressures. Like many writers of the ancient world, the evangelists wanted to write in a genre that educated people would understand and accept as true, since more and more educated and high-status people were joining the Christian movements. Thus the gospel writers aimed to write historiography (specifically biography).

Hostile critics such as Celsus might say that the evangelists had failed in their aim. Yet other educated outsiders who, for whatever reason, became interested and invested in the Christian movements apparently developed the opposite opinion. For them, the historiographical form of the gospels would have ensured that there were no formal or generic hurdles against believing their contents.

Historiographical Tropes

Generally speaking, ancient biographers could use archives full of sources; but the first gospel writer had no such luxury. When this unnamed author wrote his gospel around 70 CE, all he had, it seems, were oral and written stories (or story clusters) about Jesus. There were no archives about Jesus, the oral tradition about him was fluctuating, and most of those who personally knew Jesus had died.[55] Despite these limitations, the pioneer evangelist (often called Mark) still adopted historical discourse to produce a gospel that could count as historiography. By following the frame of this evangelist, two later imitators (often called Matthew and Luke) were even more successful in imitating historiographical discourse. Even the author of the fourth gospel (often called John)—who experimented with several different genres—made ample use of historiographical tropes.[56]

Perhaps the most important historiographical trope is objectification, or presenting an event as if it occurred in space and time. Not all events are objective in this fashion. In fact, a great deal of what occurs in human experience cannot be precisely described as an external event. Dreams, visions, perceptions of divine intervention, and so on are deeply personal and idiosyncratic experiences. Nevertheless, humans regularly tell stories about them. In the very act of narration, an event is objectified or described as if it were experienced externally, in time and space, and would be able to be seen by others in the same way.

A good example of objectification is the description of Jesus's resurrection appearances. In origin, these appearances were perhaps visions experienced by early Christians either individually or in a group setting. Yet these visions came to be described as palpable events that occurred in space and time. Eventually, Jesus's luminous body seen in visions became more solid in the act of historiographical retellings. Despite its ability to walk through walls, the body began to be depicted as "flesh and bone" (Luke 24:39), able to be poked and prodded by eyewitnesses—including the famous "doubting Thomas" (John 20:24–28).

There are other historicizing tropes that increase the "reality effect" of the gospels.[57] Synchrony, for instance, is the mention of famous persons who lived at the same time as the depicted hero. The third evangelist, for instance, mentioned the governor of Syria, Quirinius, as a contemporary of Jesus (Luke 2:2). This author wrongly dated the rule of Quirinius by about a decade, but the very mention of him as a well-known ruler (along with the then universally known "Caesar Augustus") increased the realism of his tale.

A similar trope might be called syntopy, the mention of real and familiar places. The evangelists placed Jesus in Galilee under the administration of a historical Jewish king (Herod Antipas). The third evangelist intentionally clarified elements in an earlier evangelist's topography (Luke 8:26 and Mark 5:1; Luke 4:31 and Mark 1:21) and added a travel narrative showing a discrete move from Galilee to Jerusalem (Luke 9:51–19:28).[58] Other tropes include the introduction of eyewitnesses, vivid presentation (*enargeia*), alternative reports, links of causation, and (in the case of the third gospel) a preface highlighting deliberate research.

In using these tropes, the evangelists imitated the historicizing practices of Greco-Roman authors and gave the impression that they wrote historiography. I say "gave the impression" because—like all ancient historians—the evangelists used (perhaps consciously, perhaps unconsciously) the techniques of rhetoric and invention to represent what they thought happened.

Mythic Historiography

When writers included fantastical elements, they wrote what ancient authors referred to as "mythical" or "mythologized histories." This tradition of historiography, as noted earlier, was associated with Herodotus and was widespread both before and after the gospels were written. Diodorus of Sicily, for instance, was a historian of the late first century BCE. When he came to recount the life of Heracles in book 4 of his *Library of History*, he admitted that most of his material came from "myth writers" (*mythologōn*). These writers had, over the course of time, mythologized the life of Heracles to create what Diodorus called "mythologized histories" (*mythologoumenai historiai*).[59] A contemporary Greek historian, Dionysus of Halicarnassus, similarly referred to the stories about lawgivers receiving their laws from gods as "mythical histories" (*mythikōn historēmatōn*).[60]

About the same time, the geographer Strabo did not accept prose writers who composed stories "in the guise of history" (*en historias schēmati*) without acknowledging that they wrote mythography (*mythographian*).[61] He referred specifically to the account of Andromeda threatened by the sea monster off the coast of Joppa in Palestine.[62] In the same passage, Strabo commended the historian Theopompus for expressly acknowledging that he had included *mythoi* in his historiography. Strabo noted that the historians Herodotus, Ctesias, and Hellanicus also included *mythoi*, though without admitting it.[63] Josephus, a Jewish historian and contemporary of the evangelists, also complained that many historians turned to fantastical tales (*mythologein*) to win a reputation as successful historians.[64]

Writers such as Strabo, Diodorus, and Josephus indicate that—although a conceptual difference between mythography and historiography was generally maintained—many stories could blend mythographical and historiographical elements. What resulted was a form of historiography that we might call—following the ancients—"mythic historiography."[65] To be clear, mythic historiography might have been rejected by historians wishing to pose as strict (in the Thucydidean tradition). Nevertheless, mythic historiography was still a widespread form of historiography that proved both entertaining and successful.[66]

I propose that educated non-Christian readers in the Greco-Roman world would have viewed the gospels as something like mythical historiographies—records of actually occurring events that nonetheless included fantastical elements. For this reason, some readers (such as Celsus) denigrated the gospels. Yet for the very same reason, other readers may have been attracted to them. There was at the time an independent interest in the literature of paradoxography, or wonder tales.[67] Literature that recounted unusual events especially about eastern sages would not have been automatically rejected as unhistorical.

Even as the evangelists recounted the awe-inspiring wonders of their hero, they managed to keep their stories within the flexible bounds of historiography. They were thus able to provide the best of both worlds: an entertaining narrative that, for all its marvels, still appeared to be a record of actual events. In other words, even as the evangelists preserved fantastical elements (*to mythōdes*) in their narratives, they maintained a kind of baseline plausibility to gesture toward the cultured readers of their time.

Mythologizing and Historicizing

Why did the evangelists put their narratives in historiographical form? They did so to maximize their plausibility or—what amounts to the same thing—to make them function as true discourse. The evangelists did this in accordance with a widespread impulse in the culture of their time, what I call the historicizing impulse.

Ancient Greeks and Romans were led to historicize their mythography because they viewed it as a record of the past. Over the course of time, however, the description of past events had been distorted to add a divine aura to ancient deeds. Great heroes, it was thought, were given divine parents to explain the magnificence of their accomplishments. Battles along rivers were turned into the one-on-one combats of heroes and river gods. In the fourth century BCE, the Greek writer Palaephatus made the general remark, "The poets and story writers [*logographoi*] have converted some events into unbelievable and incredible tales in order to inspire human wonder."[68] Closer to the time of the gospels, Strabo opined that "the tellers of *mythoi*, and most of all Homer, do not tell *mythoi* in all they say, but for the most part weave in *mythoi* as supplementary material [*prosmytheuousi*]."[69] A generation or so after the evangelists, Pausanias observed, "The same people who enjoy listening to mythical tales [*mythologēmasin*] are naturally disposed to invest them with fantastical elements [*epiterateuesthai*]."[70] As a result of this basic supposition (that stories are mythicized or made more fantastical over time), ancient literary critics thought they could historicize mythography and in this way "restore" it to its original form.

Now whether this mythicization of stories actually happened—at least on any large scale—is a matter of debate. Yet there is a case of mythologizing that will provide an instructive digression here. It comes from a satire, but the satire pokes fun at common assumptions about how mythical or fantastical stories originate.

Lucian of Samosata, by his own report, witnessed the death of Peregrinus, a holy man who, in imitation of Heracles, threw himself into a bonfire after the Olympic Games of 165 CE. As Lucian journeyed home from this well-attended spectacle, he encountered many people still hurrying to watch Peregrinus torch himself. Lucian felt obliged to inform them that the deed had been accomplished. Yet to certain people who pestered him with questions, Lucian spiced up the tale. He said that as Peregrinus flung himself into the fire, there was an earthquake and a bellowing sound from the ground. Then, from the midst of the flames sprung a vulture that squawked in a loud voice, "I am through with the earth! To Olympus I fare!" (Peregrinus had earlier called himself the "Phoenix," the famous resurrected bird that rose from its funeral pyre.)

To be sure, Lucian admitted that he was just playing a dirty trick on some gullible tourists. But not long afterward, he encountered a venerable old man who with a solemn air told him that he had seen Peregrinus ascend from the fire in the form of a vulture.[71] Lucian was flabbergasted. Here he was hearing his own fiction reported back to him as eye-witnessed fact!

Now this account, even if it is itself fiction, illustrates important points about how mythologization was thought to work. First, storytellers had a reputation for adding wondrous elements to a tale, which increased its entertainment value. Second, even if originally gullible people accepted the tale, its widespread repetition could also convince people who were less naive. A traditional tale often became important for social identity. When this occurred, even wise and experienced people could defend its truth value.

Third, an exciting and memorable tale could spread with lightning speed. It was not only the deep past that took on a mythical cast but recent events as well, especially if they were perceived as pivotal or fitting an ancient paradigm (in this case, the immolation of Heracles).[72] Finally, the historical existence of the person in the story did not prevent the story itself from being mythologized. The historians of Alexander the Great, to use another example, were famous (or infamous) for presenting this king as the superhuman son of Zeus within a generation of his death (in 323 BCE).

Despite the extremes of mythologization, some ancients believed that a historical core could be recovered from mythography. Historians who dealt with mythography generally believed that they could restore this core. They performed this act of restoration by reinterpreting the fantastical elements of mythography to conform more to the standards of historiography.

A good example of this phenomenon was the widespread historicizing of the Trojan War. This war was partially recounted in the epic known as Homer's *Iliad*. This epic, despite many fantastical elements, was widely taken to describe historical events.[73] Indeed, Greek historians came to date the Trojan War with astounding precision. After a ten-year struggle, the city of Troy fell in 1184 BCE.[74] The main hero of the *Iliad* is Achilles, son of the sea goddess Thetis. This particular detail was considered fantastical, but Achilles himself was not. Origen pointed out that although some people doubted that Achilles's mother was a sea goddess, still "everyone believes" the historicity of the Trojan War.[75]

To restore the historical nature of Homer's account, historians reinterpreted details of the epic. According to Homer, Achilles battled with a river god. In the view of the historian Hellanicus of Lesbos (fifth century BCE), however, the river was not a being who fought Achilles but a particular river (the Scamander) that became swollen as Achilles fought alongside it.[76]

On this general topic, Lucian made an important observation: "People are still induced to believe Homer, although he wrote most things about Achilles in a fantastical way [*pros to mythōdes*]. These people assume that only one piece of evidence suffices for proof: that Homer did not write about a living man. For this reason they find no reason for him to lie."[77]

In hindsight, this reasoning seems off the mark (the fact that Achilles had died and could no longer benefit from being glorified does not actually support his historicity). Nevertheless, the reasoning reveals a pattern of thought prevalent in the first and second centuries CE. The ancients were willing to believe the historicity of their mythography, and they were fairly confident that they could distinguish the mythical elements from the historical core. Therefore, to make the *mythoi* believable, experienced historians could put them back "into historical form" (*en historias schēmati*).[78]

A Principle of Historicization

As early as the late fourth century BCE, Palaephatus developed a basic principle of historicization.[79] It can be called "the principle of uniformity." Briefly stated, it says that anything that exists now existed in the past and will continue to exist in the future. In other words, there was no past age of unicorns when trees grew from clouds and the sky was green. Likewise, no age of ant men and talking rabbits in cufflink jackets will arise in the future. There is one single space-time continuum, we might say, in which events are always governed by the same physical forces.

For the ancients, the principle of uniformity did not exclude divine intervention.[80] God or the gods could still cause phenomena, but phenomena followed regular laws. Miracles could still happen, to be sure, but they were not viewed as violations of nature. They designated divinely caused events that—because they were unusual and magnificent—inspired wonder or fear. To quote the author of *Airs Waters Places* (written about 400 BCE), "I too am quite ready to admit that these phenomena [the inflictions of disease] are caused by god, but I take the same view about all phenomena and hold that no single phenomenon is more or less divine in origin than any other. All are uniform, and all may be divine, but each phenomenon obeys a law, and natural law knows no exceptions."[81]

Given the principle of uniformity, many fantastical events in mythography could not be accepted. There could, for instance, be no talking snake in a primeval garden or a one-eyed giant on a faraway island or mermaids in the deep blue sea. But what, then, did one do with *mythoi* that regularly featured such fantastical beings? Like many historians, Palaephatus believed that every story represented a past event distorted by repeated retellings. Yet the distortions could be undone. By assuming the principle of uniformity, one could reconstruct the past events that inspired the incredible tales.

For example, there is a *mythos* about a maiden named Callisto being turned into a bear. Palaephatus had a simple, if tragic, explanation for how this story arose. One day, the young girl went hunting, stumbled upon a bear in a grove of trees, and was eaten alive. Her companions saw Callisto going into the grove and—not long afterward—the bear lumbering out. When they later searched for the girl, she was nowhere to be found. Thus they reported the *mythos* that she had been turned into a bear.[82]

A major problem arose when *mythoi* represented events about which all other sources and memories had perished. In this case, there was no secure check against the machinations of a historicizer. Nothing could be judged by external criteria. Only internal criteria, determined by a culturally defined sense of what is plausible, came into play. In these cases, the historicizer removed the overly fantastic elements, rendering the remaining events "ordinary," even if trite.

For instance, Palaephatus claimed that the centaurs (the horse-human hybrids of Greek mythology) were in origin the men who first rode horses. From a distance—perhaps as the sun was setting—dumbfounded bystanders thought that they beheld men with the legs and bodies of horses.[83]

Further Examples of Historicization

We turn to examples of historicization closer to the time when the gospels were written. In the late first century BCE, Dionysius of Halicarnassus reported two stories of Heracles in Italy. The first he called a "mythical account" (*mythikos logos*).[84] The second he named "truer" (*alēthesteros*) and "in the form of history" (*en historias schēmati*).[85]

In the first account, Heracles works alone to drive a herd of cattle across Italy to accomplish one of his Twelve Labors. He falls asleep in a certain field. A local monster named Cacus steals some of Heracles's cattle by driving them backward into a cave. Heracles discovers the theft when the cattle low within the cave. He kills Cacus with his club and rips off the rocky roof of the cave.

In the "historical" account, Heracles is the general of a large army that marches through Italy. Cacus is a local chieftain who dwells with his savage people among rocky fortresses. When Cacus hears that Heracles's army is encamped on a nearby plain, he equips his soldiers to attack Heracles's men as they sleep. Cacus and his comrades capture much booty. Later, however, Cacus is besieged in one of his fortresses and slain.[86]

One can see how elements in the second "historical" story correspond to parts of the "mythical" account. Heracles changes from a lone ranger to a powerful general; his nap in the field corresponds to his army sleeping on the plain; the stolen cattle correspond to the plunder taken by Cacus's men; and the rocky fortress (later demolished) corresponds to Cacus's original cave. Whoever historicized the *mythos* (perhaps Dionysius himself) made a significant effort to reinterpret the original story and make it more plausible in relation to the geopolitical conditions of the time. In essence, Heracles the maverick demigod becomes a model Roman general.

Plutarch is another example of someone who intentionally pressed *mythoi* into the form of history. He wrote a series of biographies in which he paired and compared Greek and Roman heroes. One pair was the *Life of Theseus* and the *Life of Romulus*. Romulus was the founder of Rome, and Theseus was the Greek hero who joined together the smaller Athenian townships to create the city of Athens.

If Theseus and Romulus existed in ancient times, their stories were so transformed that they ceased—even to ancient readers—to seem historical. According to the *mythos,* Theseus had to defeat the Minotaur (a man with a bull's head) in a giant maze. As a child, Romulus was suckled by a she-wolf and was later raptured to heaven in a thunderstorm. Educated readers had trouble believing that these events happened (see chapter 12).

There were ways, however, of massaging away these fantastical elements. The she-wolf, said Plutarch, was actually a loose woman appropriately named "Wolfina," and the Minotaur was simply a savage slaveholder named Taurus ("Bull"). He had a dungeon called the "Labyrinth." He was called "Minotaur" ("Minos's bull") because he was also a general of King Minos on Crete.[87]

To be sure, not every historicizer had to change the content of mythography to make it into historiography. When Diodorus of Sicily recounted the life of Heracles (*Library of History* 4), he chose not to remove the fantastical elements. He let the fabulous features stand to honor the superior strength of Heracles, who was the son of a god and widely worshiped as a god himself. The divine identity of Heracles—which most people in the ancient world affirmed in some sense—loosened the strictures of historiography, allowing more fabulous events to be plausibly recorded. It is not that in ancient times the laws of nature were different; it is that Heracles the son of the chief deity was different, and therefore miracles about him could still count as historical.

Historicization and the Gospels

The evangelists were both similar to and different from these historicizers. They were different in that, by and large, they did not need to historicize their narratives of Jesus. Jesus performed many human, or human-like, activities; and many of his miracles could stand because of assumptions about his divine nature. Admittedly one could argue that the author of Mark's story about Jesus crucified by the Roman ruler Pontius Pilate (Mark 15) was a historicization of Paul's account of Christ slain by ruling daimons (middling beings between humans and gods; 1 Cor. 2:8). (I will address this theory in chapter 1.) In the main, however, the evangelists seemed to have inherited stories of Jesus who lived and died as a human figure, even if certain elements of his life would have already seemed fantastical to outsiders.

Yet there is an underlying similarity in the way the evangelists and the Greco-Roman historicizers operated. Like the historicizers, the evangelists did not let the stories of Jesus appear as fables. They deliberately put the life of Jesus into historiographical form. They did so, I propose, for the same motives that contemporary Greco-Roman historians historicized their mythography: to make their narratives seem as plausible as possible.

Roadmap

This thesis will be worked out in the comparisons that follow. Before diving into my comparisons, however, I turn to distinguish my approach from modern Jesus Myth Theory (chapter 1). This discussion will allow me to present further reflections on my purpose and theory of comparison (chapter 2). After a general introduction to the evangelists and their counterparts (mainly Greek historians and biographers), I will turn to examine major gospel stories and story patterns (incarnation, miracles, disappearances, and so on), to show how they conform to the mythic historiography of the early Roman Empire (chapters 3–15). The book concludes with reflections on myth and historiography in the modern world, specifically why modern Christian believers still consider the gospels' presumed historicity as a necessary support of Christian truth.

Further Reading

Carlo Brillante, "History and the Historical Interpretation of Myth," in *Approaches to Greek Myth*, ed. Lowell Edmunds (Baltimore: Johns Hopkins University Press, 1990), 93–138.

Richard Buxton, *Imaginary Greece: The Contexts of Mythology* (Cambridge: Cambridge University Press, 1994).

Paul Cartledge, *The Greeks: A Portrait of Self and Others*, 2d ed. (Oxford: Oxford University Press, 2002), 18–35.

Georges Dumézil, *Archaic Roman Religion*, vol. 1 (Chicago: University of Chicago Press, 1970), 60–78.

Matthew Fox, *Roman Historical Myths: The Regal Period in Augustan Literature* (Oxford, UK: Clarendon, 1996), 43–45.

Emilio Gabba, "True Historiography and False Historiography in Classical Antiquity," *Journal of Roman Studies* 71 (1981): 50–62.

Hans-Joachim Gehrke, "Myth, Historiography, and Collective Identity: Uses of the Past in Ancient Greece and Beyond," in *The Historian's Craft in the Age of Herodotus*, ed. Nino Luraghi (Oxford: Oxford University Press, 2001), 286–313.

Alan Griffiths, "Myth in Historiography," in *A Companion to Greek Mythology*, ed. Ken Dowden and Niall Livingstone (Malden, MA: Wiley-Blackwell, 2011), 195–208.

Albert Henrichs, "Demythologizing the Past, Mythicizing the Present: Myth, Historiography, and the Supernatural at the Dawn of the Hellenistic Period," in *From Myth to Reason? Studies in the Development of Greek Thought*, ed. Richard Buxton (Oxford: Oxford University Press, 1999), 223–48.

Michael Herren, *The Anatomy of Myth: The Art of Interpretation from the Presocratics to the Church Fathers* (Oxford: Oxford University Press, 2017).

Dieter Hertel, "The Myth of History: The Case of Troy," in *A Companion to Greek Mythology*, ed. Ken Dowden and Niall Livingstone (Malden, MA: Wiley-Blackwell, 2011), 425–42.

Carolyn Higbie, "Hellenistic Mythographers," in *Cambridge Companion to Greek Mythology*, ed. Roger D. Woodard (Cambridge: Cambridge University Press, 2007), 237–54.

Bruce Lincoln, *Theorizing Myth: Narrative, Ideology, Scholarship* (Chicago: University of Chicago Press, 1999).

John Marincola, *Authority and Tradition in Ancient Historiography* (Cambridge: Cambridge University Press, 1997), 117–27.

J. L. Moles, "Truth and Untruth in Herodotus and Thucydides," in *Lies and Fiction in the Ancient World*, ed. Christopher Gill and T. P. Wiseman (Austin: University of Texas Press, 1993), 88–121.

Vinciane Pirenne-Delforge, "Under Which Conditions Did the Greeks 'Believe' in Their Myths? The Religious Criteria of Adherence," in *Antike Mythen: Medien, Transformationen und Konstruktionen*, ed. Ueli Dill and Christine Walde (Berlin: de Gruyter, 2009), 38–54.

Suzanne Saïd, "Myth and Historiography," in *A Companion to Greek and Roman Historiography*, ed. John Marincola, vol. 1 (Malden, MA: Blackwell, 2007), 76–88.

Kenton L. Sparks, "The Problem of Myth in Ancient Historiography," in *Rethinking the Foundations: Historiography in the Ancient World and in the Bible; Essays in Honour of John Van Seters*, ed. Steven L. McKenzie and Thomas Römer (Berlin: de Gruyter, 2000), 269–80.

Jean-Pierre Vernant, "Forms of Belief and Rationality in Greece," in *Agon, Logos, Polis: The Greek Achievement and Its Aftermath*, ed. Johann P. Arnason and Peter Murphy (Stuttgart: Franz Steiner, 2001), 118–26.

M. J. Wheeldon, "True Stories: the Reception of Historiography in Antiquity," in *History as Text: The Writing of Ancient History*, ed. Averil Cameron (Chapel Hill: University of North Carolina Press, 1989), 33–63.

T. P. Wiseman, "Historiography, Poetry, and *Annales*," in *Clio and the Poets: Augustan Poetry and the Traditions of Ancient Historiography*, ed. David Levene and D. P. Nelis (Leiden: Brill, 2014), 331–62.

Nick Wyatt, "The Mythic Mind Revisited: Myth and Historiography, or Myth versus Historiography, a Continuing Problem in Biblical Studies," *Scandinavian Journal of the Old Testament* 22 (2008): 161–75.

CHAPTER ONE

JESUS MYTH THEORY

> To speak of the Gospel writers as presenting or intending
> to present the historical Jesus transports them in an
> exegetical time machine to the Enlightenment.
> —*John P. Meier*[1]

Before I launch my comparisons of mythic historiography in both the gospels and Greco-Roman literature, it will be helpful to discuss my theory of comparison. To prepare for this task, I first offer some examples of how comparison ought not to be done. I explore in particular a kind of comparison that features heavily among votaries of a particular viewpoint that has gained currency in recent years, namely, Jesus Myth Theory. Jesus Myth theorists (or, for short, mythicists) use the modern critical study of the gospels to pose the question, Is Jesus mythical (by which they mean *nonexisting*) or historical?

This kind of binary (either/or) thinking is unhelpful. According to the broad consensus of biblical scholarship, Jesus lived as a first-century Jew in Galilee and was crucified in Judea. At the same time, the four gospels, from a modern point of view, present a basically mythic portrait of Jesus. According to their composite picture, Jesus is the incarnation of a pre-existent deity. He is born from a virgin and becomes a sage by age twelve.

As an adult, he can exorcize superhuman foes and heal by word alone. He walks on the sea, multiplies bread, and raises people from the dead. He himself walks out of his grave with a body that can pass through walls, transport itself across great distances, and disappear into thin air. According to the book of Acts, Jesus finally departs from earth by levitating high into the sky and disappearing in the clouds.

Critical scholars of the New Testament recognize that when reading these stories, they are not reading historiography in the modern sense. The historiography of Jesus can be mined—with much labor and ingenuity—from the pages of the New Testament, but the documents are not themselves doing what modern people typically call historiography.

Still, there is a vast difference between rejecting the historical nature of the gospels and denying Jesus's existence. One can say that the gospel stories of Jesus are "mythic" while at the same time believing that Jesus existed as a first-century Jew. One simply must acknowledge that the Jesus whom early Christians *remembered* and *described* in the gospels was already a figure creatively imagined by Christians as someone more than human—and in that sense mythicized.

But mythicists say more. Not only was Jesus constructed in particular ways by early Christians, he actually *did not exist* or—by exerting no influence—*functionally* did not exist. It is this theory that I address here, with special attention to its (implicit or explicit) notions of comparison.

Mythicists and Fundamentalists

Shortly before the British New Testament scholar Maurice Casey died, he wrote a book called *Jesus: Evidence and Argument or Mythicist Myths?*[2] In this work, he chiefly dealt with recent, nonscholarly mythicists. He successfully showed that most of them were responding to their previous Fundamentalist views of Jesus. For this group of mythicists, scholarship functions more or less as a form of exorcism. They use the tropes of historical argument to try to cast out their own Beelzebub: the Fundamentalist version(s) of Jesus. Strictly speaking, this Jesus is not identical to the Jesus of the gospels or to the Jesus of historiography; he is a fluid figure imagined by modern Christians but one who usually stands in the way of modern secular values. To the degree that mythicists are successful in exorcizing this Jesus, they succeed in dispelling a phantom from their own tormented past (though the daimon often returns—seven times as strong).

Such is Casey's argument; and it is basically persuasive. From a strictly logical point of view, however, one cannot undermine a theory solely by pointing out that it springs from the psychological wounds of people who feel (or felt) themselves crucified by Fundamentalist ideology. Trying to explain (away) a theory on the basis of an opponent's past experiences and underlying psychology often works brilliantly; but it is insufficient as an argument. It may in fact be true that Jesus Myth Theory is completely born of seething resentment and (un)spoken rage against Fundamentalist Christianity, but it is not for that reason wrong. Like any theory, it must first be judged intellectually by its own merits. Is it the most probable view based on the data we possess? Or is it invalid due to actual mistakes in logic, misguided theories of truth, and skewed scholarly methods?

If we are to take Jesus Myth Theory seriously, we need to engage with its most serious proponents. Former Fundamentalists with no scholarly training in biblical studies should not be exalted as exemplars or shot down as easy targets. To provide the fairest assessment, the work of genuine scholars with real training in the New Testament and Mediterranean antiquity should be investigated. For the purposes of this chapter, I have chosen three qualified mythicists from different times and religious backgrounds. Each one denies, or comes close to denying, the historical existence of Jesus. The first is Bruno Bauer, a nineteenth-century German of Lutheran background. The second is an Irish Catholic scholar of the Dominican Order, Thomas L. Brodie. The third is Richard Carrier, a contemporary American atheist raised in a liberal Methodist tradition.

Bruno Bauer

Bruno Bauer, the son of a porcelain painter, was born in 1809 in Eisenberg, Germany. He studied at the University of Berlin, where he became an ardent follower of the philosopher G. W. F. Hegel. Hegel promoted a philosophy with deeply religious dimensions. I cannot hope to explain this philosophy in any depth here. I will, however, sketch its basic outlines in order to illumine Bauer's intellectual project.

Human minds, Hegel taught, are finite expressions of an Absolute Spirit (or Mind). The Absolute Spirit comes to self-realization through the working of human minds who arrive at self-consciousness. Humans who realize the infinitude of their own consciousness simultaneously annul and transcend themselves by identifying with the greater fullness of Absolute Spirit. In a poetic vein, Hegel wrote, "It is of the very nature of Spirit to know itself as eternal, to liberate itself so as to form those *finite flashes of light which make the individual consciousness,* and then to collect itself again out of this finitude and comprehend itself, and in this way the *knowledge* of its essence and *consequently* the divine self-consciousness appear in finite consciousness. Out of the ferment of finitude, and while it changes itself into foam, Spirit rises like a vapor."[3]

Bauer in his early period believed that Hegel's philosophy could be harmonized with Christian thought. In fact, he considered Hegel's philosophy to be Christianity's true meaning. Christianity is about attaining the consciousness of the Infinite. One man—the god-man Jesus—had realized his unity with infinite Self-consciousness, and now this realization was in principle open to all.

Bauer began with a traditional Protestant (and anti-Jewish) model for the gospels. Old Testament religion with its externalized, lawmaking deity was depicted as the problem. The gospels, which presented a law-free religion and a man who attained identity with God through his self-consciousness, provided the solution. Judaism proposed an absolute separation between a transcendent God and the human individual; Christianity identified God and one human consciousness.

Yet as Bauer's thought developed, he began to see that the gospels that spoke of the god-man were equally part of the problem. Realizing one's infinity through self-consciousness is open to all. Hence the gospels erred by portraying the realization as achieved by only one individual. This individual, conceived of as unique, became the basis for yet another legalistic, monotheistic religion that ironically came to function much like Bauer's Judaism. The Jesus of the gospels thus represented humankind's self-consciousness—though alienated from itself.

These daring and dangerous thoughts Bauer developed in four books published seriatim. In 1840, he published his *Critique of the Gospel History of John.* In this book, he argued that the gospel of John gives no information about the historical Jesus. Rather, it portrays the reflective messianic ideal of a later Christian community. This view about John's gospel was nothing new by Bauer's time. The fourth gospel was already considered to be a book of theology and theological symbols rather than historiography in the modern sense.

Yet Bauer went further. He advanced to critique what were considered more "historical" gospels. These were the Synoptics—namely, the gospels according to Mark, Matthew, and Luke. Between 1841 and 1842, Bauer published his three-volume *Critique of the Gospel History of the Synoptics* (the third volume was called *Critique of the Gospel History of the Synoptics and John*). In these books, Bauer systematically went through Synoptic stories to show that theological, not historical, concerns governed them all. The evangelists were not writing historiography. Rather, Jesus was created by the evangelists to address early Christian needs.

Originally, Bauer believed that the idea of the Messiah preexisted Jesus. Christians extracted the Messianic idea from Jewish prophetic literature and applied it to Jesus. In his study of the Synoptics, however, Bauer insisted that the concept of the Messiah or Christ actually arose in early Christian communities.[4] Jesus was not the Messiah and never claimed to be. His identity as Christ was constructed in early Christian communities that were formed much later than Jesus. Strictly speaking, then, when the evangelists talked about Jesus, they were not talking about a historical individual. They were referring to a symbolic representation of their own inner life and communal consciousness. Bauer put it this way: "In prophecy as well as in its fulfillment, the Messiah was only an ideal product of religious consciousness; as a given perceptible individual he did not exist."[5]

In the first two volumes of Bauer's *Gospel History*, he did not deny the historicity of Jesus. He still considered it plausible that a historical individual arose apart from the conceptions later applied to him. By his third volume, however, Bauer had grown deeply skeptical. He wrote, "If a man named Jesus existed, if this Jesus gave the impetus for a revolution that in the name of Christ shook the world and gave it a new form, then this much is known: that his self-consciousness was not disfigured and pulled to pieces through the dogmatic decrees of the gospel Christ." By this time, Bauer had grown disgusted with the Christian invention of Christ: "The gospel Christ considered as a real, historical appearance is an appearance before which humankind must shudder, a being that can only inspire dread and horror!"[6]

Yet even at this point, Bauer—who vigorously denounced "the gospel Christ"—did not consistently deny the historical existence of Jesus. He still left the matter open. If Jesus existed, Bauer proposed, he was a man who lived on a higher plane than the legalistic religion of his day (Judaism) as well as the legalistic religion that would invent and uphold the messianic idea (Christianity). In Bauer's view, Jesus and the later Christian idea of Christ had nothing to do with each other. Thus Bauer wanted to shift the question: "The question with which our time is so occupied—whether this man Jesus is the historical Christ—we have answered by showing that everything that the historical Christ is, everything that is said about him, everything that we know about him belongs to the world of representation and precisely Christian representation and so has nothing to do with a man who belonged to the real world. The question is answered by being struck out for all time."[7] Even here, Bauer's position is not an unqualified denial of Jesus's existence. Jesus's existence is seemingly insignificant or at least inaccessible. The point is that the "historical Jesus" is *not* the subject of the gospels—or their cause. All that we can learn from the gospels is the later Christian idea of Christ. To explain the gospels—and Christianity itself—the historical man called "Jesus" was simply unneeded.

Bauer's ideas were dangerous for his time, and he paid dearly for them. When his books on the gospels were being published, Bauer was teaching at the University of Bonn as a state employee. His colleagues at Bonn were not, by all accounts, happy to have a Christ-hater and suspected atheist in their midst. At some point, Bauer seems to have contemplated resigning and devoting himself solely to writing. Yet he decided to stay on in order to test how the university and the government would respond to his ideas. In a letter dated March 31, 1840, Bauer wrote, "The day will come when I will stand resolutely against the entire theological world. Only then, so I believe, will I be in my right place, to which I have been persistently impelled by the pressures and struggles during the past six years."[8]

So Bauer prepared for a showdown. He expected a confrontation of what he thought was pure science and freedom of thought versus dogmatism and the state control of ideas. Bauer stirred the hornet's nest by

sending the first volume of his *Gospel History of the Synoptics* to the conserva-
tive minister of culture, Johann Eichorn. The Prussian Ministry of Culture
offered Bauer a research pension if he would give up his teaching post.
Bauer refused.[9]

In August 1841, Eichorn asked the theological faculties of the six Prussian universities to advise him on Bauer's orthodoxy and whether he should
retain his teaching license.[10] Only one university—Bonn—definitively opposed Bauer. The University of Königsberg favored his retention. The
other faculties proved ambivalent. Nevertheless, Bauer had made powerful enemies. In March 1842, by order of the king, Friedrich Wilhelm II,
Bauer's teaching license was revoked.

Bauer gambled and—from the viewpoint of his career at least—lost.
The radical nature of his books, combined with their disdainful tone, cost
Bauer his livelihood. In the wake of the battle, Bauer tried to promote
himself as something of an academic martyr. He published some explosive
tracts on the radical and anti-Christian nature of Hegel's thought. In the
end, however, Bauer mainly impacted a small circle of freethinking Hege-
lians. As his views about early Christian literature became more and more
radical, Bauer lost a good deal of respectability. Unable to support himself
by his books, he turned to other pursuits such as farming.

Five years before Bauer died, he published *Christ and the Caesars: The Origin of Christianity from Greek Culture in Its Roman Form* (1877).[11] In it, he argued
that Christianity originated not from Palestine but from Alexandria and
Rome. The Alexandrian philosopher Philo provided the metaphysical basis for the Christ idea by connecting the Logos of Heraclitus with Plato's
World Soul. On the other side of the Mediterranean, the Roman philosopher Seneca created the notion of the all-enduring god-man as a model
for human morality. Christians concocted their savior from Greek and Roman models. What this means for the historical Jesus is again left in the
air. The point is that Jesus did not *need* to exist for Christianity to be born.

To conclude, Bauer opposed the gospel version of Christ even as he ironically conformed to it. Bauer compelled his own crucifixion by flipping the
tables of traditional Christian theology. He seems to have expected that
the sacrifice of his career would spark an apocalypse of political revolution
and educational reform. In his lifetime, a new era of reason and academic
freedom would dawn. Bauer was the seer, the forerunner, the one whose

self-consciousness had attained maturity, the new Christ figure who was inevitably despised.

One could argue that Bauer's work did eventually pave the way for more academic freedom in Germany and around the world. Unfortunately for Bauer, at least, he never saw the fruits of his labor. The wilder and more extreme Bauer's books became, the more he was simply ignored as a recluse and a crank. Arnold Ruge, a former friend of Bauer's, offered this evaluation: "Indeed, Bauer is the complete and therefore the last heretic, but he is also, as such, *the last theologian*. He denies the whole of theology, he hates the unspeakable theologians, he punishes them horribly; but he does this with the fanaticism of theology, even if in opposition; he is fanatic for atheism, he is superstitiously unbelieving."[12]

The connection of Jesus Myth Theory to militant (anti)religious atheism is a theme that persists to this day. Yet even those who despise or continue to ignore Bauer at present cannot deny that he was a well-trained and intellectually gifted scholar. Whatever his motivations, Bauer's work on John and the Synoptics foreshadowed later work that became generally accepted. Although the four gospels are often mined for perceived historical facts, they are now widely recognized as largely theological and literary documents that reflect the conflicts and conceptions of later Christian communities. Regardless of how much reliable memory and tradition was involved in the gospel portraits of Jesus, he remains largely a construction inspired by human needs and the ever-adapting, ever-creative religious imagination.[13]

Thomas L. Brodie

Father Thomas L. Brodie (born in 1943) is an Irish Catholic priest and biblical scholar. Since the early 1970s, he has believed that Jesus was not a historical person. Yet Brodie only publicly revealed this view in his 2012 book *Beyond the Quest for the Historical Jesus: Memoir of a Discovery*. Within two months of its publication, Brodie's own religious order (the Dominicans) issued sanctions against him. He was asked to withdraw from Christian ministry and all forms of teaching and writing. After lengthy investigations, it was determined that his book was "imprudent and dangerous."[14] The sanctions on his teaching remain.

How did Brodie reach his "dangerous" conclusions? While teaching in the late 1960s, he adopted the view that the patriarchs and prophets of the Old Testament were not historical figures but literary creations. This view is hardly considered radical today. The kind of documents present in the Hebrew Bible make it clear that they are not designed to be modern academic histories. They are highly literary narratives that transmit cultural knowledge and religious instruction. With regard to their literary form, the gospels are in basic continuity with Hebrew Bible stories. Nevertheless, even critical scholars tend to assume and even protect the historicity of New Testament characters. There is still a theologically motivated division drawn between the two testaments, and this line can sometimes be expressed by saying that—whatever the truth about Abraham, Moses, and Elijah—the gospels represent real historical figures.

In the early 1970s, Brodie noticed that the details of Jesus's life could be reconstructed from texts in the Hebrew Bible. As he put it, "In testing the Gospels, essentially every strand concerning the life of Jesus consistently yielded clear signs of being dependent on older writings—on the epistles, and on the Old Testament, especially in its Greek version [the Septuagint]."[15] Brodie concluded not only that Jesus as a historical man did not need to exist but also that Jesus did not in fact exist. In this respect, Jesus was just like Abraham or Moses or Elijah—a literary figure who nevertheless made a large impact. Late in Brodie's career, he noticed the same phenomenon with regard to Paul. The details of Paul's letters and life story in Acts were literary transformations of texts in the Septuagint. In a flash came the same realization: Paul, too, did not exist.

In this way Brodie, a devoted Catholic priest and well-traveled scholar, found himself denying the existence of the two central figures in early Christianity. Although Brodie is aware that other Christians are horrified by his conclusions, his personal faith has continued strong. One reasonably inquires, how does he reconcile the nonhistoricity of Jesus with his devout faith? Brodie puts it this way: "It is possible, then, to maintain essentially the same gospel accounts, rituals and devotions as before, not because they reflect specific events of the past, but because they use life-like stories set in ancient times to evoke the deepest truth about past, present and future. The old narratives may be read as if they were true, because they are true, but not literally. In fact, freedom from fretting about history provides an opportunity to appreciate the depth of what the stories are saying."[16]

Somewhat earlier in *Beyond the Quest*, Brodie reflects, "'Art,' 'fiction,' and 'imagination' may at first suggest something unreal, but in fact they can be the surest guides to the deepest truth. . . . Art at its best can reach to the core of the truth, and symbols do likewise. The word 'fiction' is ambiguous. It can indicate what is untrue; but it can also refer to a writing which, though not historical, is a searing depiction of reality, of radical truth, and the Gospels are a supreme example of such writing."[17]

Brodie, now in his eighth decade, continues to believe in Christ in a way that is both rich and enduring. He has taught the gospels off and on for more than forty years. He has published and lectured on Paul's writings. He was instrumental in organizing an institute for biblical studies at the University of Limerick in Ireland. When all is said and done, Brodie has been a productive scholar and has lived a model Christian life.

But is he right about the nonhistoricity of Jesus? In all fairness, Brodie is right about many things. He is right, for instance, to question whether the evangelists offer anything like reliable historiography. Their knowledge of Palestinian geography might be like Vergil's knowledge of Trojan geography (that is, based on reports, not experience).[18] Their social memory generated about Jesus does not necessarily mean that there was a man behind the memory.[19] Their use of oral tradition is often presumed and unverifiable (since all oral knowledge has perished).[20] Furthermore, Brodie is right that the description of Jesus in early Jewish and Roman authors does not provide any more information than what is in the gospels. (It is likely that these writers depended on the gospels.)[21] In the end, historians cannot give us anything but what Brodie calls a "matchstick" Jesus—a mere flicker that distracts from the brilliant light of Christ.[22]

Like Bauer, however, Brodie tends to make logical leaps from detailed literary parallels to historical dependence. Bauer's parallels came from Seneca and Philo. Brodie uses bits and pieces of the Septuagint to reconstruct Jesus's life; then he asks us to believe that Jesus's life is actually derived from readings of the Septuagint. The parallels are not sloppy but often mind-bending in their complexity. Brodie graphs these parallels in long, maze-like charts.[23]

Yet even when Brodie performs this detailed work, he does not seem to be fully aware that the genetic connections between the Septuagint and the gospels are connections that he *imagines* rather than simply discovers. Yet even assuming that the parallels are "objective," and granting that they are precise and detailed, they still do not prove actual dependence.

Although Brodie uses criteria for assessing historical dependence,[24] his ability to see biblical texts transformed into each other is basically intuitive. Often the transformation of texts is so thorough that it is almost undetectable. At any rate, few other scholars have detected the intricate dependencies that Brodie observes. They cannot see them, Brodie might urge, because the transformations of the biblical text are so mind-bogglingly complex. Yet if they are so complex, then how does Brodie himself recognize them? He admits that he is an intuitive thinker.[25] One needs Brodie's intuitive brain, it seems, to observe the causative links that he sees.

This point deserves emphasis. Brodie's writing career spans some thirty years. During this time, he has hammered away at the same themes of literary imitation in seven books and over two dozen articles. In the guild of New Testament studies, Brodie's basically intuitive methods and conclusions about dependence have not attained even minimal consent. The present writer is not aware of anyone who uses Brodie's methods to deny the historical existence of Jesus and/or Paul. Such a conclusion, at any rate, would be a non sequitur.

Like other Jesus Myth theorists, Brodie shows a strange attraction to extremes. It is absolutely true that the Septuagint sheds light on Jesus. It is absolutely true that the evangelists imitated biblical stories to construct their portraits of Jesus. Yet these facts do not make Jesus an entirely literary creation. With the gospel construction of Jesus, we have to deal with a number of factors including literary imitation and previous oral and written sources, along with (it must be admitted) creative invention on the part of the evangelists. Using literary imitation as a totalizing explanation for the data is in the end simplistic. In historiography, we might say, there is no single explanation for anything—let alone for so complex a figure as Jesus.

In the game of historiography, it is rarely *either/or*. We do not need to choose whether Jesus is entirely historical *or* entirely literary. By making us choose, Brodie introduces a false opposition. The fact is that Jesus in the gospels is neither pure historiography nor pure mythography. Even if the Christ of the gospels is pure myth, Jesus may still have existed—or at least his existence is the most plausible hypothesis to explain the gospels as literary products.[26]

Richard Carrier

Richard Carrier is an American writer born in 1969. His religious background was not Fundamentalist but liberal Methodist. He attended Sunday school but did not undergo a thorough education in either Bible or church history. At age fifteen, he became a philosophical Daoist after picking up the Daodejing in a bookstore. By age twenty-one, he had shifted into secular humanism. In 2008, at the age of thirty-nine, Carrier was awarded a Ph.D. at Columbia University. His dissertation was entitled "Attitudes toward the Natural Philosopher in the Early Roman Empire (100 BC to 313 AD)."

While growing up, Carrier was not religiously unmusical. In his Daoist phase, in fact, Carrier had profound visions. He describes one of these in a testimony posted on the website infidels.org. On a midnight voyage under the starry sky, Carrier recalls,

> I fell so deeply into the clear, total immersion in the real that I left my body and my soul expanded to the size of the universe, so that I could at one thought perceive, almost "feel," everything that existed in perfect and total clarity. It was like undergoing a Vulcan Mind Meld with God. Naturally, words cannot do justice to something like this. It cannot really be described, only experienced, or hinted at. What did I see? A beautiful, vast, harmonious and wonderful universe all at peace with the Tao. There was plenty of life scattered like tiny seeds everywhere, but no supernatural beings, no gods or demons or souls floating about, no heaven or hell. Just a perfect, complete universe, with no need for anything more. The experience was absolutely real to me. There was nothing about it that would suggest it was a dream or a mere flight of imagination.[27]

Later Carrier would refer to his "Taoist mystical experience of an obviously hallucinatory nature."[28] The language reflects his conversion from Daoism to atheism, a radical shift that occurred in his early twenties. As he describes the experience, the conversion was sparked by revisiting his Christian roots. An associate encouraged him to read the Bible from cover to cover. Carrier obediently did so, using the New International Version translation (produced chiefly by Evangelical scholars). "When I finished the last page," Carrier reported, "though alone in my room I declared aloud: 'Yep, I'm an atheist.'"

Carrier's atheism can be described as a virulent hatred of the biblical God. Certainly Yahweh, the ancient Jewish deity, does not jibe with Carrier's modern humanistic sensibilities. According to Carrier's characteristically heated language, the God of the Old Testament is a "demonic monster . . . worthy of universal condemnation, not worship. He who thinks he can do whatever he wants because he can is as loathesome [sic] and untrustworthy as any psychopath." (Interestingly, Carrier's interpretation of Yahweh as a daimon accords with ancient gnostic Christian views.)

In a later essay, Carrier reports a vision in which he fought with a daimon (Yahweh?) who was trying to crush his chest. This experience he felt to be "absolutely real": "I was certainly awake, probably in a hypnagogic state [an altered state of consciousness between sleeping and waking]. I could see and feel the demon sitting on me, preventing me from breathing, but when I 'punched' it, it vanished."[29]

Carrier was astounded by the vision, because he never believed in daimons and never imagined a creature remotely similar to what he saw. He left open whether it was a hallucination or a "supernatural encounter."[30] Was Yahweh striking back?

To Carrier it seemed inconceivable that he was the only one, as he put it, "who noticed what a total baloney cock-up the Bible was, the only one who could see that all the evidence, and the simple process of well-thought logic, led to the conclusion that there was no god, or certainly none around here."[31]

Carrier's cavalier dismissal of the Bible and animosity toward the biblical deity would not seem to predispose him for careful biblical scholarship. Despite his considerable acumen, Carrier's thinking is rationalistic, black and white, and seemingly untouched by developments in postmodern philosophy over the past thirty years.[32]

Although Carrier's experience of Christian Fundamentalism seems to have come after his childhood, it had a powerful impact on his frame of mind. Once he declared himself an atheist, his relation to Christians and Christianity radically changed. "For the first time, rather than being merely constantly pestered, I was being called names, and having hellfire wished upon me. It was a rude awakening."[33]

Carrier's frustration was expressed not only against Christians but also against Christ (or what Carrier took to be the biblical Christ). "Jesus himself tells everyone I am damned," Carrier remarks, "and if the most informed, wise and compassionate being in the universe condemns me utterly, deeming me worthy of unquenchable fire and immortal worms, far be it for any mortal to have a kinder opinion of me."[34]

Currently Carrier is a religious believer in "a science-based secular humanism rooted in a metaphysical naturalism."[35] He portrays himself as a kind of crusader fighting for the truth of secular humanism, an apostle—or antiapostle—responding to the extremes of Fundamentalism with equally extreme views. Carrier's scholarship exists, it would seem, to prove Christianity (or Carrier's understanding of it) wrong.

With such a foregone conclusion, one is rightly cautious about Carrier's academic work. On the other hand, he uses seemingly scholarly methods and arguments to deny the historicity of Jesus. He is a trained scholar, even if he exists on the fringes of the academic guild.

Whatever Carrier's motivations, if his claims are to be opposed, it must be on the level of careful argument. In the present discussion, I focus on his academic book *On the Historicity of Jesus: Why We Have Reason to Doubt* (2014). In this work, Carrier does not completely deny Jesus's existence. In fact, he concedes that there is a one in three "prior probability" that Jesus existed. Still, it is fairly clear that Carrier supports the nonexistence hypothesis. I cannot address all the material in the volume (a hefty 618-page tome); instead, I select some of his major arguments for individual treatment.

The Hero Pattern

Carrier frequently appeals to what is called "the hero pattern." This pattern was explored by Otto Rank in Germany (1909) and more thoroughly by Lord Raglan in England (1934). Raglan's pattern includes twenty-two events in a kind of abstract heroic "life":

1. The hero's mother is a royal virgin.
2. His father is a king and
3. Often a near relative of his mother.
4. The circumstances of his conception are unusual, and
5. He is also reputed to be the son of a god.
6. At birth an attempt is made, usually by his father or his maternal grandfather, to kill him, but
7. He is spirited away and
8. Reared by foster parents in a far country.
9. We are told nothing of his childhood, but
10. On reaching manhood, he returns or goes to his future kingdom.
11. After a victory over the king and/or a giant, dragon, or wild beast,
12. He marries a princess, often the daughter of his predecessor, and
13. Becomes king.
14. For a time he reigns uneventfully and
15. Prescribes laws, but
16. Later he loses favor with the gods and/or his subjects and
17. Is driven from the throne and city, after which
18. He meets with a mysterious death,
19. Often at the top of a hill.
20. His children, if any, do not succeed him.
21. His body is not buried, but nevertheless
22. He has one or more holy sepulchers.[36]

Although it is enticing to apply this pattern to Jesus (a task that Raglan avoided but that Carrier takes up), its theoretical value is questionable. Even if it gives an air of universality, this pattern is hardly cross-cultural. It is based on European heroes and specifically the myth of Oedipus. Raglan based his work on James George Frazer's notion that a king-killing ritual lies behind the pattern. Yet such a cross-cultural ritual never seems to have existed.

There are yet deeper problems. Although no hero perfectly conforms to the pattern, the pattern itself encourages mythicists to hunt for similarities between incredibly wide-ranging figures, skating over differences based on locality, time, and culture. Claimed similarities are sometimes forced (the fudge factor). Carrier avers, for instance, that though Jesus failed to marry a princess, he took the church as his bride.[37] Yet here we are on the level of Christian allegory, at second remove from the gospel stories.[38]

In the case of Jesus, moreover, the pattern ignores major elements of his life. What would Jesus be without his incarnation, his works of wonder, the resurrection, and so on? Other elements of Raglan's pattern contradict the gospel accounts. Jesus's mother was a peasant. His father or grandfather did not try to kill him. He was not raised by foster parents. Jesus did not attain his kingdom on earth (in one version, he denied that his kingdom was of this world; John 18:36). He did not lose favor among those who killed him. His killers, depicted as elite Jews and Romans, never actually favored him. Finally, all gospel stories agree that Jesus was buried.

It is unlikely, then, that the gospel writers thought of this or any other holistic pattern to construct their narratives about Jesus. Instead, they called to mind their own native (Jewish) mythology. If there is any mythology historically connected to early Christian mythology, most scholars would opt for Jewish lore. Yet in this case we encounter the same problem. No matter how similar two stories may be, we do not know if story "x" ever caused Christian story "y"—and it is simplistic to think so.

The Sky Daimon Hypothesis

Carrier turns to another argument, which I will call the *sky daimon hypothesis*. According to this argument, the original myth of Christ, devised by Paul, was that Christ was an angelic being crucified by daimons in the sky (or, as Carrier repeatedly and anachronistically says, in "outer space"). As a consequence, Christ was never incarnated and never led a human life. The gospel writers later used this myth to construct their stories of a human character, namely, Jesus, crucified by the Roman authorities outside Jerusalem.[39]

To be sure, Paul says that the "rulers of this age" crucified "the Lord of glory" (1 Cor. 2:8), and these rulers are probably daimonic agents. One should not exclude the view, however, that we have a double entendre: "rulers" refers to both human and daimonic persons.[40] It is the Romans, after all, who used the punishment of crucifixion. Daimons were not known for this method of execution. How the daimons actually affixed a spiritual being to a spiritual cross and how this spiritual being could die is not explained. Only in post-Pauline literature (Col. 2:15; Eph. 6:12, *Nature of the Rulers* [Nag Hammadi Library II.4]), it seems, do we have a focus on exclusively daimonic rulers.

Yet even if Paul viewed Jesus as crucified by daimonic rulers, he says nothing about the crucifixion occurring in the sky. Carrier takes his sky-crucifixion narrative from a text significantly later than Paul, namely, the *Ascension of Isaiah.* This text, or the relevant portion of it (called the "Vision of Isaiah"), was originally written in Greek, although the Greek version is now lost. This original version is dated to the early second century—at least half a century after Paul lived. Carrier at one point speculates that an earlier version of the text was available to Paul.[41] His speculation is baseless—an attempt to down-date a text to serve an argument.

In the *Ascension of Isaiah,* the idea that Jesus was crucified in the sky is hardly explicit. Carrier must omit a long section in the text (11:2–21) that tells of the birth of Christ and his crucifixion in Jerusalem. He omits it because he considers it to be something added later. It is true that chapter 11:2–22 is lacking in surviving Latin and Slavonic versions of the *Ascension of Isaiah.* Yet the Ethiopic version contains it, and there is a Coptic fragment of the passage. The editor of the most recent critical edition of the *Ascension of Isaiah,* Enrico Norelli, convincingly argues that 11:2–22 was part of the original (Greek) text.[42] Carrier did not address any of Norelli's arguments.

Yet even if we accept the omission of 11:2–21, Carrier's argument is without foundation. In the *Ascension of Isaiah,* Jesus descends from a multi-tiered heaven in angelic form to destroy the angels of death. He finally takes on a human form and descends "into the world." The "world," in context, can only mean the world in which humans dwell, namely, earth. On earth, then, the angels crucify Christ. They crucify him "on a tree"—not in the sky. Trees do not grow in the sky. Likewise, crosses do not hover in the heavens; they are sunk in the soil. The angels suppose that Christ is a man of flesh. Men of flesh dwell on earth. If Jesus was floating around in the lower heavens, the angels would not have mistaken him for a man of flesh.[43] Thus, even if we admit the *Ascension of Isaiah* as a text relevant for understanding Paul's mythic conception of Jesus, a close reading of the text undercuts Carrier's hypothesis.

Dying and Rising Gods

Carrier repeatedly makes an appeal to James George Frazer's category of "dying and rising gods."[44] As his showcase example, he highlights the Mesopotamian myth of Inanna (dated from about 1900 to 1600 BCE). Carrier leaves unexplained, however, how this extremely ancient story could have actually influenced the gospel writers in Syria, Palestine, and Rome from 70 to 100 CE.[45]

In the early twentieth century, the theory of "dying and rising gods" proved enticing to many scholars. Today, the category is now defunct insofar as it designates a god strictly identified with the seasonal growth cycle. The fact is, few Mediterranean gods actually die; even fewer die and rise. It is rare, moreover, for a deity's resurrection to cause the earth's fertility.

To be sure, *a few* gods die; and of these, *some* of them return, in some fashion, to life. Yet they do so for all sorts of reasons and in all sorts of ways. Mythicists such as Carrier fixate on abstract similarities. As a result, they often ignore or paste over important differences in the stories.

Today, there is hardly any agreement on whether other ancient Mediterranean deities rise in a way analogous to Christ. When, however, we narrow the focus solely on gods who *die*, there is a consensus that *some* divinities perish in ways just as tragic as Christ. Attis, lover of Cybele, bleeds to death after cutting off his genitals. Osiris, husband of Isis, is locked in a coffin and later sliced to pieces. Heracles is poisoned and burnt alive on a pyre.[46] The infant Dionysus is dismembered, boiled, roasted, and gulped down by the Titans.[47] The chief point of similarity between Christ and these deities is *not* that they rise again but that they suffer. Their suffering is not just any suffering but the calamitous, shameful, even grotesque suffering that excites both wonder and pity.

It is possible, as Jaime Alvar has recently argued, that the suffering of the gods provided a model of suffering and triumph for their human worshipers. Suffering is arguably the fundamental human experience, and suffering gods are perhaps the most human. They undergo human experiences (even death), thus allowing humans to participate in divine experiences (the triumph over pain and death). Triumph over human destiny is made possible through divine suffering. Alvar observes, "That is why the [Greek] mysteries [rites performed in secret] needed divinities who had had some experience of something like the human condition, had themselves lived historically, so that they could function as models. Their adherents might suffer pain and torment, but with the god's aid they could overcome them. Their individual successes were partial victories over destiny (and potentially over the established order) and made them worthy to join the eternal company of the gods."[48]

Therefore, on the theme of divine suffering and (partial) victory over death, there is a general parallel aligning Christ with dying deities.

Nevertheless, some of the gods said to "die" actually disappear; and the gods said to "rise" do so in ways different from Christ. In the case of Attis, for instance, there are many variants in his mythology. Even if we took account of all them, in none of them does Attis actually rise from the dead. At best his body is preserved without decay. His hair is allowed to grow and his pinky to twitch.[49]

In a ritual known to have been practiced in Rome, the pine tree was portrayed as the symbol of Attis. The god is represented by the tree wreathed with wool and sprinkled with violets. The fact that this tree, though cut down, remains green indicates that Attis survives *in* death (to use the formula of Giulia Sfameni Gasparro),[50] not that he was raised *from* the dead.

Osiris, unlike Attis, is raised from the dead—but in a peculiar way. He returns to life to become lord of the netherworld. The spirit of Jesus temporarily invades the underworld, according to Christian mythology (see in particular the *Gospel of Nicodemus*), but the resurrected Jesus ascends to heaven. So Jesus is raised to life on earth, then goes to heaven; Osiris is raised to life in the realm of the dead and remains there to rule. Carrier's remark that both Christ and Osiris "both end up living as lords in heaven" is simply false.[51]

We might also point out that none of the dying gods die of their own free will. Adonis is gored by a bore. Osiris is fooled. Attis is driven mad. Baal is slaughtered in a climactic battle. Inanna is the only one to initiate her own death by entering the gates of the underworld. Yet one cannot say that she accepted being stripped of her powers (and her clothes); she was outwitted by the netherworldly queen Ereshkigal. Only the Christian deity gives up his life of his own accord. This single act changes the meaning of his death. He dies (in Pauline language) "for us" or "for our sins." His death is a conscious sacrifice, an act of substitution. This factor alone makes the *mythos* of Christ's death significantly different from other dying and rising deities.

It also alters the meaning of Christ's resurrection. Christ dies for his people, and he is raised for them as well. The worshipers of Attis, Baal, and Osiris benefited, it seems, from the new life of their deities. Yet in none of these cases is the purpose explicitly to give life to a community of committed believers. Christ's resurrection is only the beginning of a general resurrection of all those "in Christ." Although separated by centuries or even millennia, his resurrection is the model for theirs. This is not a pattern of cyclical renewal but a decisive event that leads to a mass resurrection of believers.

Nonexistent Heroes

Finally, Carrier makes the point that some ancient heroes—even those featured in biographies—never existed. He gives the example of Romulus, first king of Rome, and Daniel, the Jewish sage said to have lived in the Babylonian court.[52] Carrier fails to note that ancient Romans never seemed to have questioned the existence of Romulus. Likewise, Jews in antiquity apparently never denied that Daniel lived. It is modern historians, people with little to no investment in these heroic characters, who so readily detect their fictionality.

Nevertheless, let us address Carrier's point and compare a historicized fictional character with Jesus. I propose that we choose a more contested example—a figure whom modern scholars would not so easily dismiss as unhistorical. I refer to Homer, the reputed author of the *Iliad* and the *Odyssey*, whom Greeks widely considered to be their finest poet.

A great scholar of classical antiquity, Martin L. West, argued that Homer was fictitious. West made this judgment on several grounds. First, the name of the poet is not securely attested until 520 BCE. If the poems were composed in the late eighth century (the traditional dating), then there is a two-hundred-year period in which we do not know to whom—if anyone—the poems were ascribed. West himself believed that the poems, which were in circulation about 630 BCE, were anonymous until about 520 BCE. He added the point that "Homer" is an unusual Greek name—something that Greeks themselves recognized. Those who were called "Homer" in later antiquity (beginning in the fourth century BCE) seemed to have been named after the poet.

West concluded that Homer was an invention of a roving guild of poets known as the "Homeridai." This name may have originally meant "those who met in assembly." Their guild was active in the late 500s BCE. From their name, they invented an ancestor and founder, namely, Homer. The Homeridai circled the Mediterranean world spreading Homer's fame as the finest of Greek poets. In so doing, these singers and reciters established their own far-flung fame and authority. In short, Homer's name was invented to signify "authoritative (Greek) poetry," and those who recited it benefited by the matchless legacy of their "ancestor."

West summed up his conclusion as follows: from the late sixth century BCE, "Homer becomes an object of historical curiosity, literary criticism, and biographical romance, and the almost complete absence of reference to him in the preceding 150 years rapidly gives way to a great abundance of reference. Homer had been invented long before as the eponym of the Homeridai, but now he was invented again as a figure of real flesh and blood and intellect. It was probably at this period that he became established as a school text, as the author that every gentleman's son would most benefit from studying."[53]

Is it possible to make similar arguments to prove the nonexistence of Jesus? First of all, we observe that the name Jesus was not an uncommon name but an exceedingly popular name among Jews in antiquity (it was the Greek form of Joshua).[54] Second, the name Jesus is attested by the earliest Christian writer, Paul, some twenty—not two hundred—years after Jesus's death. A name and a human character to go with it could not have been invented in this short period without invoking suspicion.

Finally, Paul, for all his focus on a superhuman Christ, also considered Jesus to be a real human being. Jesus was "born of woman" and was "of the seed of David" (Gal. 4:4; Rom. 1:3). He had a real human mother with a real human ancestor. This lack of correspondence with Homer indicates that one should take the historicity of Jesus more seriously as a hypothesis.

Given the historical data we possess, and current structures of plausibility, there is little reason to think that Jesus never lived.

Conclusion

"It is extraordinary," Casey remarks, "that mythicists claim that many events in the life of Jesus have happened somewhere else before, and that none of his teachings were original."[55] Strictly speaking, mythicists who make this claim are correct. Time and time again, the biblical maxim proves true: "There is nothing new under the sun" (Eccles. 1:9). No single deed or saying of Jesus is unique in the sense of being without parallel—because nothing in human history is without parallel.

If the mythicist databank is world mythology ranging from about 1800 BCE to 100 CE, then any creative mythicist can chalk up a host of parallels to Jesus. It is simply a matter of blasting Jesus's life into small enough bits that represent single actions or motifs stripped of narrative context. Jesus was born from a virgin, Attis was born from a virgin; Jesus brought baptism of fire, Zoroaster (Zarathustra) brought baptism of fire; Jesus rose from the dead, Osiris rose from the dead; and so on. The gospels do not go back to original, unique experiences, the argument runs, and thus they are not historical.

Never mind that these parallels come from radically different times and cultures; never mind that they are shorn of their context and mean almost nothing as individual units; never mind that the parallels never add up to a coherent story that looks anything like the portraits of Jesus in the gospels—the parallels, in shards, are there. And if the parallels are there, then nothing in the gospels is genuine, or—going even farther—Jesus must not have existed. Needless to say, this sloppy logic is hardly compelling. So why, we might ask, do mythicists constantly repeat it?

Casey was probably correct. By and large, mythicists consciously or subconsciously try to oppose Fundamentalist Christian narratives about the nature and identity of Jesus. At the same time, it is important to understand *why* Casey was correct. It has to do with how historical discourse functions in modern culture. Christian apologists argue that the gospel stories are true because they are "historical" (meaning: they happened in space and time). Mythicists such as Carrier turn the tables. Jesus is not historical, so the gospel stories cannot be true. By removing him from history, mythicists suppose that they can deprive Christ of his power and his very reality. They not only deny the so-called supernatural—the virgin birth, the miracles, the resurrection, and so on; they deny the fact of Jesus's existence. Yet they make the same assumption as the Fundamentalists— that what is deemed "historical" reveals the "real" and manifests what is "true." Hence removing Jesus from history is the quickest way to undercut "gospel truth."

It seems that both Christian supporters of the "historical Jesus" and their mythicist opponents have an equally questionable view of myth and history. They both basically tend to represent myth as false and history as true. A fairer view would demand that both mythography and historiography be seen as works of the human imagination (and in this respect fictional). Historiography needs to be *imagined* just as much as myth. I will return to this point in this book's conclusion.

A trained historian might claim that historiography is the work of the disciplined imagination while *mythos* represents the imagination run amok. Yet again, this binary model does not really work in actual practice. It is rare when dealing with ancient heroes to find one represented as either pure fiction (utterly fantastical) or purely historical (utterly "normal"). The two kinds of representations are always mixed. It is true that ancient intellectuals such as Plutarch tried to historicize mythic heroes such as Theseus and Romulus. Yet the end product was never pure historiography, at least in the modern sense. It was mythic historiography: a kind of writing in which ancient intellectuals experienced the truth of their cultural heritage while supposing they had risen above the folly of popular credulity.

Further Reading

Mary Beard, "The Roman and the Foreign: The Cult of the 'Great Mother' in Imperial Rome," in *Shamanism, Historiography, and the State,* ed. Nicholas Thomas and Caroline Humphrey (Ann Arbor: University of Michigan Press, 1994), 164–90.

Philippe Borgeaud, *Mother of the Gods: From Cybele to the Virgin Mary,* trans. Lysa Hochroth (Baltimore: Johns Hopkins University Press, 2005).

Susan Elliot, *Cutting Too Close for Comfort: Paul's Letter to the Galatians in Its Anatolian Cultic Context,* Journal for the Study of the New Testament Supplement Series 248 (London: T&T Clark, 2003).

J. C. L. Gibson, "The Last Enemy," *Scottish Journal of Theology* 32 (1979): 151–69.

Maria Grazia Lancellotti, *Attis: Between Myth and Historiography: King, Priest and God,* Religions in the Graeco-Roman World 149 (Leiden: Brill, 2002).

Dale B. Martin, *Slavery as Salvation: The Metaphor of Slavery in Pauline Christianity* (New Haven, CT: Yale University Press, 1990), 50–60.

Tryggve N. D. Mettinger, *The Riddle of Resurrection: "Dying and Rising Gods" in the Ancient Near East* (Stockholm: Almquist & Wiksell, 2001).

J. C. O'Neill, *The Bible's Authority: A Portrait Gallery of Thinkers from Lessing to Bultmann* (Edinburgh: T&T Clark, 1991), 152–54.

Lynn E. Roller, *In Search of God the Mother: The Cult of Anatolian Cybele* (Berkeley: University of California Press, 1999).

Jonathan Z. Smith, *Drudgery Divine: On the Comparison of Early Christianities and the Religions of Late Antiquity* (London: School of Oriental and African Studies, 1990).

Mark S. Smith, *Origins of Biblical Monotheism: Israel's Polytheistic Background and the Ugaritic Texts* (New York: Oxford University Press, 2001), 110–20.

CHAPTER TWO

A THEORY OF COMPARISON

The issue of difference has been all but forgotten.
—*Jonathan Z. Smith*[1]

To understand how mythic historiographies work, they must be compared in a way that is both thoughtful and sound. In chapter 1, I presented some instances of unsound comparison in my discussion of Jesus Myth Theory. In short, mythicists tend to genetically connect words and motifs for religious (or antireligious) ends. Often their zeal induces them to ignore or paste over differences in cultural setting and storyline.

Seeing similarities is not problematic in itself. It is the *type* of similarities and how comparativists deal with them that sometimes prove problematic. Similarities that are isolated and superficial often conceal greater differences. What is worse, superficial similarities are sometimes employed to prove historical causation. Yet individual words, phrases, and ideas that are similar (in some respect) are not necessarily genetically related. Similarities, no matter how precise, never amount to causation.

It is comparativists who see, and then posit, similarities between stories for their own intellectual ends. The similarities may have existed in the past, but the past is gone and, apart from a time machine, cannot be experienced again. The loss of the past, however, is not paralyzing. Comparativists are welcome to make a statement about how two similar events, words, stories, or settings related in the past; but they must first acknowledge that *they* first see the similarities and then posit the relation. Whether the relation corresponds to a real connection in the past then becomes a matter for debate. Not everyone sees similarity or sees it in the same way. This is one reason why there are different—sometimes radically different—reconstructions of the past.

All similarities, furthermore, must be contextualized. If a posited similarity is between *mythoi* in two different texts, then one must situate the texts in their sociocultural settings. When were the texts written? Where were they written? Who wrote them? For what purposes? Do they belong to the same culture or sphere of cultural codes? And so forth.

Only after this contextual work has been done can one even think about positing a relation between stories. The relation, moreover, is not always that the author of text B knew and copied text A. Sometimes the authors of texts A and B depended on another text, C, or perhaps they saw the same event X or heard a similar oral report Y or belonged to common culture Z.

Most connections between stories leave no paper trail. Large distances of space and time and moth holes in the historical record make constructing causative relations between texts almost impossible and more often jejune. We need to think of the relations between the gospels and Greek lore more as dynamic cultural interaction: the complex, random, conscious and unconscious events of learning that occur when people interact and engage in practices of socialization.

Mimesis

The model of dynamic cultural interaction is different from what Dennis R. MacDonald calls "mimesis criticism."[2] *Mimesis* is a term designating the conscious imitation of a text by the writer of another text. MacDonald imagines that one author had a specific text in hand that he or she imitated in the production of a new *mythos* or mythic variant. Mimesis is generally accepted when it comes to the Jewish scriptures. (The evangelists advertised their connection to previous Jewish texts.) The question of whether the evangelists expressly imitated classical poets such as Homer or Vergil is more controversial.

MacDonald presents six criteria for establishing mimesis:

1. The accessibility of a model text for imitation
2. Whether other ancient authors imitated the model text in question (analogy)
3. The density of parallels between the proposed model text and imitation
4. The order of parallels between the two texts (sequence)
5. The use of distinctive mimetic flags by the imitator (such as a significant name)
6. Changes or transformations introduced to adapt the model text (emulation).[3]

MacDonald uses these criteria to chart—sometimes quite literally—a host of parallels between texts that he believes are genetically connected.

Since MacDonald's method has already been criticized in print, my own assessment can be brief.[4] First of all, MacDonald's method makes his thesis about mimesis largely unfalsifiable. A broad range of imagined similarities can be construed as imitation, and an equally broad range of differences can be construed as emulation. So MacDonald can posit similarity when he wants and explain away differences by the notion of emulation. Margaret Mitchell calls this the "'have your cake and eat it too' methodology."[5]

The second problem is the fudge factor. MacDonald creatively rearranges and tweaks most of his parallels in order to fit the structure of his (often extensive) lists and charts.[6] One example is Jesus walking on water (Mark 6:48). MacDonald compares this passage with Homer's *Iliad* 24.340–46 and *Odyssey* 5.43–55.[7] But in these Homeric passages, Hermes and Athena never actually walk on water; they fly over it.

Third, MacDonald does not consistently apply all his criteria. Sometimes only density and sequence are applied. Occasionally only a single criterion is applied, such as emulation.[8] If only select criteria are applied, however, there is too much left to subjective judgments. To be sure, creativity and imagination are good qualities in a scholar. Yet if the imagination is not disciplined and controlled by stricter guidelines, it veers into a kind of solipsistic dogmatism.[9]

Fourth, sometimes the parallels that MacDonald points out are trite. The fact that Odysseus was on a floating island and Jesus on a floating boat, for example, is not very significant.[10] What else would a seaworthy boat do? As Umberto Eco points out, from a certain point of view, almost everything "bears relationships of analogy, contiguity, and similarity to everything else."[11] The question is, which similarities are significant? The significant similarities are not always the ones that can be explained by means of direct imitation.

This brings me to perhaps the key problem with mimesis criticism: it exists primarily to make genetic connections between texts. MacDonald boasts that he discovers dense parallels in texts that correspond in order and sequence. Yet no amount of similarity between texts can prove a genetic connection. In his recent work *The Gospels and Homer* (2015), MacDonald quotes Francis Cairns: "It is all too easy to suppose that imitation is present where it is not, or, where it is present, to make incorrect identifications of sources."[12] One wonders if MacDonald has sufficiently heeded this warning. He rarely expresses uncertainty about his method; and when legitimately criticized on direct and specific points, he continues unrepentant.

Naturally, the evangelists knew Homeric mythology and so could have been influenced by it in various ways. Indeed, virtually everyone in antiquity knew Homer, from the great orators to the washerwoman who cleaned the sheets. They heard Homer performed, saw Homeric scenes in paintings, and witnessed Homeric plots in plays. The thesis that the evangelists sat down to adapt precise written passages of Homer like elite poets is, however, unlikely. If imitation occurred, it did not occur in this bookish fashion. There were many more common ways for people in antiquity to absorb and adapt cultural lore.

In fairness to MacDonald, it is impressive how Homeric texts have saturated his imagination. He replicates, in a sense, the imaginations of ancient scholars who knew Homer like the back of their hand. Moreover, he successfully shows that early Christian texts are best read against the backdrop of culturally pervasive Greco-Roman lore. In his terms, the cultural context of early Christian narratives "was as profoundly Hellenistic as it was Jewish."[13]

Nevertheless, the goal of comparison is never simply to trace links between words or ideas in texts. It is to compare whole stories, structures of thought, and discursive practices. If scholars want to posit historical interaction between stories, they should think less about genetic relations between texts and more about shared cultural conceptions communicated through a broad array of cultural media.

A Shared Culture

Greek *mythoi* were the mass media when the gospels were written in the late first century CE. *Mythoi* were reflected in virtually all the cultural venues available: sculpture, painting, pantomime, hymn, novels, coins, gems, mosaics, plays, athletic events—even executions.[14] The Christian writer Tertullian (early third century CE), for instance, saw condemned criminals "dance out the stories of myth" in theatrical spectacles. He claimed to have seen a criminal burned alive like Heracles on a pyre and Pluto (god of the underworld) haul corpses out of the arena.[15] Condemned Christian women also played the role of Dirce, a Theban queen tied to the horns of a bull and dragged to her death.[16]

Every person in the ancient Mediterranean recognized the heroes Achilles, Heracles, and Theseus, just as virtually everyone in America today recognizes Superman, Batman, and the Hulk. If one is to understand the myth of Captain America, one must understand the mythmaking of American culture. In the same way, if one is to understand the practice of early Christian mythmaking, one must understand it in the larger context of Hellenistic culture.

Here "culture" refers specifically to a system of inherited and socially constructed patterns of thought and practices by which people communicate and develop their various bodies of knowledge. These bodies of knowledge were social creations transmitted by various traditions of language, artistry, and civic rituals in the various cities of the Greco-Roman world.

To be sure, there was no monolithic culture in the ancient Mediterranean. The lands bound together by the Roman Empire formed what we would call a multicultural society with many competing religious ideas and ideologies. Distinct local cultures of the Mediterranean blended because these cultures were fairly weakly bounded and subject to constant change.[17]

Subcultures can also blend by virtue of their relation to a dominant culture. In the ancient Mediterranean world, the dominant culture was not, by and large, the culture of the reigning power (Rome) but a basically Greek (Hellenistic) culture that had been ingrained at least since the time of Alexander the Great (died 323 BCE). Indeed, Greek lore was so compelling that the conquering Romans largely let themselves be intellectually colonized. In the famous lines of the Roman poet Horace: "Conquered Greece her conqueror subdued, and Rome grew polished, who till then was rude."[18]

Due to the ubiquitous patterns and practices of Hellenistic culture, there was a widespread sense that, as the Roman historian Tacitus remarked, "all things were connected."[19] Politically, lands from London to Memphis, from Spain to Syria, were bound together by the same Roman administration. Economically, paved roads and shipping routes across the Mediterranean united three continents. Linguistically, most citizens of the empire spoke Greek as the common tongue. Even in the "boondocks" of rural Galilee, there remained a dominant cultural ethos privileging the values, art, language, and lore of ancient ("classical") Greece. What united learned peoples in the provinces was a shared educational system and repertoire of stories, poems, and speeches that virtually every person of culture knew.[20]

Josephus, a late first-century CE Jewish historian, claimed that Greeks and Jews were distinguished from each other more by their geography than by their practices.[21] He also insisted that Greeks borrowed heavily from Jewish traditions. This historian assumed that Jewish culture was older than Greek culture—and many Jews concurred. As a consequence, Jews felt no hesitation adapting a Greek cultural idea or story if they considered it, in its "original" form, their own. So, for example, philosophically inclined Jews more readily adapted the Platonic belief in a central divine being because they thought that Plato had learned it from Moses.

Since gospel stories arose when Greek *mythoi* were the dominant cultural lore, it is not strange to think that this lore shaped the formation of Jesus narratives. Working out the nature of this shaping is tricky in part because Christians throughout the centuries had a habit of denying outside cultural influences—particularly when it came to the creation of putatively inspired texts. Yet historically we know that Hellenistic culture was never really "outside" Christianity. It was already "inside" the minds of the earliest Christians because it was the culture in which they all were raised. Greek mythology was part of the "pre-understanding" of all those who lived in Hellenistic culture—including Jews and Christians.

To be sure, early Jews and Christians developed their own subcultures, which sometimes assumed an oppositional stance toward the dominant culture. Yet these subcultures were still enmeshed in the dominant culture and competitively adapted its ideas and practices. Even the rigorist Jewish Essenes, who sequestered themselves in the Judean desert, employed astrological, calendrical, organizational, and scribal practices common to the Hellenistic world.

Many, if not most, Greek ideas about the world, human beings, and the divine were simply taken for granted by Jews and Christians. It was assumed that the earth formed the center of the universe and was encircled by seven planets. It was assumed that males were in charge of the family and that respectable women ought to cloister themselves at home. It was assumed that the state gods desired animal sacrifice and punished those who polluted their temples. Likewise, it was assumed that there was a past heroic age when powerful heroes roamed the earth and giants ravaged it. Such assumptions formed a set of givens shaping how the world, divine beings, and society were perceived.

At the same time, most of these basic notions about cosmic and social reality did not need to be explicitly taught. People who grew up in ancient Mediterranean culture would have absorbed these ideas through the more indirect means of socialization. Socialization comprises all the unconscious learning that humans undergo since childhood by interacting with different social groups. As a result of socialization, human beings come to share assumptions that allow them to communicate and experience phenomena in a basically similar way.[22]

In this sense, early Jews and Christians were inevitably influenced by the dominant cultural lore. Greek mythic discourses were part of the mainstream, urban culture to which most early Christians belonged. If Christians were socialized in predominantly Greek cultural environments, it is no surprise that they were shaped by the dominant stories. Some of the influence would have been consciously experienced through the educational system. Other influences would have been absorbed by attending plays, viewing works of art, hearing poetry, and simply conversing on a daily basis with Hellenized peoples in the many marketplaces of ideas.

Gospel Genre

It is time to offer some historical and literary contextualization of the writers I will compare. First I deal with the thorny question of gospel genre. Prior to reading an unfamiliar text, it is logical to ask what kind of literature one is dealing with. For ancient texts, this is often a difficult question to answer. Literary genre is a fluid category, and texts can inhabit multiple genres.[23] In the end, genre is more of a literary strategy than something set in stone. That said, there is a rough consensus that the gospels best approximate ancient biographical (or *bios*) literature.[24] We can define biography as a form of historiography focusing on the life and character of a single person.[25]

The ancients could distinguish between biographies and more traditional historiography. In a work of historiography, the writer was expected to present a coherent series of political events in which significant historical actors played. A biographer, by contrast, could focus on microdetails and anecdotes to illustrate an individual's character.[26] No ancient writers of biography would deny, however, that they spoke of real historical events and persons who lived in space and time. Many biographers, moreover, worked hard to give their works a historical cast. They described real places, mentioned precise times, referred to contemporary monuments, and so on.

Even though the evangelists wrote biographies, it would be incorrect to call their products "historiography" in the modern sense. The evangelists used ancient historiographical tropes to depict their (divine) savior, whom they worshiped as a deity. Granted, of course, the Jesus of the gospels seems to be human for the most part (he can walk, talk, eat, and so on). But appearances can be deceiving. One eventually discovers that he is a divine being manifest in flesh, and the point of the texts is in part to make his higher nature known in a kind of intellectual epiphany.

The Evangelists

Who were the evangelists? What was their social class and level of education? The popular stereotype is to think of them as plain fishermen who barely knew how to scrawl their own names. The gospels themselves prove otherwise. The evangelists might not have been as educated as Vergil, as accomplished as Plato, or as savvy as Euripides, but they were not country bumpkins. Careful study throughout the centuries has shown that the gospels, if at times unpolished, are works of literary sophistication. Those who produced them were educated and sophisticated writers.

Churchgoers are often instructed that the gospels were written by eyewitnesses or those who knew them. In fact, the gospel writers are all second- and third-generation Christians, none of whom claimed to be apostles or intimates of Jesus. None of them, it seems, attached their names to their work or clarified their sources. (The titles "According to Mark," "According to Matthew," and so on are second-century additions.) As skilled writers with a measure of rhetorical training, they were not interested in neutral reporting and did not use modern historiographical methods to compose their works.

Indeed, historiographical reporting as we know it today was hardly possible in the late first century CE. There were no eyewitness accounts of Jesus's childhood, minutes of his speeches, diary entries, newspaper clippings, sound recordings, photographs, or paintings of Jesus. All that the gospel writers had at their disposal were oral and written sources for Jesus's sayings, accounts of his miracles, and (increasingly) stories of his postmortem appearances in Judea and Galilee. None of these collections of stories and sayings formed a complete narrative. Thus the evangelists exercised considerable ingenuity in the creation of their stories.

Who were the intended audiences of the gospels? It seems that the gospels were primarily aimed to strengthen the faith of Christian insiders. Yet their historiographical cast indicates that the evangelists aimed at a secondary, broader readership of outsiders who, for various reasons, became interested in the Christian movements. The social locations of both the primary and secondary audiences were probably diverse. Certainly not every reader would be considered "lower class."[27] The gospel according to Luke is addressed to "Theophilus," who is probably a rich, Gentile patron belonging to a Christian community.

The gospels are straightforward and simple in their diction and style— a fact that proved embarrassing to later Christian intellectuals. Yet the very prosaic nature of the gospels can be understood as a trope of historiographical discourse. According to ancient authors, the language of historiography is supposed to be "plain and unadorned" (*nuda*),[28] "easy and flowing" (*fusum atque tractum*),[29] without the use of "unknown and out-of-

the-way words."[30] When history was told in clear prose without poetic ornament, "truth" distinguished itself from *mythos*.[31] Accordingly, the gospels
were written in the common speech of the day (called *Koinē*) so that people
of every level of education—or even none at all—could understand their
recitation.

All the gospel writers are, finally, anonymous. Why they chose to remain
anonymous is unknown, but the gospels are not for this reason unique.
Other authors—among them Plato, Plutarch, Lucian, and Porphyry—
also wrote works in which they did not name themselves. The anonymity did not necessarily mean that the authors were particularly humble
or that the gospels were community products. The gospels were written
by individuals with their own peculiar emphases and tendencies. By the
second century, they were connected to named individuals thought to be
related to the apostles. Yet these names are secondary. When I refer to
them (Mark, Matthew, Luke, and John), I aim solely to designate texts, not
persons.

As for what we know about the contents and emphases of each gospel, it
is better to treat them singly.

Mark

The gospel of Mark is the first (surviving) historiographical narrative of
Jesus's life. Where the author of this text received his material is uncer-
tain. Even where he wrote is unknown, although most scholars, following
church tradition, select the cities of either Rome or Alexandria.[32] If one
desires to discern how and why the author wrote, one's only refuge is the
text itself.

Mark was written around the time that the Jewish temple went up in
flames in the summer of 70 CE. Scholars zero in on this date because
Mark placed a prophecy in the mouth of Jesus professing that "every
stone" in the temple complex would be thrown down (Mark 13:2). As it
turns out, the Romans cast down most of the stones—but they left one
wall to indicate the glory of what once was. This wall, called the "Western"
or "Wailing Wall," stands even today as a testimony to the glory of the
ancient temple mount. The theory, then, is that the author of Mark knew
about the destruction of the temple in 70 CE but not in the kind of precise

detail that emerged in the aftermath of the war. Otherwise, he would have known about the surviving wall and would not have placed a demonstrably incorrect prophecy into the mouth of Jesus.

The year 70 CE was over forty years after Jesus's death. Most of the disciples and eyewitnesses of Jesus's ministry had died, and apparently no full-scale narrative of Jesus's life had been written. The author of Mark wrote to highlight Jesus as the suffering Messiah. He is probably responsible for the selection and ordering of the gospel's material, if not most of its contents.

Early in the gospel, the author of Mark depicts Jesus as a miracle worker. Only as the story unfolds do his disciples intuit that he is someone greater than human. To these disciples, Mark's Jesus tells the mysteries of the kingdom. To those outside, he speaks in parables with veiled meanings.

Jesus's most common miracle in Mark is driving out daimons (or exorcism). The daimons know exactly who they are dealing with: the Messiah and son of God. When Jesus's disciples belatedly get the message, Jesus strictly forbids them to unveil his identity. Only at the very end—in his trial—does Jesus publicly reveal that he is the Messiah. He pays for the revelation with his life. Yet after he is crucified and buried, his body disappears from the tomb. A young man tells female disciples that Jesus will appear in Galilee, but the women run away and tell nothing to anyone.

Matthew

Since the author of Matthew used Mark as a source, his work is frequently dated ten to fifteen years after Mark (thus 80–85 CE). The author of Matthew closely followed (indeed, paraphrased) the narrative of Mark, though he added a set of speeches mostly from a collection of Jesus's sayings (called "Q").

The author of Matthew is unknown, but he is typically viewed as an educated Jew who became a follower of Jesus. He is often given a community—usually in Antioch, a large urban metropolis in ancient Syria, or alternatively a city in Upper Galilee. In both places, Jews had long been established, and Christian communities flourished in the late first century. Even so, the identity of the author's community remains obscure, and one wholly depends on the gospel text to construct it. As with the other gospel writers, the author does not care to tell why he wrote. Yet from his text it is clear that he wanted to present Jesus as the Messiah, the greatest prophet, and Israel's rightful king.

Matthew is not only Mark rewritten but refashioned as a more complete biography. A birth narrative is supplied for Jesus, although still nothing is said about his childhood. The charismatic miracle worker becomes a teacher of Torah, a sage giving sermons. Five homilies given by Jesus portray him as the new Moses, giver of the five books of the Law. Far from coming to abolish the Law, Jesus arrives to fulfill it. This teacher does not tell secrets, and he is not overly concerned to keep his Messianic identity secret.

Jesus's increasingly heated conflicts with the Jewish leaders are thought to mirror the later conflicts between Jewish believers in Jesus and other Jews in the late first century CE. The author's insistence that Jesus fulfilled Hebrew prophecy may have been born of his will to oppose fellow Jews who denied that Jesus, a Galilean peasant, was the royal son of David come to deliver Israel from its sins. Salvation does not come immediately. Even the resurrection does not bring about Jesus's rule on earth. Before that happens, the good news must be preached to all nations. The preachers are the apostles whom the resurrected Jesus commissions on a mountain in Galilee.

Luke

The writer of the third gospel probably wrote between 85 and 95 CE, though perhaps somewhat later. His location is also unknown. Scholars conjecture that he lived in a city somewhere in the eastern Roman Empire, possibly Asia Minor (modern Turkey). As for the author himself, some scholars have called him the only Gentile evangelist. Yet his deep knowledge of Jewish texts and traditions suggests an early formation in the synagogue. By the time of writing, the author was a follower of Jesus writing for a presumably Gentile Christian patron.

Judging by the historiographical gestures in the preface, the author of Luke was evidently trying to play the part of a historiographer.[33] He gives the impression that he researched traditions handed down by eyewitnesses. These claims seem formulaic and are not justified by precise details (such as the names of the eyewitnesses and their actual relation to

Jesus). Scholars can trace the writer's sources, and they do not appear to be eyewitnesses. These sources include Mark, "Q," and an additional oral or written source sometimes called "L."

The Jesus of the third gospel is given both a birth narrative and a story detailing a childhood event. The adult Jesus works with a strong sense of mission and divine purpose. His aim is to reach out primarily to the poor and the outcasts of society (lepers, women, foreigners, and so on). He criticizes wealth and luxury like a Cynic philosopher. He travels a great deal, spreading his mainly moral message and summons to repent. When Jesus is arrested and killed, the author accentuates Jesus's innocence. After Jesus is resurrected, he appears solely in Jerusalem and its environs. His commission to spread the gospel to the ends of the earth indicates that he has become the savior of the world.

John

Written probably in stages in the last decade of the first century, the fourth gospel too comes without a name. Scholars disagree on where to place it. Church tradition vouches for Ephesus (in eastern Turkey), but more recent researchers are inclined to place it somewhere in Syria or Palestine. Its sources probably included a separate "Signs Source" for Jesus's miracles. All of Jesus's miracles are called "signs," and there are precisely seven of them. No exorcisms are included. The culminating sign — the resurrection of Jesus's friend Lazarus — is not mentioned in any other gospel.

It is disputed whether the author of the fourth gospel knew the previous three (called "Synoptic gospels," since they share a basic plot and point of view). If he knew one or more of them, he considerably revised the storyline as well as the character of Jesus. The account of Jesus's birth is passed over. Jesus appears as a god in flesh. He tells virtually no parables but offers long monologues. Instead of preaching God's kingdom, Jesus preaches mainly about himself and his own significance. This significance is summed up in the famous "I am" sayings ("I am the bread of life," "I am the gate," "I am the truth," and so on).

Jesus's focus on his own divinity leads him into vitriolic conflict with "the Jews" (or "Judeans") of his time. When Jesus is arrested and killed, he does not seem to suffer. He remains in perfect control until he sovereignly releases his spirit. When Jesus returns to manifest himself to his disciples, he appears in a transformed body. Some of the disciples fail to recognize him, but they eventually worship him. The purpose of this gospel is for readers—predominantly Gentile at this point—to believe that Jesus is the Messiah and son of God (John 20:31).

Greco-Roman Writers

I will mainly compare the gospels with Greco-Roman writers of mythic historiography. I cannot formally introduce here every Greco-Roman author cited in the chapters that follow, but I can briefly discuss the main authors whose stories I compare.[34]

Diodorus

Diodorus was a Sicilian born in Agyrium (modern Agira) in the early first century BCE. He composed a *Library of History* forty books in length, fifteen of which survive complete. His history ranges from the beginning of the world to the Roman conquest of Britain in 54 BCE. Diodorus performed research in Egypt sometime between 60 and 57 BCE. He worked in Rome for a longer period and used Latin historians as sources. All told, he worked a total of thirty years compiling his history, which was published around 30 BCE. Unlike previous authors, he took the mythical period of world history seriously and devoted the first six books of his *Library* to world events that occurred before the Trojan War.[35] Diodorus aimed to provide readers with a succinct and comprehensive world history that would allow them to forgo extensive reading of earlier authors.

Plutarch

Plutarch was born around 45 CE and lived until the early 120s. His birthplace was Chaeronea in northern Boeotia (central Greece). He spent lengthy periods of his life in Rome, where he became friends with several leading citizens and won his citizenship. In later life, he became a priest at the shrine to Apollo at Delphi (also in central Greece). He was among the most prolific of ancient writers, writing some 227 works of philosophy, morality, rhetoric, biography, and history, many of which unfortunately do not survive. His philosophical interests shine out clearly in his *Lives*. The *Lives* probably belong to the period after 96 CE (the death of the tyrannical emperor Domitian).[36] He wrote individual *Lives*, of which four survive, and others in pairs, always comparing famous Greeks with notable Romans. Twenty-two pairs are extant today and show the general confluence and compatibility of Greek and Roman culture. Plutarch's *Lives* exemplify the flexible nature of biography, as they include elements of historiography, rhetoric, and moral reflection.[37]

Suetonius

Gaius Suetonius Tranquillus was born about 69 CE. A professional scholar and writer, he held secretarial posts under the emperors Trajan (ruled 98–117 CE) and Hadrian (ruled 117–38 CE). Little is known about his life apart from personal references in his work and correspondence with his friend and patron Pliny the Younger. Suetonius appears to have been dismissed from office by Hadrian in 121 or 122 CE, and the date of his death is unknown.

Much of Suetonius's work was biographical, including the large volume *On Illustrious Men*, now lost except for fragments. His most famous work, *Lives of the Caesars* (published about 125 CE), contained twelve biographies, beginning with that of Julius Caesar and continuing until the life of Domitian. Suetonius presented a lively story, and this, together with his simple, flowing style, ensured him a wide readership. His accounts of Julius Caesar and Augustus are the most detailed; the quality of the other *Lives* suffers probably as a result of his dismissal from the imperial service with its access to archives and libraries.[38]

Philostratus

Flavius Philostratus was born about 170 CE. He studied rhetoric at Athens and then went to Rome to become part of the circle of Julia Domna, wife of the emperor Septimius Severus (ruled 193–211 CE). Philostratus survived the turbulent end of the Severan dynasty, continued to write and publish, and died about 250. His interest in biography is demonstrated by his *Lives of the Sophists,* a collection of short biographies detailing the lives of professional orators and their craft.

In the early years of the third century, Philostratus received from the empress Julia certain documents with a request that he write an account of Apollonius, a first-century CE Pythagorean philosopher and mystic from Tyana in southeastern Turkey. An active teacher and religious reformer, Apollonius traveled all over the known world, and Philostratus used these travels as a backdrop for relating his many speeches and wonders. Apollonius lived until about 100 CE. The *Life of Apollonius* was probably published shortly after 217 CE. Philostratus intended to show that Apollonius was no mere quack or magician but a true holy man worthy of worship.[39]

Iamblichus

Iamblichus was born around 240 CE in the city of Chalcis by the Belus River (in modern northwestern Syria). Probably he studied with the Neoplatonist philosopher Porphyry in Rome before setting up his own philosophical school in Apamea of Syria. He wrote the ten-volume *Compendium of Pythagorean Doctrine* as a kind of introduction to the Platonic mode of living. The first volume, *On the Pythagorean Way of Life,* survives and offers a plethora of biographical information about one of Greece's greatest sages, namely, Pythagoras (late sixth century BCE). To write his biography, Iamblichus used a range of earlier sources, some of which date back to the fourth century BCE. Iamblichus aimed to portray Pythagoras as the model for the best kind of moral, political, and philosophical life—a divine sage and archetype of Hellenic wisdom.[40]

Conclusion: The Third Factor

To compare stories, one must not only contextualize them historically and literarily but also "self-contextualize" by revealing one's own interests and purpose for comparison. This discussion is essential because two objects are always compared in relation to a third factor governed by the comparativist's own interests.[41]

In this book, I am primarily interested in the question of why the gospels seemed true to their earliest readers. My thesis, already stated in the introduction, is that the gospels seemed true because they were written in historiographical discourse with historiographical tropes that gave the impression of historicity. Thus the third factor of my comparisons is the historiographical form used by both classical and Christian authors to maximize the plausibility of their stories. I will primarily compare stories (as opposed to ideas or motifs) and in particular stories called *mythic historiography,* as defined in the introduction.

Ultimately what I want to affirm is that the similarity between select gospel and Greco-Roman stories is due to a similarity in cultural setting.[42] In the late first century CE, historiography was considered to be a discourse communicating "real" objects of knowledge. Both the evangelists and other writers of mythic historiography felt the same cultural pressures to employ historiographical rhetoric to give the sense that they spoke of "real"—and thus true—events.

To sum up, my theory of comparison is based neither on the idea of genetic connection between texts nor on some kind of psychic unity of humankind. Rather, it is based on structural similarities of learned patterns of thought rooted in a shared (Greek) language and (Hellenistic) culture. This shared culture affected not only the *content* of certain stories but also *how* they were told in the late first and early second centuries CE. At this time, biographers and historiographers tended to (re)describe their *mythoi* in historical form to maximize their plausibility. The gospel writers, by using the tropes of historiography, performed an analogous cultural practice as they composed their stories, some of which we will now explore.

Further Reading

Dale C. Allison, *The Historical Christ and the Theological Jesus* (Grand Rapids, MI: Eerdmans, 2009), 8–22.

Mark Chancey, *Greco-Roman Culture and the Galilee of Jesus* (Cambridge: Cambridge University Press, 2006).

Richard A. Horsley, *The Liberation of Christmas: The Infancy Narratives in Social Context* (New York: Crossroad, 1988), 162–72.

Arnaldo Momigliano, *The Development of Greek Biography,* exp. ed. (Cambridge, MA: Harvard University Press, 1993).

Paul Roscoe, "The Comparative Method," in *The Blackwell Companion to the Study of Religion,* ed. Robert A. Segal (Oxford, UK: Blackwell, 2006), 25–46.

Samuel Sandmel, "Parallelomania," *Journal of Biblical Literature* 81 (1962): 1–13.

Robert Segal, "Comparative Method," in *Vocabulary for the Study of Religion,* ed. Robert Segal and Kocku von Stuckrad, 3 vols. (Leiden: Brill, 2015), 1:305–14.

Susan Stephens, "Hellenistic Culture," in *The Oxford Handbook of Hellenic Studies,* ed. George Boys-Stones (Oxford: Oxford University Press, 2009), 86–97.

Charles Talbert, *What Is a Gospel? The Genre of the Canonical Gospels* (Philadelphia: Fortress, 1977).

L. Michael White, and John T. Fitzgerald. "Quod est Comparandum: The Problem of Parallels," in *Early Christianity and Classical Culture: Comparative Studies in Honor of Abraham J. Malherbe,* ed. John T. Fitzgerald, Thomas H. Olbricht, and L. Michael White (Leiden: Brill, 2003), 13–40.

Tim Whitmarsh, "Hellenism," in *The Oxford Handbook of Roman Studies,* ed. Alessandro Barchiesi and Walter Scheidel (Oxford: Oxford University Press, 2009), 728–47.

CHAPTER THREE

INCARNATION

The idea of the incarnation linked the substance of the myth, the nature
of deity itself, to a historical event, a historical person.
—*Wolfhart Panneberg*[1]

The Logos Becomes Flesh

It may seem strange to start with the fourth (and latest) gospel, but it
contains a story referring to what is oldest in time—in fact, before time
itself began. I refer to the story still celebrated during the high holy days of
Christmas: the incarnation, or "enfleshment" of Christ as a preexisting deity. "The Word [Greek: *Logos*] became flesh" (John 1:14) is one of the most
celebrated verses in the gospels, yet it contains many puzzles. Since there
is no birth narrative in the fourth gospel, the Logos could have appeared
in flesh as a fully formed adult. The flesh, that is, might not have been normal human flesh that is born and grows. Jesus is never shown eating in the
fourth gospel, and when he is offered food, he says, "My food and drink is
to do the will of him who sent me" (John 4:34). Jesus's insistence that his
disciples must eat his flesh to be saved (John 6:55–56) raises further questions about the nature of his flesh, especially when Jesus goes on to remark,
"The flesh profits nothing" (John 6:63).

In short, incarnation in the fourth gospel is not a simple idea. Empirically speaking, it is impossible to see and to fathom in terms of modern

physics (what kind of body would a god have anyway?). In this chapter, I am solely concerned with incarnation as it is narrated in ancient literature. For my purposes, *incarnation* refers to the strange and often undefined union of divinity and humanity narrated in the life of an individual person.

Stories of incarnation hardly sound historical to contemporary readers. In 1977, a group of English theologians published *The Myth of God Incarnate* to show that it was no longer appropriate to believe in the historicity of the Christian account(s) of incarnation.[2] For most people today—even most Christians—a literal incarnation falls outside the bounds of believability. In modern Christian lingo, incarnation has largely become a metaphor: "God was in Christ," and by following Christ's example, every Christian can "incarnate" the presence of God.

Yet in the ancient world, the incarnation of deities and daimons was not necessarily implausible and certainly not impossible. Gods were not invisible. They had their own "super bodies" unlike human bodies in size and voice. According to Homer, the body of Ares covers seven acres when he falls, and Hera, queen of the gods, causes the tops of trees to tremble when she walks.[3]

At the same time, these massive gods could appear, if temporarily, in human flesh—and not merely as a disguise. Having real flesh was presumably necessary for having sex with humans, a delight that the gods regularly enjoyed. According to Hermetic theology, blessed daimons were incarnated in Egyptian pharaohs.[4] The Jewish writer Philo speculated that a daimonic being was incarnated into the Jewish prince of Egypt, Moses.[5] Poets celebrated the incarnation of divine beings in Roman emperors. Biographers also found ways to speak of incarnate gods who came into this world to become philosophers and holy men.

Sophia and Hermes

Appealing to native Jewish mythology, commentators often compare the incarnate Logos with the figure of Wisdom. Wisdom is a female being who existed with God before the world began. She was the means of creation, as is the Logos in the fourth gospel (Prov. 8; John 1:3). She tried to dwell among humans but—like the goddess Justice in Greek mythology[6]—was driven away by human sin (Sirach 24; 1 Enoch 42). The Logos also came to his own people, but his own did not receive him (John 1:11). By making Wisdom into Logos, the author of John may have been translating Jewish mythology into Greek terms. Jesus as Logos expressed the thought and mind of the father deity, just like Wisdom of old. But Wisdom, according to Jewish mythology, was never made flesh.

In the Hellenistic world, it was more common to conceive of the Logos as the god Hermes.[7] Hermes was called Logos not only because his works expressed the reason of God but also because he was the *interpreting* god. He explained the will of his father, Zeus. Christ the Logos is also a god, intimately related to the high God. When John's Logos takes on flesh, his mission is specifically to interpret or explain his divine father (John 1:1, 18).

Zeus often sent his son Hermes on missions. One of these missions was to create the world.[8] In the Hermetic myth called *Korē Kosmou,* Hermes is assigned the task of creating human bodies.[9] As a god, Hermes has human form; yet there are certain "historical missions" in which he assumes a tangible human body.

In a Homeric myth, Zeus once sent Hermes down to escort Priam, king of Troy. Priam was traveling into the enemy (Greek) camp to retrieve and ransom the body of his son Hector. Without divine protection from Hermes, Priam would not have survived. So Hermes assumed the form of a young nobleman, his downy beard just sprouting from his face. He took Priam's hand, led him to the beached ships of the Greeks, and ensured his safe return.[10]

Hermes also became manifest in a distinctly historical figure. Around 30 BCE, the Roman poet Horace told of terrible prodigies afflicting the city of Rome: snow squalls, lightning electrifying the citadel, and the yellow Tiber overrunning its banks. The Romans were terrified at the signs of divine wrath and supposed that the age of Pyrrha had returned (the time of the great flood). The people were afflicted by a horrible curse. Warring Romans battled not their enemies but themselves. In desperation, the poet asked, "What divinity are the people to call upon to restore the fortunes of their collapsing power? . . . To whom will Jupiter [the Roman Zeus] give the task of atoning for the crime?" As candidates, Horace considered Apollo wrapped in a cloud, smiling Venus, and blood-stained Mars. Surprisingly, he settled on the "winged son of kindly Maia," or Mercury (the Roman Hermes). Fitting it was for this divinity to lay down his wings and "take on the shape of a young man on earth"—no less than the Roman emperor Augustus. What was initially introduced as hypothetical in the poem swiftly becomes reality. Mercury did indeed come to earth and arrived in space and time as the flesh-and-blood emperor. The historical emperor was really Hermes clothed in flesh. Thus all the benefactions of Augustus were really the gifts of a god. The poet duly prayed to the descended deity: "May it be long before you return to heaven; may you dwell happily with Romulus's folk [the Romans] for many a year, and may no breeze come too soon and carry you on high [to heaven], alienated by our sins."[11]

Although this particular myth owes much to Horace's fancy, it is worth taking seriously. It well exemplifies how an ancient Mediterranean person conceived of an extraordinary benefactor in mythic terms. The benefactor is not a normal human being but a subordinate deity who arrives in flesh. He comes from heaven in a time of crisis. By virtue of his divine nature, he becomes a leader or king. He brings peace on earth, a purifying act of atonement, and then rises—all too swiftly—back to his heavenly home.[12]

Humans themselves could not atone for their crime. Therefore a god, agent of the high God, performs it for them. In Horace's poem, the crime is not specified, but it probably refers to Rome's civil wars (which raged intermittently from 88 to 31 BCE). The poet traced back these civil wars to an earlier, primeval crime: the death of Ilia (mother of Romulus and Remus).

To atone for the ancient crime, Mercury came in human form, obeying the commands of his divine father. He came as ruler and peace bringer.[13] For Horace, Mercury was not just a poet's patron or a tradesman's deity. He was the one bringing reconciliation, truces, and terminations of civil war; he was the preservation—indeed salvation—of the Roman people. He was incarnated, moreover, in a real, well-known, historical human being mentioned in the third gospel: Caesar Augustus.

Pythagoras

A myth of incarnation also appears in Greek biographical literature. The three surviving biographies of the philosopher Pythagoras all refer to him as the incarnation of the god Apollo. These biographies were written by Diogenes Laertius (late second or early third century CE), the philosopher Porphyry (late third century CE), and Porphyry's student Iamblichus (early fourth century CE). Each of these authors incorporates—and sometimes mechanically copies—earlier biographical traditions that date back to the fourth century BCE.[14]

The earliest known biographies of Pythagoras were written by Aristoxenus (about 370–322 BCE) and Dicaearchus (about 350–285 BCE).[15] Aristoxenus was from southern Italy, and Dicaearchus was from Sicily—two key sites of Pythagoras's ministry. Both men were trained in the school of Aristotle. Although their biographies do not survive, their materials were earnestly read and recycled. It was said that Aristoxenus interviewed the last remaining disciples of Pythagoras,[16] and Cicero calls Dicaearchus "the most accomplished historian [*historikōtatos*]."[17] Both men wrote their biographies in the late fourth century BCE, about a century after Pythagoras's death.

In the meantime, Pythagoras's life story had become mythic historiography. The Platonist Heraclides of Pontus (390–322 BCE) told a tale about Pythagoras's previous incarnations.[18] Aristotle (384–322 BCE) composed a list of Pythagoras's miracles.[19] The philosopher could talk to animals including a bear, a bull, and an eagle. Multiple witnesses attested that Pythagoras was addressed by a river (or rather a river god) as he forded the channel. It was Aristotle in his work *On the Pythagoreans* who wrote that the people of Croton (a town in southern Italy and a key site of Pythagoras's ministry) believed that he was the incarnation of Apollo.[20] This tradition can thus be dated to the fourth century BCE.

Following this tradition, Diogenes, Porphyry, and Iamblichus all present the disciples of Pythagoras as confessing that their master is Apollo incarnate.[21] Since the time of Pythagoras, Apollo was one of the most popular Olympian deities worshiped throughout the Roman Empire. He was associated with music, youthful beauty (as signified by his long hair), and prophecy. Music was one of the pastimes of Pythagoras; he was called "long-haired," and his powers to divine the future were a matter of awe.[22] All these traits made Pythagoras seem Apolline. Yet his disciples said more: Pythagoras was Apollo in flesh. The god had come to earth, in the words of Iamblichus, "for the benefit and amendment of mortal life, to grant mortal nature the saving spark of happiness and philosophy."[23]

Iamblichus modified the tradition in accordance with his own theology. He preferred the view that Pythagoras was a kindly daimon.[24] For Platonists, daimons are typically benevolent beings, and especially worthy daimons can be incarnated to help the human race. To support this view, Iamblichus quoted Aristotle: "Of rational living creatures, one is god, a second is human, and the third is like Pythagoras."[25] This third or middling type of being is probably a daimon.[26]

Yet earlier biographical traditions had no problem depicting Pythagoras as a fully fledged god in flesh. Iamblichus reported a Pythagorean creedal question (*akousma*) with its correct answer: "'Who are you Pythagoras?' For they confess that he is the Hyperborean Apollo."[27]

Hyperborea

Who was this Hyperborean Apollo? Here we see a *mythos* subtly slide into historical discourse. Originally, Hyperborea was the mythical land beyond the North Wind (called *Boreas* in Greek). The poet Pindar wrote, "Neither by ship nor by foot could you find the wondrous way to the Hyperborean assembly."[28] According to Herodotus, Hyperborea existed beyond the tribe of one-eyed Arimaspians and the gold-guarding griffins.[29] It was a land of perfect climate, inhabited by a mythical people, to whom Apollo gave both laws and learning.[30]

In historiographical literature, however, Hyperborea could become an actual place. The geographer Strabo argued that the Hyperboreans were simply the people who lived farthest north.[31] In part, Strabo was following Hellanicus (491 – 405 BCE) who placed the Hyperboreans beyond the "Riphaean Mountains" (perhaps the Ural Mountains in Russia).[32]

Abaris

One particular Hyperborean came to visit Pythagoras. His name was Abaris. Abaris was said to be a priest of the Hyperborean Apollo.[33] He wrote oracles—or oracles were attributed to him—which existed as real documents in antiquity. His mission was to travel throughout Greece and Italy in order to collect gold for the temple of Hyperborean Apollo.

How does one travel from a mythical land? According to widespread tradition, Abaris was given Apollo's arrow, which he apparently rode like a rocket through the sky.[34] The arrow was quite large, for it was used by the towering Apollo himself to kill the Cyclopes (one-eyed monsters who populate Greek mythology).[35] The historian Herodotus mentioned the arrow but reported (perhaps rationalizing) that Abaris carried the arrow rather than being carried by it.

Yet in Porphyry's biography of Pythagoras, Abaris appears riding on his arrow over rivers, seas, and other impassable places.[36] Iamblichus reports the same tradition. Yet he distances himself by saying, "as the story goes" (*hōs logos*).[37] Iamblichus was not prepared to vouch for the arrow as a means of fabulous transport. He identified Abaris as a Scythian. Scythia, as opposed to Hyperborea, was undisputedly known geography (what is today southern Russia and Ukraine).

In Italy, Abaris encountered Pythagoras. After noticing his dignified bearing and certain secret tokens of Apollo, Abaris came to believe (*pisteusas*) that Pythagoras was Apollo incarnate.[38] As a sign of recognition, Abaris gave Pythagoras his wondrous arrow.[39] Pythagoras received the token without any sign of surprise. He understood exactly why Abaris gave it to him (or, one should say, "returned" it to him). Pythagoras drew Abaris aside privately (*idiai*), drew up the hem of his robe, and revealed to Abaris his golden thigh. Pythagoras was in fact Apollo and privately proved it. Gold is the flesh not of humans but of gods. As the metal that does not rust, it is the emblem of a deity's eternity.[40]

As further confirmation, Pythagoras listed from memory each of the sacred objects lying in the Hyperborean Apollo's temple. He explained to Abaris that he arrived on earth for the healing and benefit of the human race. He took human form so as not to frighten people by his higher nature and so lose the harvest of his advent. Pythagoras bid Abaris to stay with him as a close disciple, and on him he bestowed his deepest teachings.[41]

Olympia

In addition to the private revelation of Pythagoras's divinity, there was also a public one set in another place and time. It occurred in Olympia in the Greek Peloponnese at the celebration of the Olympic Games. The timing is significant, since the four-year interval of the Olympic Games (called the "Olympiad") was the basic unit of the Greek dating system. For instance, Iamblichus wrote that Pythagoras "arrived in Italy in the sixty-second Olympiad, in which Eryxias of Chalcis won the footrace."[42] Such precision is characteristic of historiographical discourse.

The accounts of Pythagoras's Olympic epiphany are various but share a basic plot. Pythagoras was in the stands, or what is once called "the theater." As he stood up to watch an event—or perhaps to cheer—bystanders caught sight of something strange. Shining from beneath his robe was his golden thigh, temporarily exposed before the robe slid back into place.[43] Alternatively, Plutarch says that the thigh was exposed as Pythagoras walked past an assembled crowd at the Games.[44]

What is striking about this revelation is not so much the shining thigh itself but how pedestrian was its manifestation. Pythagoras is normally depicted as rather solemn and secretive about his identity. Yet here, as if by accident, his thigh is publicly, if briefly, exposed. The circumstantial nature of the revelation contributes to its reality effect. The accounts do not say how the bystanders reacted. It was sufficient that there be multiple eyewitnesses to confirm it.

Caesarea Philippi

The multiple witnesses to the epiphany and especially the revelation to Abaris are comparable to two consecutive episodes in the Synoptic gospels. At the midpoint of Jesus's ministry, he withdrew with his disciples to the suburbs of Caesarea Philippi. The very act of setting the story in a concrete town adds the impression of historicity. The town was named after Philip the tetrarch, a minor potentate mentioned in the gospels (Mark 6:17; Matt. 14:3). In this quiet spot, nestled to the southwest of Mount Hermon, the hero privately addressed his followers and poignantly asked, "Who do you say that I am?"

Peter, self-made spokesman, answered correctly: "You are the Messiah" (Mark 8:29). The author of Matthew clarified the divine identity of the Messiah by having Peter add, "son of the living God" (Matt. 16:16). Jesus privately confirmed Peter's judgment, declaring it a divine revelation. "Blessed are you, Simon bar Jona, for flesh and blood did not reveal this to you but my father in the heavens" (Matt. 16:16–17). Despite the importance of the revelation, Jesus ordered his disciples to tell no one (Mark 8:30; Matt. 16:20).

Transfiguration

Precisely at this juncture, Jesus decided to manifest his glory. Jesus's closest disciples had already intuited his divine identity, and now it was time to show it. He drew them aside privately (*kat' idian*) and took them up a high mountain (Matt. 17:1). On the summit, Jesus's body was transfigured before them; Moses and Elijah appeared around him like deified saints, Jesus's face shone like the sun god Helios, and the disciples worshiped him (Matt. 17:2–3).

The sublimity of the story is only broken by one silly remark of Peter: "Rabbi, it is good for us to be here. Now we will make three tents, one for you, one for Moses, and one for Elijah" (Mark 9:5). The remark is consistent with the character of Peter, who is typically portrayed as a man whose mouth runs ahead of his mind. At any rate, Peter is duly silenced by a heavenly voice, which once again confirms Jesus's divinity: "This is my beloved son; hear him!" (Mark 9:7). The circumstantial detail of Peter's remark again adds to the historiographical flavor of the tale.

Oddly, Jesus's transfiguration is never again referred to in the Synoptic biographies. Some scholars propose that the episode was originally a vision of the resurrected Christ later shifted back into Jesus's ministry.[45] Whether or not this was the case, it is striking how the vision is described in historical terms. It is set in a place (a high mountain, perhaps Mount Hermon near Caesarea Philippi), in a narrative sequence of cause and effect (Peter's correct answer about Jesus's divinity leads to its concrete revelation), portrayed before multiple witnesses, one of whom—the disciple Peter—appears embarrassingly foolish.

The historicity of the transfiguration is later upheld by an impersonator of Peter's character. This author, writing an epistle in the early second century, portrays himself as the elderly apostle Peter about to die (2 Pet. 1:13–14). Before he does so, however, he relates some old "memories" in opposition to competing Christian teachers. "We did not follow cleverly devised *mythoi*," he says, "when we made known to you the power and presence of our Lord Jesus Christ. Rather, we became beholders of his majesty. For he received glory and honor from the father God when so great a voice was conveyed to him by the majestic glory: 'This is my son, my beloved; he is the one in whom I am well pleased.' And this voice we ourselves heard conveyed from heaven when we were with him on the holy mountain" (2 Pet. 1:16–18).

This is the earliest known reception of the transfiguration story. It is telling that the author first denies that it is a *mythos*. The reader can only suspect that it was perceived to be exactly that. It is, after all, a story about divine light shining through Jesus's body accompanied by a voice from heaven. The account has all the tropes of an epiphany common to mythology (overwhelming light, the response of fear or awe, a declaration of divinity), yet it is still portrayed as any other event in the life of a seemingly historical figure.[46]

Notice "Peter's" insistence on apparently real geography: the epiphany occurs on "the holy mountain." Mountains were typical sites for epiphanies. One could argue, in fact, that Jesus's mountaintop transfiguration is an imaginative adaptation of Moses's transfiguration on Mount Sinai.[47] Moses even appears with Jesus on the mountain, as if the Synoptic writers were "citing" the previous tale. Yet "Peter" insists on a real, physical mount of transfiguration. (It was later identified with the rounded peak of Mount Tabor in Galilee.) The author of 2 Peter also emphasizes the real (auditory) experience of himself and the other eyewitnesses. "Peter" is no longer an embarrassing chatterbox. He is an apostle whose real "experience" and eyewitness "memory" cannot be written off as subjective fantasy.[48]

The use of the plural in "we became beholders of his majesty" is a known technique for making an account seem objective. The author gives the impression that "different people have had the same experience or seen the same thing."[49] The technique recalls the saying in the prologue of John, "We beheld his glory" (1:14), as well as the opening of the letter called 1 John: "What was from the beginning, what we have heard, what we have seen with our eyes, what we have beheld, and our hands have touched concerning the Logos of life" (1:1–2). In writing this way, these authors effectively ventriloquize the so-called witnesses of the transfiguration, witnesses who supposedly saw divinity beaming through Jesus's flesh.

Confession and Epiphany

Abaris is the sacred and reliable witness to Pythagoras's epiphany. In the surviving literature, we never hear his own voice (or a fictionalized rendition of it). There are, however, other points of overlap worth considering. In the Synoptic gospels, a pattern of confession plus epiphany resembles the structure of the Abaris report. First, Peter confesses the divine identity of Jesus ("son of the living God"); then, in a blaze of glory, Jesus reveals his deity on a mountain (the transfiguration). In both cases, it is a close disciple who intuits the divinity of the god in flesh. The confession of this disciple is followed by the revelation of the hero's divinity in the form of a token. In both cases, the token has something to do with the hero's body. Some feature of the hero's body, normally hidden, is suddenly exposed. The flesh of the hero is real but somehow unlike normal human flesh. The flesh of the deity shines or has a golden luster. The shiny flesh indicates the divinity of the hero, a divinity attested by multiple witnesses.

The Abaris and Synoptic stories feature a private revelation of divinity. Yet by being narrativized as historiography, the revelation is in fact "made public" to any and all who peruse the account. All readers, no matter their state of initiation, are brought into the secret. The veil is lifted, and readers have a sense that they have also seen the superhuman. The witnesses that are added to the story only supplement the imagined notion that the readers behold the event itself.

The transparency of Jesus's flesh is analogous to the supposed transparency of historical discourse itself. The Evangelical commentator F. F. Bruce glossed "the Word became flesh" to mean "the revelation [of God] became history."[50] There is no sense that the reader must see through a cloud of *mythoi* or subjective, fallible memories to witness the glory of Christ.

The author of Luke has the disciples see the transfiguration after awaking from sleep. But he quickly erases their haziness with the comment, "they had become fully awake" (Luke 9:32). The disciples are not dreaming. The experience is portrayed as objective and real. With the disciples, the reader can share in the impression of objectivity. What could not be seen with empirical eyes and what could only be unveiled to the most advanced initiates suddenly becomes public knowledge seen with the most powerful eye—that of the imagination. In short, what appears to be largely subjective literary invention takes the form of historiography, a straightforward and matter-of-fact form of discourse.

Conclusion

Although the embodiment of rationality, the Logos is not above *mythos*. He is the quintessential mythical being: subordinate to a higher God, the Logos is sent into the world to act on and react to other human beings. Little is said, or can be said, about the Logos in his prehuman state. Only when he is objectified, narrativized, and historicized can his story be told. The Logos become flesh is actually the Logos made into historiography. The unspeakable revelation is inscribed on paper with ink; the divine Word becomes human words. And all the while, readers are given the impression that they have met the divine one himself and have become witnesses of his glory.

Yet what readers actually meet is a literary creation of evangelists who took the unspeakable and put it into the prosaic words of historical discourse. In so doing, these literary artists were not alone. The admirers of Pythagoras narrativized the epiphany of his divine (Apolline) identity. They included in their biographies the secret revelation of his divinity to a close disciple in a way strikingly similar to the transfiguration and its preceding episode. What we are dealing with here is not historiography or *mythos* in simple terms but mythic historiography written in the interests of confirming and even recapitulating the experience of epiphany in the minds of future readers.

Further Reading

François Bovon, "The First Christologies: From Exaltation to Incarnation, or from Easter to Christmas," in *Jesus Christ Today: Studies of Christology in Various Contexts,* ed. Stuart George Hall (Berlin: de Gruyter, 2009), 27–43.

Daniel Boyarin, *The Jewish Gospels: The Story of the Jewish Christ* (New York: New Press, 2013).

Courtney Friesen, *Reading Dionysus: Euripides' Bacchae and the Cultural Contestations of Greeks, Romans, Jews, and Christians* (Tübingen: Mohr Siebeck, 2015).

Joshua W. Jipp, *Divine Visitations and Hospitality to Strangers in Luke-Acts: An Interpretation of the Malta Episode in Acts 28:1–10,* Novum Testamentum Supplement 153 (Leiden: Brill, 2013).

Bruce Louden, *Homer's Odyssey and the Near East* (Cambridge: Cambridge University Press, 2011), chapters 2 and 12.

Charles H. Talbert, *The Development of Christology during the First Hundred Years and Other Essays on Early Christian Christology* (Leiden: Brill, 2011).

CHAPTER FOUR

GENEALOGY

The variation and extent of the genealogies of heroes, demigods, and
other men makes their exposition hard to understand.
—*Diodorus of Sicily*[1]

Two of the greatest works of Greek mythology come in the form of genealogy: Hesiod's *Theogony* (early seventh century BCE) and the *Catalogue of
Women* (mid-sixth century BCE). The former treats the genealogy of gods,
the latter of heroes.[2] In Homer's *Iliad* and *Odyssey*, the heroes cite their genealogies, often before engaging in mortal combat.[3] When prose literature
came to fruition, Greeks organized their most ancient historiographies by
genealogy. The historian Hecataeus of Miletus wrote his *Genealogies* of famous heroes around 500 BCE. Around the same time, the Jews edited the
many genealogies of Genesis as a prologue to their national history.[4]

In imitation of Genesis, the author of Matthew began his gospel with a
genealogy: "A scroll of the generation of Messiah Jesus, son of David, son
of Abraham. Abraham fathered Isaac, Isaac fathered Jacob"—and so on
for a list of several dozen names (Matt. 1:1–17). To many modern readers,
genealogies make not only dry reading but the worst kind of fiction. They
presume that the right to rule and the privilege of honor are guaranteed by
blood, notions that have all but perished in the West.

For different reasons, modern people have the experience of Plato's philosopher, who cannot understand why people preen themselves on pedigree. People make a great song about their wealthy ancestors without seeming to realize that everyone's ancestry is mixed, tainted, and tangled—full of characters both base and noble, rich and poor, white and black, depending on how far back one goes. Thus Plato considered it "absurd when people solemnly recount their twenty-five ancestors that go back to Heracles." If the lineage is taken in other directions, inevitably paupers, wackos, and criminals crop up in other branches of the family tree.[5]

Despite such criticism, the historian Polybius (200–118 BCE) indicated that genealogies were popular among ancient readers. He categorized genealogy as a kind of historiography that attracts people who enjoy a good story.[6] Hippias of Elis (ca. 443–399 BCE), a famous sophist portrayed by Plato, found that the Spartans delighted most in genealogies of men and heroes.[7] Tracing the lineage of heroes fostered a sense of pride in the Spartans' civic history.

Genealogies were a popular way to organize *mythoi* in the era of the gospels. The famous mythological handbook ascribed to the librarian of Augustus, Hyginus, was originally called *Genealogies*. Its Greek counterpart, the *Library of Mythology* (ascribed to Apollodorus of Athens) organizes its material by genealogies.[8] This is the best-known work of mythography today, in large part because it survives almost complete. Genealogies are also characteristic of biographical literature since great generals and kings often claimed a divine ancestry.[9]

Another genealogy of Jesus appears in the gospel according to Luke (not at the beginning but as a more direct preface to Jesus's ministry). Famously, the Lukan and Matthean genealogies do not agree. Luke features forty-one generations intervening between David and Jesus, while Matthew has only twenty-six. In some parts of Luke's genealogy, he also has different individuals posing as Jesus's ancestors. In fact, with the exception of two names, all the persons between King David and Joseph (Jesus's reputed father) are different in the Lukan and Matthean genealogies.[10]

These radical disagreements were deeply problematic, since genealogical correctness was a sign of historical accuracy. Hecataeus complained that the tales of the Greeks are "many and absurd." It may be that the tales of heroic lineages were absurd because they were so many.[11] Josephus chided the historians Hellanicus and Acusilaus when their genealogies did not coincide.[12] Such disagreements undermined their status as good historians. If they could not correctly work out the ancestors of a famous person, what other historical data did they get wrong? And yet the point of a genealogy is to show that an author was at least trying—despite inaccuracies—to use the tropes of historiography.

Mythos and Genealogy

Genealogies show that the line between *mythos* and historiography is often quite thin. About 100 BCE, the grammarian Asclepiades of Myrlea divided the historical part of grammar into three categories: the true, the seemingly true, and the false. There is only one kind of false history, said Asclepiades, and that is genealogy. It is genealogy that he expressly called "mythic history" (*muthikē historia*).[13] In his system, genealogies were even less true than the stories presented in comedy and mime.

In the late first century CE, the author of the letter now called "1 Timothy" associated genealogizing with mythmaking. He sternly commanded his young, if fictive, charge, "Pay no attention to *mythoi* and endless genealogies" (1 Tim. 1:4).[14] Here *mythoi* evidently refer to false stories.

Why would an ancient reader associate genealogy with falsehoods? Genealogies—although ostensibly about flesh-and-blood relationships—are constructs expressing human claims to status. In the ancient world, pedigree mattered much more than it does today. People of noble blood could make a claim to royal honor with all its wealth and power. Elite males spent a great deal of time and money "discovering" and advertising their noble ancestors.[15] So much stress was placed on genealogy that the matter became fit for satire. In the parody of Homer known as *The Battle of the Frogs and Mice* (*Batrachomyomachia*), a frog asks a mouse, "Who are you, stranger? Whence do you come to this shore? And who is the one who begot you?" (line 13).

Royalty and divinity were linked, since the gods also ruled. At an early stage, royal bloodlines were infused with divinity. The kings of Sparta declared their right to rule by tracing their lines back to Heracles, son of Zeus.[16] The kings of Alba Longa in Italy tracked their line to the Trojan demigod Aeneas.[17] The Jews traced their royal line back to King David, to whom Yahweh declared, "You are my son, today I have begotten you" (Ps. 2:7).

The historian Hecataeus "connected his paternal line to a god as his six-teenth ancestor."[18] Herodotus, who reported this fact, was not impressed but rather amused. He was of the opinion that the names and roles of the gods had only been invented some four hundred years prior to his time.[19] Hecataeus's genealogizing was both inventive and self-serving.

To give a more humorous example of genealogical construction, the character Amphitheus in Aristophanes's play *Acharnians* (425 BCE) boldly proclaims before a state assembly, "I'm immortal. For Amphitheus was son of Demeter and Triptolemus, and to him was born Celeus, and Celeus married Phaenarete my grandmother, of whom Lycinus was born, and being his son, I'm immortal. . . . But though immortal, gentleman, I have no travel money."[20]

Of course this a play, not a history book. Yet Aristophanes's exaggerated display of genealogical misuse mocked real historiographical practice. Am-phitheus's genealogy appeals to several well-known Athenian (specifically Eleusinian) ancestors. Triptolemus, for instance, was widely credited with introducing grain agriculture (somewhat like Johnny Appleseed). Celeus was associated with the founding of Demeter's cult in Eleusis (a suburb of Athens).

Yet the content of Amphitheus's genealogy remains ridiculous, since it is missing several generations. Celeus—assuming that he is historical—lived hundreds of years earlier in the age of heroes, so he could not have mar-ried Amphitheus's grandmother. By chance, Amphitheus might have had a grandmother with the same name as the Eleusinian princess, but they were hardly the same person.

Genealogy is thus a good example of mythic historiography. It poses as historical fact—an authoritative list of names supposedly excerpted from an ancient archive. Yet the names are sometimes little more than ciphers, and the persons they designate can be mythic through and through. Some ancestors listed go far beyond the range of reasonable memory and archi-val verification; thus their real existence cannot be investigated. Contra-dictions can be ironed out, and synchronies with real historical events can be inserted. Despite genealogies' appearance of accuracy, however, they are basically fictive, rhetorically engineered products designed to generate concrete social effects. In the case of Amphitheus, although he is deathless, he lacks travel money. He reports his lengthy ancestry for a reasonable goal: to apply for a state grant.

Not by coincidence, the author of Matthew's genealogy is also missing several generations. It begins with Abraham, descends through King David, and ends with Jesus. Yet when it lists the Israelite kings, it omits four of them.[21] These kings are deleted, it seems, to construct a pattern of three sets of fourteen generations: from Abraham to David, from David to the Babylonian Exile, and from the Exile to Jesus (Matt. 1:17). Yet the period from the Exile to Jesus (almost six hundred years) is too long for fourteen generations, so probably the author (or his source) omitted names here as well. In addition to these problems, the author's math simply does not add up. There are actually only thirteen generations in his first and third groupings, not fourteen.

Assuming the initial hearers of Matthew were not immediately aware of these problems, the triple-fourteen pattern showcases the work of divine providence, an enduring trope of ancient—especially Jewish—historiography. The message is, God has been with Israel from the beginning and has timed everything precisely. The goal of the genealogy is social: form sustainable communities that recognize Jesus as the rightful king. Accuracy need only be apparent rather than real. Apart from major figures such as David and Abraham, at any rate, the authors of Matthew and Luke could not agree on Jesus's actual ancestors.

Kings and Gods

Matthew made Jesus the son of kings. The author of Luke went farther by tracing Jesus's genealogy back to the Jewish deity (Luke 3:38). Yet kings and gods are the traditional ancestors of heroes. In Homer's *Iliad*, the hero Aeneas boasts that he is descended from Zeus through Dardanus (ancestor of the Trojan royal family). Aeneas is even more directly related to Zeus because he was the son of Aphrodite (the child of Zeus, according to Homeric tradition).[22]

Aeneas's genealogy became important during Jesus's lifetime because the Julian family (including Julius Caesar and his heirs) claimed to have descended from Aeneas's son Julus (or Iulus). The claim appears in a speech that the young Julius supposedly made on the occasion of his Aunt Julia's funeral: "On her mother's side Julia, my aunt, was sprung from kings, and on her father's side connected with the immortal gods. For the Marcian kings (Marcia was her mother's name) descended from Ancus Marcius [the fourth king of Rome], and the Julian clan, to whom my family belongs, descended from Venus [the Greek Aphrodite]. Therefore in our family is the sanctity of kings, who have supreme power among humans, and the venerability of the gods, to whose power kings themselves are subject."[23]

Cicero complained that Roman historiography was falsified by such eulogies, since they contained "fake genealogies" (*genera falsa*).[24] The Roman historian Livy made a similar point in his history: "I believe that memory is savaged in funeral eulogies [*funebribus laudibus*] . . . as long as certain families draw to themselves the glory and honor of historic deeds by a deceiving lie."[25]

Yet the young Caesar, if he ever gave this speech (or something like it), probably believed in the truth of his genealogy. To increase his clout, at any rate, he put *mythos* into historical (specifically, genealogical) form. Masterfully, he combined into a single ancestry both his royal and divine lines. The Julian clan was thus able to enjoy the benefits of both bloodlines. This is a fine example of mythic historiography. Roman mythology with its divine ancestors is presented as historical fact.

Closer to the period when the gospels were written, the Roman emperor Galba (who briefly ruled in 69 CE) displayed a family tree in which he traced his paternal ancestry to Jupiter (the Roman version of Zeus).[26] Tracing one's line to the king of the gods was certainly an effective tool for someone wanting to rule the civilized world. The later emperor Vespasian (ruled 69–79 CE) took a more relaxed attitude toward genealogies. He knew that his origins were humble, so when certain men tried to trace his line to a companion of Heracles, he simply laughed at them for their pains.[27]

According to the author of Matthew, Jesus's prestigious ancestors were David, the most famous Israelite king, and Abraham, the founder of the Jewish nation. By listing these ancestors, the author tied the story of Jesus to Israel's national myths. He constructed Jesus's claim to royal power, as well as his ability to found a new Israel full of Gentile believers (Abraham himself originally being a Chaldean Gentile).

Assuming for the moment that Abraham was a historical figure, one can grant that Jesus (a Jew) was his descendant. Technically, however, any Jew could claim to be a child of Abraham. Tracing Jesus's line through King David was a bolder claim. Historically speaking, however, Matthew's claim is as little justified as Aeneas being the descendant of King Dardanus or Julius Caesar being the descendant of King Ancus Marcius. Jesus's Davidic ancestry is a mythic claim with a culturally specific meaning for Jews and proselytes: accept the rightful king!

The tracing of Jesus's line to David resembles a claim made in the *Alexander Romance*. Although called a "romance" today, this work presents itself as a biography.[28] In it, the most magnificent Greek king—Alexander the Great—is made the son of the last native pharaoh (Nectanebo II, ruled 360–342 BCE). Although the Greek *Alexander Romance* is dated to the third century CE, this particular genealogical construction probably dates back to Ptolemaic times (323–33 BCE).[29] During this period, Greek kings, heirs of Alexander, took control of Egypt. They had no more right to rule there than did the Persians before them. Yet by linking Alexander to the last native pharaoh, the Ptolemies could stake their claim to rule.

Matthew's claim that Jesus was the rightful ruler of Israel was no less bold. To be sure, the author of Matthew meant it as a historical claim, but it is driven by his confession that Jesus is the Messiah (the expected Anointed One or Jewish king); Jesus must be a Davidic descendant to qualify for this role.

It would seem to be an obvious problem for Matthew that he traces Jesus's lineage through Joseph, even though Joseph is not, by most accounts, Jesus's biological father. Joseph may be the descendant of King David, but if Jesus is not actually the child of Joseph (Matt. 1:20), it is difficult to see how Jesus can literally be a descendant of David.

Yet when we compare other mythic genealogies, these kinds of hitches did not seem bothersome to the ancients. The Greek biographer Plutarch, for instance, fleshed out the genealogy of Alexander the Great. Plutarch recorded the common tradition that Alexander, through his father, Philip, was a descendant of the god Heracles. One would think that this impressive genealogy would be ruined by the fact that, according to widespread perception—and Plutarch's own report—Philip was not Alexander's biological father. Plutarch himself narrated that Zeus impregnated Alexander's mother, Olympias; and Olympias supposedly acknowledged this point directly to the adult Alexander.[30]

Yet these conflicting reports did not seem to impose cognitive dissonance. A concept of dual paternity was possible. As most people in the ancient world knew (and perhaps believed on some level), Alexander's real father was the high God Zeus, though he was also the "son of Philip." Likewise, Jesus's real father was, according to Matthew, the Jewish deity Yahweh (sometimes identified with Zeus), but Jesus is specifically the Messiah due to his Davidic ancestry through Joseph.

Neither Plutarch nor Matthew made the (to us) obvious objection: you cannot have your cake and eat it too! Either the hero claims the royal ancestry of his human father, or he leans solely on his divine paternity—but not both. Evidently, however, the ancients did not think like modern critics. A hero could claim both divine paternity and the prestige of his human "father's" ancestry—despite the fact that, in the latter case, there was no actual biological link.[31]

Conclusion

Whether one is tracing the genealogy of Alexander the Great, Julius Caesar, the emperor Galba, or Jesus, we circle back to a fundamental point: the ancients had an interest in presenting their mythography in historical form. And genealogies, even if mythic to the core, seemed supremely historical. They are simple, authoritative lists of supposedly "real" flesh-and-blood ancestors—or so they present themselves.

In our terms, we can reclassify gospel genealogizing as a form of mythic historiography. Though the story wears the guise of historiography, it proves (as so often) to derive largely from human invention. Jesus's real father was probably a simple builder or handyman (*tektōn;* Mark 6:3) in an out-of-the-way Jewish village. Yet to establish Jesus's political legitimacy and authority, the authors of Luke and Matthew paid close attention to *mythoi* and lengthy genealogies. In doing so, they could not agree on names, but they indicated something more important by independently showing their debts to a common intellectual culture. In this culture, a hero's status was greatly augmented by pointing to well-known ancestors posing as both royal and divine.

Further Reading

David Aune, *The New Testament in Its Literary Environment* (Philadelphia: Westminster, 1987), 121–22.

Claude Calame, "Spartan Genealogies: The Mythological Representation of a Spatial Organisation," in *Interpretations of Greek Mythology*, ed. Jan Bremmer (London: Croom Helm, 1987), 153–86.

J. C. Carrière, "Du myth a l'histoire. Généalogies héroïques," in *Généalogies mythiques*, ed. Danièle Auger and Suzanne Saïd (Nanterre: Center for Mythological Research, 1998), 47–84.

Detlev Fehling, *Herodotus and His Sources: Citation, Invention, Narrative Art*, trans. J. G. Howie (Leeds, UK: Francis Cairns, 1989), 179–84.

Robert L. Fowler, "Genealogical Thinking, Hesiod's *Catalogue,* and the Creation of the Hellenes," *Proceedings of the Cambridge Philological Society* 44 (1998): 1–19.

Christian Jacob, "L'ordre généalogique: Entre le mythe et l'histoire," in *Transcrire les mythologies: Tradition, écriture, historicité,* ed. Marcel Detienne (Paris: Albin Michel, 1994), 169–202.

Marshall D. Johnson, *The Purpose of the Biblical Genealogies, with Special Reference to the Setting of the Genealogies of Jesus,* 2d ed. (Cambridge: Cambridge University Press, 1988).

W. S. Kurz, "Luke 3:23–38 and Greco-Roman Biblical Genealogies," in *Luke-Acts: New Perspectives from the Society of Biblical Literature Seminar,* ed. Charles Talbert (New York: Crossroad, 1984), 169–87.

Rosalind Thomas, "Genealogy and the Genealogists," in *Greek and Roman Historiography,* ed. John Marincola (Oxford: Oxford University Press, 2011), 72–99.

CHAPTER FIVE

DIVINE CONCEPTION

Since myth as form was never questioned, ancient criticism varied
according to its content: to offer a more pious version of the mythical
gods or to transform the heroes into historical characters.
—*Paul Veyne*[1]

In one of the first attempts to compare Jesus with other ancient Mediterranean heroes, the philosopher Celsus (about 180 CE) pointed out that
Jesus was not alone in his divine conception. Ancient *mythoi* also attributed
a divine begetting to the Greek heroes Perseus, Amphion, Aeacus, and
Minos. Yet there were many others who demonstrated their divine origin
by their wondrous deeds and beneficent works.[2] Celsus even poked fun at
the Christian birth narrative, depicting it as a run-of-the-mill Mediterranean *mythos:* "Was Jesus's mother beautiful, and did god have sex with her
due to her beauty?"[3]

Since the days of Celsus, comparisons of divine conceptions have repeatedly run aground because they have attempted to make (or strongly
imply) genetic links between the divine birth of Jesus and other Mediterranean gods and heroes. In Greek mythology (so it is thought), divine conception is literal and common, whereas in Jewish lore, divine conception
is infrequent and figurative. Although the Israelite king (Ps. 2:7; 1 Sam.

7:14), collective Israel (Exod. 4:22; Deut. 14:1; Hos. 11:1), and the righteous man (Sir. 4:10; Wisd. 2:18) are all called "sons of god" in Jewish literature, this is usually understood in a figurative sense.[4] Thus many interpreters—and not a few critics of Christianity—have deduced that early Christians must have borrowed a tradition of divine conception from Greco-Roman sources, either as a result of their gradual Hellenization or in a rhetorical attempt to render their message more persuasive to Gentiles.

To do serious comparative work, however, one needs to go beyond both the search for genetic links (many of which are banal and impossible to prove) and the religiously motivated attempt to sever those links (ensuring that the divinely conceived Jesus is "unique"). It is not that the evangelists *borrowed* from the stories of Perseus, Heracles, or Minos to present their idea of divine conception. Stories of divine conception were culturally common coin in the ancient Mediterranean world and could be independently imagined and updated in distinct ways.

Gods Do Not Have Sex

The author of Luke expressed the "mechanics" of divine birth in subtle and culturally plausible language. In the passage commonly known as the "Annunciation" (Luke 1:26–38), the angel Gabriel announces to Mary that she will have a son. Then the young—but betrothed—girl asks a rather awkward question: "How will this be—since I do not know a man?" (1:34). Such a question puts a nervous smile on the face of the reader since it could function as an innocent prelude to "divine sex education." Gabriel is put in a bind, since he is now forced to explain to an adolescent girl exactly where divine babies come from. Thankfully, the author of Luke provides him with a tactful and poetically pleasing response:

> Sacred breath will come upon you,
> and power of the Most High will overshadow you;
>> and so the child to be born will be called "sacred,"
>> a son of god. (Luke 1:35)

Such delicate and seemingly indeterminate language allowed the author to present his narrative of Jesus's divine birth as plausible historiography.

He deliberately distanced himself from stories of sexually produced demigods that he, like other urbane members of his culture, deemed fantastical and unworthy of God.[5]

Luke's mythic historiography was widely appreciated in its time. Beginning in the early second century CE, Christian apologists extolled the nonsexual nature of Jesus's conception. The author of Luke shared with philosophers of his day a theological presupposition: God (or the gods) do not have sex, since sex involves passion (that is, emotional fluctuation), and passion is perceived to be an evil.

Celsus, as we have seen, based this supposition on a Platonic maxim: "By nature, God does not love [or feel sexual attraction for] a perishable body."[6] Accordingly, when in other ancient stories the gods are depicted as enjoying sexual intercourse, such accounts were perceived as mythical (*mythōdes*).

A witness to this attitude is the historian Dionysius of Halicarnassus (late first century BCE). Dionysius wrote that the historian Thucydides differed from early historians "by his exclusion of all mythical material and his refusal to make his history an instrument for deceiving and captivating the common people, as all his predecessors had done when they narrated stories about . . . the semidivine offspring of divine and mortal sex and other stories that appear unbelievable [*apistous*] and quite stupid [*anoēton*] in view of our life today [*tōi kath' hēmas biōi*]."[7]

Sharing this attitude, Christian apologists throughout the ages have differentiated Greek "mythical" accounts from their own mythistorical stories of divine conception. According to Justin Martyr, for instance, the Logos (that is, Jesus) was conceived "without sexual union." He later affirmed that the Logos was born "not through sexual intercourse but through power."[8] Justin's language of divine "power" (*dynamis*) directly recalls the language of the Lukan evangelist.

This evangelist's theologically tactful avoidance of sexual encounter did not mean that Jesus the divinely conceived hero was unique. The third evangelist was not the only author to adapt a mythic template to historiography. He was part of a broader cultural trend. As attitudes toward divine sex changed by the first century CE, so did stories told about divinely caused births.

Plutarch and Divine Conception

One such story we learn from Luke's contemporary, the biographer Plutarch. Significantly, Plutarch used similar language and a similar pattern of thought when he spoke of Plato's divine conception.[9] Careful comparison with Plutarch will indicate that the Lukan author was in accord with the sensibilities of contemporary writers who eschewed the anthropomorphism of divine-human sex.[10]

In Plutarch's dialogue *Table Talk*, Tyndares the Lacedaemonian remarks that fathering a child seems opposed to divine incorruptibility because it involves emotional and physical fluctuation in God.[11] This logic goes back to Plato's famous "rules" or "patterns" (*typoi*) for theology. The first rule is that God is good, and the second is that God does not change.[12]

Tyndares goes on to make a remark derived from Plato's dialogue the *Timaeus:* "I take courage when I hear Plato himself [say concerning] the father and maker of the world and other generated beings . . . [that these beings] do not come to be through semen, to be sure, but by another power of god, who engendered in matter the productive principle by which it [the world and the things made in it] suffered passion and changed."[13]

The language is careful—and for good reason. Plutarch wrote in his treatise *To the Unlearned Prince* (§5), "For it is neither probable nor fitting that God is, as some philosophers [namely, the Stoics] say, mingled with matter." Plutarch agreed with Celsus that the imperishable God did not love a perishable (female) body and could not be linked with it. Thus it is not God who directly interacted with matter—only God's power. God's power—a term used to defer God's unqualified presence—is made the means of his generative activity.

Plutarch illustrated the productivity of this "other power of God" by a quote from the poet Sophocles: "The crisscrossing of the winds escapes the notice of the hen, except when she lets fall a chick!" The idea here—popular in the ancient world—is that the hen is not made pregnant by male seed but by a more subtle power transmitted in or by the winds.[14] The word for "wind" that Plutarch used is *anemos*, whereas in his *Life of Numa*, he uses the more flexible term *pneuma* (wind/breath/spirit).

In the latter biography, Plutarch related the tradition that Numa (Rome's second king) enjoyed a "divine marriage" with the nymph Egeria.

Although as a biographer, Plutarch felt obliged to relate this story, as a Platonist and man of learning, he squirmed. He cringed to think that a woodland goddess would physically gratify herself with a human male. The truth of the story, he said, is that Numa's virtuous *soul* gave pleasure to Egeria. Nothing bodily was involved.[15]

Although Plutarch found it reasonable that God loves human beings and joins company with people who are good, holy, and self-controlled, he denied that a god would engage in sexual gratification with a human body, however lovely. Plutarch, in short, was uncomfortable with anthropomorphized gods having sex with mortal women. For him, such stories were not theologically correct and thus not credible. Speaking of divine conception in terms of *pneuma* was a philosophically respectable—because nonsexual—way of relating the reality of divine conception.

Plato Conceived

Plutarch's moral and theological sensibilities were formed by the (then widespread) philosophy of Platonism. Ironically, Platonists passed on a story that their own founder (Plato) was son of the god Apollo. Thus by a strange twist of fate, Platonists found themselves in this pickle: their founding father explicitly taught that deities (1) do not have uncontrolled emotions and (2) do not change. Sex involves radical emotional changes and other bodily fluctuations. A Platonic god, therefore, cannot have sex. Soon after Plato's death, however, his mother, Perictione, was coupled with Apollo.[16] In the face of this dilemma, Plutarch employed a rationalizing strategy mirrored in the gospel according to Luke: (1) he denied that Apollo actually had sex with Perictione, and (2) he argued that the deity caused the conception in a nonsexual way.

The mechanics of divine conception were relatively simple. No penetration and ejaculation were involved—only the pumping of divine "power" (*dynamis*) and "breath" (*pneuma*). The language is close to what one finds in Luke. It is "not impossible," Plutarch wrote, "for divine breath [*pneuma*] to approach a woman and engender certain productive principles." Elsewhere he remarked that it is "by a different power [*dynamis*] that God engendered in matter its productive principle."[17]

For the author of Luke, God's breath and power operated to produce Jesus. The angel tells Mary, "sacred breath [*pneuma*] will come upon you, and power [*dynamis*] of the Most High will overshadow you" (Luke 1:35). In this passage, "breath" (sometimes translated "spirit") and "power" are exactly the terms used by Plutarch. The usage of the terms is also similar: they are the means of divine conception. To conceive Jesus, Mary does not need to "know" a man, and God does not need to penetrate a woman (at least not like a man). For both the evangelist and Plutarch, sex has been rooted out of the story to make a *mythos* of divine conception fit the modes and codes of historiographical discourse.

Pneuma and Power

To be sure, the words "breath" and "power" do not forbid some kind of physical engagement between deity and a human female. In the ancient world, *pneuma* could cause pregnancy because it was widely thought to be the active element in semen. According to Aristotle, for instance, *pneuma* is the hot air in semen that makes it foam and turn white.[18] *Pneuma*, said Aristotle, contains *dynamis* and allows male semen to perform its generative function.[19] By using the terms *pneuma* and *dynamis* in the context of conception, Luke and Plutarch probably drew on the "scientific" resonance of these terms.

If divine breath was assumed to penetrate the mothers of Jesus and Plato, it did so like air seeping through their pores. In antiquity, the motion of air was felt to be a good analogy for how the divine comes into contact with a human female to make her pregnant.[20] Think of the wind fertilizing the chicken egg in Sophocles. Wind is invisible, but its effects are powerful. Moreover, wind is not anthropomorphic. It does not take any shape at all. Thus wind or breath cannot make contact with the human body in a sexual fashion. In this way, both Mary and Perictione (Plato's mother) could preserve their purity, and *mythoi* could assume the form of historiography.

Comparing Techniques

The author of Luke and Plutarch, as late first-century historians, evidently shared similar intellectual dispositions.[21] Accordingly, they rejected an anthropomorphic and sexual understanding of divine conception. Even so, they did not reject the *possibility* of such a conception for their respective heroes (Plato and Jesus).

Both authors apparently received their stories of divine conception from previous tradition. As creative writers, both probably improved on these traditions in order to make them theologically sophisticated, plausible, and seemingly "historical" to the cultured readers of their day.

This is not an argument that the evangelist "borrowed" from Plutarch or from other historicized Greek myths. The similarities between Luke and Plutarch are not due to a genetic link but to a shared intellectual culture. It was a common, culturally shaped set of theological conceptions that shaped what would be appropriate and plausible in a story of divine conception.

The third evangelist and Plutarch were also working with similar assumptions about *mythos* and historiography. For both authors, tales of anthropomorphic gods mating with human women could only be "mythical." (So, one might add, would stories about "sons of god" mating with human women in Genesis 6.)[22] Nevertheless, both authors crafted stories of divine begetting that are coded as "historiography" (an account of actual and believable events) as it was understood in the late first century CE.

What makes "historiography" is not "the facts" objectively recorded but a culturally informed framework of plausibility about what *could* happen. Although a few educated persons in the late first century CE might have believed that gods take on male bodies and ejaculate semen into female vaginas, it was more believable that a breath of god could "come upon" a woman in some subtle sense and by divine power create a child in her womb.

Despite these commonalities, the third evangelist and Plutarch exemplify different styles of engagement with Greek *mythoi*. Plutarch realized that there were elements in Greek *mythoi* that are hopelessly crude and unredeemable. To use his own words, sometimes "*mythos* brashly despises what is probable."[23] At other times it is useless and morally obscene.[24] Yet Plutarch did not for these reasons eschew all *mythoi*. Rather, he skillfully rationalized and moralized *mythoi* in line with his Platonic philosophy (which he considered to be the most ancient wisdom).

Plutarch assumed that truth is symbolically contained in many *mythoi*. He presented one of his characters in a dialogue say that even "what is mythic [*to mythōdes*] gropes in some fashion after truth."[25] With reference to Egyptian mythology (*mythologia*), Plutarch said that it contains "dim, faint effluvia of the truth." Nevertheless, one needs "a sleuth-like mind" to track down those truths, a mind "that can draw important conclusions from tiny scraps of evidence."[26] Plutarch himself was a model for these "sleuth-like" interpretations.

Plutarch never laid out a single theory for interpreting *mythoi*. In general, however, one can say that he did not take them at face value. Rather, he adopted from each "what is appropriate, on the principle of likeness."[27] In the *mythos* of Plato's divine conception, what is rationally and morally appropriate for Plutarch is that Plato was (and is) the son of god. Plato, as Plutarch emphasized, proved this by his wisdom and upright character.

The author of Luke, for his part, explicitly engaged not Greek but Hebrew myth. He skillfully used the stories of Sarah (Gen. 18:1–15, 21:1–7) and Hannah (2 Sam. 1–2)—among other Jewish texts—to weave together two tales of wondrous conception (those of Jesus and John the Baptist). John the Baptist—not Heracles or Perseus—was the evangelist's explicit parallel in his birth narratives (Luke 1–2), and Jesus both imitates and emulates his putative cousin John. Even with regard to divine conception without a human father (Luke 1:34–35), there is no direct allusion to Greek *mythoi*.

The evangelist's literary practice of evasion did not mean that he did not indirectly and subconsciously emulate Greek mythic templates. As an educated writer, he presumably had a general knowledge of the many stories of divine birth in Greek lore. Nevertheless, the refusal of the author of Luke to explicitly engage the Greek "other" underscores an important point: the author, who posed as a historian, was also a Christian apologist. Although he lived in a broadly Greco-Roman culture and was thus unable to escape its influence, for religious (and other) reasons he chose to identify with the stories and traditions of his Jewish subculture. For this author, even to gesture toward "Greek" stories in any direct way would have hindered his apologetic aim: to portray Jesus as the sole divine savior and fulfiller of Israel's Messianic expectations.

Conclusion

To sum up, stories of divine conception are widely conceived of as mythic, even from an ancient point of view. Such stories were viewed as inappropriately mythic if they involved gods having sex with mortal women. Yet divine conception remained theologically important to many authors. It was important because it allowed authors to ascribe a "real" ("genetically" based) divine status to their own cultural heroes. To make stories of divine conception plausible, they were "desexed" and presented in the form of mythic historiography. This practice can be witnessed in both the Lukan evangelist and Plutarch, contemporary authors who used similar language and ideas to present a *mythos* of divine conception in a culturally credible way.

Further Reading

Hans Dieter Betz, "Credibility and Credulity in Plutarch's Life of Numa Pompilius," in *Reading Religions in the Ancient World: Essays Presented to Robert McQueen Grant on His 90th Birthday,* ed. David Aune and Robin Darling Young (Leiden: Brill, 2007), 52–54.

Luc Brisson, *How Philosophers Saved Myths: Allegorical Interpretation and Classical Mythology,* trans. Catherin Tihanyi (Chicago: University of Chicago Press, 2004), 63–71.

John J. Collins, "The Sons of God and the Daughters of Men," in *Sacred Marriages: The Divine-Human Sexual Metaphor from Sumer to Early Christianity,* ed. Martti Nissinen and Risto Uro (Winona Lake, IN: Eisenbrauns, 2008), 259–74.

John Granger Cook, *The Interpretation of the New Testament in Greco-Roman Paganism* (Tübingen: Mohr Siebeck, 2000), 28–31.

P. R. Hardie, "Plutarch and the Interpretation of Myth," *Aufstieg und Niedergang der römischen Welt,* ed. Wolfgang Haase, 33:6 (1992): 4743–87.

Andrew T. Lincoln, "'Born of the Virgin Mary': Creedal Affirmation and Critical Reading," in *Christology and Scripture: Interdisciplinary Perspectives,* ed. Andrew T. Lincoln and Angus Paddison (London: T&T Clark, 2007), 84–103.

Gerd Lüdemann, *Virgin Birth? The Real Story of Mary and Her Son Jesus,* trans. John Bowden (Harrisburg, PA: Trinity, 1998).

Robert Miller, *Born Divine: The Births of Jesus and Other Sons of God* (Santa Rosa, CA: Polebridge, 2003).

Christopher Pelling, *Plutarch and History: Eighteen Studies* (Swansea, UK: Classical Press of Wales, 2002), 171–96.

Heikki Räisänen, "Begotten by the Holy Spirit," in *Sacred Marriages: The Divine-Human Sexual Metaphor from Sumer to Early Christianity,* ed. Martti Nissinen and Risto Uro (Winona Lake, IN: Eisenbrauns, 2008), 321–44.

Charles H. Talbert, "Jesus' Birth in Luke and the Nature of Religious Language," in *Reading Luke-Acts in Its Mediterranean Milieu,* ed. Charles H. Talbert (Leiden: Brill, 2003), 79–90.

Charles H. Talbert, "Miraculous Conceptions and Births in Mediterranean Antiquity," in *The Development of Christology during the First Hundred Years and Other Essays on Early Christian Christology* (Leiden: Brill, 2011), 161–70

Andrew Welburn, *Myth of the Nativity: The Virgin Birth Re-examined* (Edinburgh: Floris Books, 2006).

CHAPTER SIX

DREAM VISIONS AND PROPHECIES

Accepted myths soon cease to function as myths: they are asserted to be
historical facts or descriptive accounts of what "really happened."
—*Northrop Frye*[1]

In the ancient world, people widely assumed that dreams could provide information about the future and how to act in the world. The science of dream interpretation was a thriving business, as evinced by surviving handbooks (such as that by Artemidorus).[2] Typically gods would
send dreams through lesser divine beings (daimons or angels). These beings would appear, sometimes in the guise of trusted friends and family, to
communicate the divine will. Sometimes the communication was obscure,
but in other cases it could be quite direct. Gods who gave commands in
dreams expected to be obeyed.

The story of Titus Latinius is a good example. It was told, Cicero said,
"by all our historians."[3] Titus, as the story goes, was a Roman peasant.
One night, he dreamed that Jupiter, king of the gods, told him to enter the
great Senate chamber and demand that the Roman Games (an important
spectacle put on by the state) be restarted. The next day, Titus neglected
the command out of fear. The second night, the same command came

again in stricter terms. When Titus still did nothing, his son suddenly took ill and died. On the third night, Jupiter told Titus that heavier punishment awaited him if he disobeyed. When Titus still hesitated, he himself fell ill with a terrible disease. He then arranged to be brought into the Senate chamber on a litter to inform the heads of state. When he did so, he was instantly cured and walked out of the chamber whole.[4]

Dream Visions

Divinely sent dream visions also occur in gospel historiography. We focus on a story in the gospel of Matthew. Jesus's father, Joseph, seeing that Mary is pregnant under unknown circumstances, is about to divorce her. Yet in a dream during the night, he learns that the Jewish deity is the father of Mary's child. In this initial epiphany, an angel (or messenger) tells Joseph that the child will save his people from their sins. In a second dream vision, Joseph is warned to flee the wrath of a wicked king by traveling to Egypt. In yet a third vision some years later, he is told to return from Egypt and settle again in the land of Israel (Matt. 1:21, 2:13, 19). In each case, obedience is never a problem for Joseph. He directly and fearlessly obeys and in this manner highlights his piety.[5]

As it turns out, parents often dream of their child's wondrous destiny in mythic historiography. Plutarch reported the dream of Olympias, mother of Alexander the Great. She saw a lightning bolt strike her womb, kindling a conflagration that spread in all directions. Her husband, Philip, dreamed that he sealed his wife's womb with the image of a ferocious lion.[6] According to the historian Dio Cassius, the pregnant mother of the future emperor Augustus dreamed that her womb "was lifted to the heavens and spread out over all the earth." That same night, her husband, Octavius, had a vision in which the "sun rose from between her thighs."[7] A noblewoman of Miletus had a vision while giving birth: she saw the sun enter her mouth, pass through her abdomen, and exit her genitals.[8] The boy she delivered became a famous prophet of Apollo.[9] In these dreams, the power and brilliance of divine children is vividly foretold.

Plutarch in his *Table Talk* mentioned a vision that is said to have appeared to Ariston, Plato's father, in his sleep. The vision forbade him to have intercourse with his wife or touch her for ten months.[10] Plutarch did not himself vouch for this story but passed it on as tradition. He also related that Alexander's father, Philip, after his dream vision, did not touch his wife, Olympias, for the months before and after she conceived.[11] The author of Matthew narrated that after Joseph's initial dream vision, he did not touch Mary until she gave birth (Matt. 1:25). In these cases, the purpose of the motif is similar: to secure the purely divine origin of the child.[12]

According to the Jewish historian Josephus (contemporary of the evangelists), Amram, father of Moses, was addressed by the Jewish deity in a dream. Yahweh told Moses that his son would free the Hebrew people from oppression.[13] Such a dream never appears in the Bible, which makes it all the more significant. The mythology of Moses became a model for the Christian hero, as we will later see.

Greek heroes too were born to be saviors. In Hesiod's *Shield*, Zeus makes Alcmene pregnant for the express purpose of producing "a protector for gods and grain-eating men."[14] Heracles's role as protector (*alktēra*) is connected to his birth name, Alcides. Similarly, Jesus's name (*Jehoshua*) etymologically means "Yahweh saves."[15]

Prophecies

In mythic historiography, the divinely conceived child is often announced by prophecies. Mnesarchus, father of Pythagoras, learned from Apollo that his wife "would bring forth a son surpassing all who previously lived in beauty and wisdom and who would be the greatest benefit to the human race."[16] An angel tells Mary, "You will conceive in your womb and bear a son, and you will name him Jesus. He will be great, and will be called the son of the Most High" (Luke 1:31–32). The specific qualities of the child are culturally determined, but their greatness is in both cases divinely assured.

The Roman biographer Suetonius narrated a prophecy about the emperor Augustus. Augustus's mother, Atia, gave birth to the future emperor on September 23, 63 BCE. As a result of the birth, her husband, Octavian, was late arriving at the Senate house in Rome. On his way, he was met by a wise old senator called Nigidius Figulus.

Nigidius was a special figure in the late Roman Republic. He was, first of all, a respected politician. He apparently renewed the ancient philosophical sect of the Pythagoreans in Italy. Finally, he was reputed to be a diviner who foretold the future. His great interest in all forms of foreign wisdom predestined him to take on the guise of an eastern prophet. He wrote a work on the interpretation of dreams (only a fragment of which survives). Better attested is his work called *Sphere,* which told the *mythoi* associated with the zodiacal constellations. Cicero called Nigidius the "most learned and most holy of men."[17] The Roman poet Lucan (39–65 CE) represented him as foretelling the future from the stars.[18] The church father Jerome (347–420 CE) called Nigidius a *magos* (for the relevance of this title, see chapter 7).[19]

It was this Nigidius who met Augustus's father on his way to the Senate house. When he inquired about Octavian's tardiness, the latter explained that his son had just been delivered. When Nigidius learned the precise time of the child's birth, he shouted out before astounded witnesses, "the ruler of the world had been born!" Octavian, afraid that his son would grow up to overthrow the Roman Republic, planned to kill the child. (Romans who were true patriots were known to kill their sons to save their country—at least according to mythic historiography.)[20] Yet Nigidius dissuaded him, remarking that it was impossible for the child to evade his imperial fate.[21]

This story has several important points of contact with the presentation of Jesus in the gospel of Luke. When Jesus's parents are in Jerusalem, they offer the customary sacrifice at the temple. Suddenly an old man emerges from the shadows of the temple courts, scoops up the child from Mary's arms, and delivers a prophecy. He addresses the Jewish deity in a prayer heard by all: "Master, now you are dismissing your servant in peace . . . for my eyes have seen your salvation, which you have prepared in the presence of all peoples, a light for revelation to the Gentiles and for glory to your people Israel" (Luke 2:29–32).

Evidently the old prophet—called Simeon—had received a revelation that he would not die before he had seen the Messiah. The Jewish Messiah was no local potentate. Jews (in particular, Jewish Christians) believed that their king would rule the world. Indeed, Simeon's prophecy put the spotlight on the Gentiles, who made up "all peoples" besides the Jews. Jesus, like the Roman emperor, would be master of the civilized world.

How Simeon knew that Jesus was the Messiah is not stated. All that the text reveals is that a sacred spirit rested on Simeon (Luke 2:25). Simeon himself is not introduced beyond the remark that he was a man both righteous and devout. Was he a priest? A local holy man? Some sort of ascetic? The reader can only speculate. The important point is that he fits the type of "elderly prophetic sage" represented by Nigidius Figulus.[22]

Did these prophecies really occur as they were presented? Were two infants publicly proclaimed as world rulers before major public buildings in capital cities some sixty years apart? The historical details are tantalizing. In both accounts, the prophet is named, the prophecy occurs before many witnesses, and (as the narrative unfolds) the prophecy proves true. Nevertheless, the prophecy of a child's future greatness is a well-known mythological motif.

Take the example of the baby Heracles in Greek mythology. After this son of Zeus strangles two serpents in his crib, his father, Amphitryon, summons the old prophet Tiresias. This blind bard makes known that Heracles will kill many monsters in the "wild west" of the Mediterranean (as it existed in ancient times). When Heracles succeeds in civilizing the world, Tiresias announced, he will dwell "in uninterrupted peace for all time" and hold a "wedding feast at the side of Zeus."[23]

In a variant myth, Alcmene, Heracles's mother, is the one who hears Tiresias's prophecy. She bids the prophet foretell the outcome of the omen (the strangling of the serpents). Tiresias reassures her, telling her to lay up in her heart the better part of what is to come. Heracles will be famous throughout the world. Alcmene will be honored among women, who will sing songs of her in days to come.[24]

It is no surprise that in the wake of Mary's miraculous conception, she sings her famous Magnificat: "Surely, from now on all generations will call me blessed!" (Luke 1:48). The song is still sung in her honor, but the language of the hymn is not taken from any memoir. It is an adaptation of the Song of Hannah in Hebrew scripture (1 Sam. 2:1–10). Here we see an important pattern in Lukan mythmaking: the author used the language of Jewish historiography to reinforce the historical vibe of his tale.

The peculiar prophecy of Tiresias to Alcmene is formally similar to Simeon's private revelation to Mary. Yet a tragic aspect is added. Simeon addresses her: "This child is destined for the falling and the rising of many in Israel, and to be a sign that will be opposed so that the inner thoughts of many will be revealed—and a sword will pierce your own soul too" (Luke 2:34–35).

Mary, like Alcmene, is blessed with a private revelation beyond that given to her husband. As it turns out, both mothers will outlive their sons, watching them die horrifying deaths. Even as a child, Jesus would cause "great anxiety" in the heart of Mary (Luke 2:48). Yet her special knowledge about the nature of her son causes her to "treasure all these things in her heart" (Luke 2:51).

Such special knowledge is not unlike Plutarch's "historical" report about Olympias, mother of Alexander the Great. Before the young Alexander went forth on his expedition to conquer the world, his mother pulled him aside. As she kissed him good-bye, she revealed the secret of his divine birth—a secret known to no one else at the time. Alexander was not the son of King Philip (his so-called father) but of Zeus. Olympias bade Alexander to perform deeds worthy of his begetting.[25]

Plutarch, for his part, denied that Olympias had sex with Zeus to produce Alexander.[26] Yet he did not deny that Alexander had a divine origin. Such an origin was proved, at any rate, by Alexander's great deeds. Raging like wildfire, he conquered an empire stretching from Bulgaria to India.

Conclusion

We have here compared stories that occurred in what the ancients considered both "historical" (concerning Alexander, Augustus, Jesus) and "mythical" times (regarding Heracles). The Greek hero Heracles is clearly categorized as mythical—especially by modern people. Yet the mythological template exemplified by Heracles played out in the lives of figures still deemed historical: Alexander the Great, Caesar Augustus, and Jesus himself. When historiography follows a mythic pattern, however, it is no longer simply a record of past events. It is what we are calling mythic historiography.

By telling the stories of great heroes as mythic historiography, ancient authors made their stories recognizable and rhetorically effective in the minds of their audiences. As we have seen, the evangelists were no exception. They used the same mythistorical patterns to highlight the transcendent greatness of their hero, even while he was a tiny baby. Yet their practices best resemble those of ancient historians who wrote historical accounts reporting supposedly real events.

Further Reading

Adela Yarbro Collins, "Mark and His Readers: The Son of God among Greeks and Romans," *Harvard Theological Review* 93 (2000): 85–100.

David Engels, "Prodigies and Religious Propaganda: Seleucus and Augustus," in *Studies in Latin Literature and Roman Historiography XV,* ed. Carl Deroux (Brussels: Latomus, 2010), 153–77.

Robin S. Lorsch, "Augustus' Conception and the Heroic Tradition," *Latomus* 56 (1997): 790–99.

Gerald Mussies, "Joseph's Dream (Matt 1,18–23) and Comparable Stories," in *Text and Testimony: Essays on New Testament and Apocryphal Literature in Honour of A. F. Klijn,* ed. Tjitze Baarda (Kampen, Netherlands: J. H. Kok, 1988), 177–86.

Charles H. Talbert, "Prophecies of Future Greatness: The Contribution of Greco-Roman Biographies to an Understanding of Luke 1:5–4:15," in *The Divine Helmsman: Studies on God's Control of Human Events, Presented to Lou H. Silberman,* ed. James L. Crenshaw and Samuel Sandmel (New York: KTAV, 1980), 129–41.

CHAPTER SEVEN

MAGI AND THE STAR

> Some 130 years before the Star of Bethlehem led the Wise Men
> to assign the savior's role to another newborn, those hopes of
> salvation centered on Mithridates.
> —*Adrienne Mayor*[1]

In the month of December, a host of Christmas pageants and Nativity displays present the Magi standing serenely by Jesus's manger. There are typically three of them, one for each of their gifts (gold, frankincense, and myrrh). Sometimes they wear crowns and are girded with a faint aura of light. Their fellow worshipers are a host of uncouth shepherds and singing angels tightly crowded in and around a lowly stable.

In Matthew's gospel, the Magi appear without shepherds, angels, or animals at a house in which the infant Jesus is about two years old. They unexpectedly arrive from the east during the latter days of Herod the Great (ruled 37–4 BCE). They start asking bystanders in Jerusalem about the newly born king of the Jews. They claim that they learned of his birth from the appearance of his star in the east. Normally Gentile astrologers did not care about the birth of Jewish royalty. Yet this king was something more.

By inquiring about a newborn king, the mysterious Magi throw the city of Jerusalem into confusion. Talk of a new regent meant that the old one had to go. Getting wind of the news, King Herod of Judea is disturbed. He quickly gathers a council of priests and scribes to ask—as if it has occurred to him for the first time—where the Messiah is to be born. They give the location as Bethlehem, citing ancient Hebrew prophecy. For the priests and scribes, the question appears to be theoretical. They show no interest in actually going to see the Christ child themselves. Herod then summons the Magi again and extracts from them the exact time of the star's appearance. Smilingly, he sends them to Bethlehem, though he secretly plans the child's death.

When the Magi exit the court, the fabled star appears again. This time, it starts acting utterly bizarrely. It moves as a disk of light for about six miles (from Jerusalem to the town of Bethlehem) until it rests over the house where the child Jesus lies. With this wondrous escort, the Magi cannot contain their joy. They meet the child in his mother's arms, bow down to the ground, and offer him three treasures. That night, they have a dream that they interpret as a warning not to return to Herod. Somehow avoiding the king altogether, they return to their country unscathed.

In yet another dream, an angel warns Joseph, the boy's apparent father, to escape into Egypt. The family hastily packs up and flees. They slip out of town just as Herod's troops burst through the gates of the town with orders to systematically slaughter every infant two years old and under (Matt. 2:1–18).

The author of Matthew is the only gospel writer to tell this tragic tale, and his sources are unknown. Influence from the Balaam tale in the Hebrew Bible is possible, given that Balaam prophesies about a king symbolized by a star.[2] Yet the author of Matthew—who takes every opportunity to mention fulfilled prophecy—fails to mention this one. Balaam, moreover, was often portrayed in a poor light, as leading Israel into illicit sex and idolatry. None of these negative connotations attach to Matthew's Magi.

Who were these Magi? Despite the Christmas hymn "We Three Kings," they were almost certainly not royal. And although they were thought to be wise, they were far more than "wise men." The word "Magi" is the plural of the Greek word *magos*, which in Matthew's day could have the meaning of "magician" or "quack." Yet—to the surprise of many Christian commentators—the second evangelist assumes nothing negative about these Magi at all. The Magi are correct about the significance of the star and laudable for coming to worship the child.

The author of Matthew seems to have understood the term *magos* in its original sense as "hereditary Persian priest." The official religion of Persia at the time was Zoroastrianism. Thus it is probably correct to identify the Magi as Zoroastrians. Many educated Greek writers identified Zoroaster as the first *magos*.[3] All Magi to come were considered to be his disciples. As the Greeks interacted with Persian culture, they had many opportunities to observe the workings of the Magi. Favorable historians depicted them as skilled prophets, dream interpreters, enchanters, and exorcists.[4]

As Zoroastrian priests, the Magi would have had their own mythology. They may have believed in a mythical savior to come, called the Saošyant. This figure was a wonderful being, a king of righteousness destined to benefit the entire world. His coming was considered to be the prelude to the time of resurrection, the dawn of the future age introducing a glorious reign of justice and peace. According to Zoroastrian myth, the Saošyant was prophesied by Zoroaster as a child of his line yet destined to be born from a virgin.[5] How this exactly worked is a complex story (and not very much like Matthew's). Yet perhaps it is no mistake that Matthew presents a virgin-born savior.

Is the Saošyant myth relevant for the author of Matthew? Zoroastrian beliefs emerged long before the first century CE. To be sure, many of the written myths related to the Saošyant postdate the gospels. Still, credible scholars of Zoroastrianism affirm that the earliest forms of the Saošyant myth would have predated Matthew. Mary Boyce, for instance, comments, "Zoroaster himself appears to have taught the doctrine of a coming Saviour; and the legend that he was to be born miraculously of the prophet's seed was perhaps fostered by devout princes . . . in south-eastern Iran." The basic story of the Saošyant's birth must "have been evolved during the prehistoric period of the faith." In its "simple, most impressive form it became, with its message of hope, one of the most influential doctrines of Zoroastrianism, affecting, it seems, . . . Jews and Christians to the west."[6]

So why did the author of Matthew introduce Magi at Jesus's birth? One cannot know for certain. Yet if he knew that the Persians prophesied a coming savior born of a virgin, it was appropriate to introduce Persian priests (the Magi) in order to confirm that a Saošyant figure had indeed come—in the person of Jesus.

The Magi in Greek Myth

Yet our focus is on the mythic historiography of the Greeks. In this literature, Magi often appear at the birth of great kings. As well-known diviners, they are best qualified to prophesy the greatness of a future ruler. Herodotus seems to have initiated this literary trend. In the first book of his *Histories,* he tells about the birth of Cyrus, widely acknowledged to have been the greatest of Persian kings.[7]

Herodotus's story can be summarized as follows. One night, King Astyages, Cyrus's grandfather (ruled 585–550 BCE), had a dream. He dreamed that water (i.e., urine) flowed from the privates of his granddaughter and flooded the whole of Asia. Immediately he called in the Magi to interpret the dream. They informed him that his granddaughter would have a son who would replace Astyages as king. The king was terrified. Adding to the terror was a second dream. He dreamed that a vine sprouted from the vagina of his granddaughter and spread across all of Asia. Opening his eyes, Astyages exploded into action. He ordered his steward Harpagus to seize his granddaughter's newly born son and destroy him.[8]

Harpagus gave the child to a shepherd with the command to expose the infant on the mountains. As it turned out, the shepherd's wife had just given birth to a stillborn son. She took one teary look at the beautiful baby Cyrus and knew that she must claim the child as her own. It was she who convinced her husband to exchange the boys. The dead child was duly exposed. Harpagus sent his agents to verify that "Cyrus" was dead.

Ten years later, the young Cyrus was playing a pretend "game of thrones." Local boys in town made him the pretend king, and Cyrus appointed them his ministers and spies. Suddenly the game became serious. When a boy of noble birth would not obey Cyrus, Cyrus had him whipped. When the noble boy's father got wind of this, he hauled the young Cyrus into the presence of the real king, Astyages. Staring at Cyrus with eagle eyes, Astyages (quite miraculously) suspected Cyrus's true identity from his voice and features. When Harpagus and the boy's shepherd "father" were called in, the truth was slowly extracted. Astyages took revenge on Harpagus by murdering his son, cooking him, and secretly serving him up to Harpagus for dinner.

Then Astyages called in the very same Magi who appeared in his presence a decade before. When he questioned them about their prophecy, they claimed that—thankfully—it had been fulfilled in the boys' harmless game. Cyrus had been made king and would not be inaugurated a second time. Astyages was relieved, and Cyrus was spared.

In this case, however, the Magi's desire to please the king led to disaster. Cyrus was sent off to Persia. Several years later, he led the Persians in open revolt against Astyages. The government was overthrown, and Astyages was deposed. A new, conquering king had come.

With regard to narrative structure, Herodotus's story foreshadows a number of elements that appear in Matthew. The Magi inform the ruling king that a child to be born will soon replace him (Matt. 2:2). In order to prevent this, the terrified king orders the child to be killed (Matt. 2:3, 13). Nevertheless, the child miraculously escapes, leading the king to take terrible revenge, a revenge that results in the death of other children.

Yet for our purposes, the key point of similarity is this: the accounts are presented as historiography. Magi, if they had become stock characters, were considered to be real persons. The stories also mention real kings and genuine circumstantial details. Cyrus did lead the Persians in revolt, and Herod was worried about losing his kingship. For fear of being overthrown, Herod executed three of his own sons. The emperor Augustus once quipped that he would rather be Herod's pig (*huos*) than Herod's son (*huios*). (The joke is funny because Jews do not slaughter pigs.)[9] That Herod killed babies as well may not be historical, but it *sounded* enough like historiography to be accepted as true.

Magi appear in yet another biographical tradition. This one features a famous Greek king, Alexander the Great. According to Plutarch, the very night that Alexander was born, the temple of Artemis at Ephesus (on the west coast of modern Turkey) was burnt to ashes. Ruling Ephesus at the time were the Persians (heirs of Cyrus). Thus it is no surprise that Magi were present in the vicinity.

These Magi did not take the conflagration lightly. They were great prophets; and they ensured that all the people of the city knew what the burning foretold. At first light, the Magi ran amok in the streets, beating their faces, crying out that disaster was destined for Asia.[10] They understood the conflagration as a sign, a sign of a future king who would one day overrun the Asian continent with his destroying armies.

In this story, the Magi, as in Matthew's tale, throw a whole city into confusion. They know the future. They know that a great king of global significance has come. Unlike Matthew's story, however, the Magi do not go to worship the new king. Like Herod, they are terrified.

Perhaps it is significant, however, that the first-century CE Roman historian Quintus Curtius presented the Magi as joyfully welcoming the adult Alexander into the royal city of Babylon. According to this account, silver altars burned frankincense (one of the gifts of the Magi, according to Matt. 2:12) as the king entered with great fanfare on a caparisoned horse. The Magi chant a hymn before Alexander to welcome their new, foreign, lord.[11] They joyfully confirm his royal privilege, just as Matthew's Magi validate the infant Jesus.

These stories were meant to be read as historiography. From a modern perspective, however, they prove rather hard to believe. The contemporary reader, for instance, will doubt that the Magi of Herodotus and Plutarch could see the future victories of Cyrus and Alexander the Great. The same reader will doubt that Persian priests traveled cross-country to worship the son of a Jewish peasant girl.

Regardless of the current implausibility of Matthew's tale, its claims to historicity helped make plausible the evangelist's essentially theological point: that Jesus really was the universal king. He came not as a destroyer of nations but as a savior of the same mythic proportions as the Saošyant.

A Star in the East

According to the evangelist, the Magi learned of Jesus's birth by the appearance of a star. Matthew's Magi are not just stargazers; they are also astrologers (like Nigidius in the previous chapter). They study the stars and read in them events of world significance. In the first-century context, none of this is surprising. By this time, the Magi were widely associated with the art of astral interpretation.

From the perspective of modern historiography, the Babylonians (also called "Chaldeans") were the real founders of astrological science. Yet ever since Cyrus conquered Babylon (in 539 BCE), there had been continuous cultural interaction between the Magi and Babylonian astrologers. Thus the Magi had time to absorb the astrological learning of the Chaldeans. Starting as early as the fourth century BCE, Greeks failed strictly to distinguish the Magi and Chaldeans. Both were perceived as priestly personnel who dared to discern the future by various means, including the stars.[12]

In Herodotus's *Histories*, the Magi are already associated with the interpretation of heavenly bodies. On the march to attack Greece, King Xerxes of Persia is shocked by a solar eclipse. To interpret the sign, he calls in the Magi, who of course inform him that the sun has set for Greece.[13] According to Cicero, the Magi interpreted a dream of King Cyrus. In the dream, Cyrus saw the sun standing at the foot of his bed. He tried to grasp the sun three times before it swirled and faded away. The Magi accurately interpreted the dream to indicate that Cyrus would rule for thirty years.[14]

Matthew's Magi saw a star, and one that seems to have been real. But was there actually a star that appeared around 7–6 BCE (according to modern estimations of Jesus's birthday)? Despite the many attempts to identify the star as a supernova, a planetary conjunction, or the appearance of Halley's Comet, Matthew's star continues to defy modern astronomical explanations.

It was, after all, no ordinary star. The text of Matthew specifically says that this heavenly body was Jesus's own personal star. The Magi report, "we saw *his* star in the east" (Matt. 2:2). The star first appears in the east, then in the west (as if the people in the west did not initially see the star in the revolving heavens). In its second appearance, the star guides the Magi as if it were a lighted spaceship. It halts and hovers directly over the house where Jesus lay (Matt. 2:9). Unlike some modern science-fiction enthusiasts, one cannot claim that this star was a flying saucer. Our best tool for understanding it is to compare other mythic historiographies.

In this literature, strange stellar phenomena often signify regime change. The phenomenon means either that a new king is to be born or that another king is going to rule. Weird astral events were thus associated with coups—events that inspired real boldness among renegades and genuine terror in rulers.[15]

The historian Pompeius Trogus wrote his *Philippic History* during the reign of Augustus (late first century BCE). In his historiography, he wrote that a "long-haired star" appeared at the birth of Mithridates VI Eupator (120–63 BCE). Mithridates was king of Pontus, south of the Black Sea. He was an immensely powerful king who sponsored the last real threat to Rome in Asia Minor (modern Turkey). As a young king, Mithridates conquered the Roman lands in western Asia Minor. For a time, he even threatened Roman Greece, proclaiming himself deliverer of the east from Roman oppression.

At the time, many people of Pontus and Asia Minor were burdened by Roman taxation and greedy governors. Mithridates was a foreign king from the east; and many locals genuinely viewed him as their deliverer. They hoped that this foreign king would free them from an oppressive power. For a time, Mithridates's victories seemed to confirm that Providence was on his side.

To such a powerful king, a stellar sign was assigned both at the time of his birth and at the time of his accession to the throne. The epitome of Trogus's historiography states, "Even the heavenly bodies in their manifestation predicted his [Mithridates's] future greatness. For in both the year in which he was born and in the year in which he began to reign, a long-haired star shone for seventy days, so that the entire sky seemed to blaze. In its greatness, it filled a quarter of the heavens, and with its brilliance it outshone the sun."[16]

Here again, this star—brighter than the sun—is no normal stellar phenomenon. Modern astronomers, whatever their ingenuity, will always fail to find a star that can fill a quarter of the heavens. It is far too bright to be plausible to modern sensibilities—but apparently not to ancient ones. We are not told how bright the star in Matthew was. It is no mistake, however, that in early Christian reception, it also outshone the sun.[17]

The chronological references in Trogus's account amplify the impression of historicity. The duration of Mithridates's star (seventy days) must have been similar to the duration of Matthew's. The Magi, tracing the star, had to travel all the way from Persia (modern Iran) to Judea (modern Israel). Such a trek would have taken several weeks. The fact that Matthew's star could move across the sky might have led some ancient interpreters to view it as another "long-haired star"—known to moderns as a comet.

Comets were widely recognized in the ancient world as harbingers of the future. According to a Hermetic text (dated anytime between the first and the third centuries CE), "Comets are appointed to become manifest as messengers and heralds of events with worldwide significance. They occupy the place below the circle of the sun. They appear when something is about to happen in the cosmos. After appearing for a few days, they return again below the circle of the sun and remain invisible. Some appear in the east, some in the north, some in the west, and some in the south. We call them 'foretellers of the future.'"[18]

Origen of Alexandria, a third-century CE Christian theologian, thought that Matthew's star was a comet. He was eager to add, however, that the comet signified good things to come, not calamities.[19] Yet if the star signified regime change, whether it was good or evil was, of course, a matter of perception.

Matthew's star had a strange feature. After the Magi visited Herod, the star is said to "go in advance" (*proagō*) of them and stop right above the house where Jesus lay (Matt. 2:9). Here modern biblical commentators balk. Even those who claim that Matthew's star represents a historical memory begin to rationalize the star when it starts moving like a spaceship. From the viewpoint of modern astronomy, no star or comet could be perceived as close enough to zoom over a particular country, let alone a small house. Stars, even supposing that they can move like modern drones, are so many millions of light-years away that they could never align themselves over a particular object on earth.

Yet one must attend to ancient, not modern, standards of plausibility. In ancient historiography, astral phenomena can act very much like Matthew's star. Josephus spoke of a sword-shaped star that hung over Jerusalem before the city was conquered in 70 CE. It was joined, Josephus added, by a comet that ominously flew over the city for a whole year.[20] These astronomical phenomena are strictly speaking impossible from a modern point of view. A comet cannot fly over a single city, and the length of its appearance now seems unrealistic. Still, there is little doubt that Josephus presented these phenomena as historical events that presaged the city's doom.

Josephus is not the only historian to report fantastical astral events. Two other ancient historians, Diodorus of Sicily and Plutarch, made reference to the so-called Torch of Timoleon. This star, said to resemble a fiery torch, "led the way"—the same verb used in Matthew—for the famous Corinthian general Timoleon around 344 BCE. At the time, Timoleon was sailing by night in a small armada from Corcyra to southern Italy.[21] Plutarch wrote that the star not only accompanied Timoleon's ships but also darted down like a meteor on precisely that part of Italy where the ships were meant to land.[22] This heavenly body was taken to signify divine help for Timoleon, as well as his future fame and glory. And the star did not lie. Timoleon went on to defeat his enemies in war and to become master of nearly all Sicily.

Now Josephus, Plutarch, and Diodorus are all well-known historical writers around the time the gospels were written. There is no doubt that their reports were meant to be taken as descriptions of past events. One should conclude no less in the case of Matthew's star. Comparison with contemporary texts indicates that this star story fell within the bounds of historiography. Today, the registers of plausibility have changed, making it reasonable to reclassify the gospel story as myth.

This reclassification is due not only to the tale's astronomical impossibilities but also to parallels in what is now called ancient mythology. For instance, Vergil's story of Aeneas and his flight from Troy is today classified by nearly everyone as a myth. It is unclear that Aeneas ever existed, and even if he did, it is hard to believe that his mother was the goddess Venus.

Yet there is a significant detail in the mythology of Aeneas that resembles Matthew's star story. According to Varro, a Roman scholar of the first century BCE, the star of Venus (representing the goddess herself) guided her son every day until he traveled from Troy to Italy. Aeneas came from the east, and he moved—along with his star—in a westward direction. Evidently, the hero could look up into the night sky and see Venus guiding him toward his promised land. When Aeneas finally reached Italy, the star miraculously disappeared.[23]

Here we are dealing with what moderns—including modern Christians—would call "myth." The star of Venus (in antiquity, the planets were called "wandering stars") does not (or does not consistently) move westward in the night sky, and it does not disappear as a result of human events. Yet those who were invested in the *mythos* of the moving star (in this case, the Roman historian Varro) apparently presented it as historiography. Today, those who have no cultural investment in the story are prone to read it as myth.

A remark of Servius, famous commentator on Vergil's *Aeneid,* is telling. Servius said that Vergil knew Varro's version of the Aeneas myth. Vergil knew, in other words, that the star of Venus guided Aeneas on his journey. Nevertheless, according to Servius, Vergil did not speak of Aeneas guided by the star because this version of the story sounded too historical (*ne aperte ponat historiam*)! Vergil omitted the guiding star because he was not writing historiography but epic poetry (what moderns would call "myth").[24]

These examples indicate that the perceived differences between myth and historiography are themselves historically conditioned. It is a matter of perception; and throughout time, perceptions of plausibility change. As a result, classifications of what counts as myth and historiography alter.

Perceptions of plausibility also fluctuate according to the expertise of the audience. What is acceptable to a popular audience (past and present) will not be acceptable to an astronomer (ancient and modern). Yet most readers of Matthew's moving star are not astronomers, so there is less of a hindrance to belief.

Modern astronomers will probably discount a story about a drone-like star. Or, if they wish to make Matthew's *mythos* seem more like historiography, they throw out the part about the star hovering over the house. Yet such historicization is wrongheaded, since the evangelist knew nothing of modern astronomy. What is plausible to this author and his contemporaries will not always be convincing to contemporary educated readers. In the end, it seems that nothing in the gospel story fell outside the boundaries of ancient mythic historiography.

Conclusion

What is the point of a mythic story made to look like (ancient) historiography? Here it is helpful to read the star of Matthew and the star of Mithridates "in conjunction." According to the gospels of both Matthew and Mithridates, the miraculous star signified regime change. More specifically, it foretold the reign of a glorious savior-king. The reaction to the star was (and is) predicated on one's relation to the coming king. The incumbent tyrants of the time—such as Herod, Rome's puppet king—feared it. But those who expected a deliverer—such as later Christians and those oppressed by Rome—exceedingly rejoiced.

Thus to persist with the question "Did these miraculous stars actually appear in the night sky thousands of years ago?" is to mistake ancient mythic historiography for modern historiography. A more interesting question is why these mythic stars appeared on the pages of texts made to look like historiography. The stars appeared to magnify particular kings. They were brilliant signs of a savior's future greatness. Historically speaking, the greatness of the kings in question was known only *after* their deeds were done and their lives lived. It is unlikely, then, that these stars ever shone in the night sky. What is more important is their shining in the imagination of those who still long for liberation.

Further Reading

Roger David Aus, "The Magi at the Birth of Cyrus and the Magi at Jesus's Birth in Matt 2:1–12," in *Religion, Literature, and Society in Ancient Israel, Formative Christianity, and Judaism* (Lanham, MD: University Press of America, 1987), 97–114.

Jan N. Bremmer, "Persian *Magoi* and the Birth of the Term 'Magic,'" in *Greek Religion and Culture, the Bible and the Ancient Near East*, Jerusalem Studies in Religion and Culture 8 (Leiden: Brill, 2008), 235–48.

Nicola Denzey, "A New Star on the Horizon: Astral Christologies and Stellar Debates in Early Christian Discourse," in *Prayer, Magic and the Stars in the Ancient and Late Antique World*, ed. Scott B. Noegel, Joel Thomas Walker, and Brandon M. Wheeler (University Park: Pennsylvania State University Press, 2003), 207–21.

John R. Hinnels, "Zoroastrian Influence on the Judaeo-Christian Tradition," *Journal of the K. R. Cama Oriental Institute* 45 (1976): 1–23.

Anders Hultgård, "The Magi and the Star—the Persian Background in Texts and Iconography," in *"Being Religious and Living through the Eyes": Studies in Religious Iconography and Iconology*, ed. Peter Schalk, Acta Universitatis Upsaliensis 14 (Uppsala: Uppsala University Library, 1998), 215–26.

Roy Kotansky, "The Star of the Magi: Lore and Science," *Annali di storia dell'esegesi* 24 (2007): 379–421.

Gerard Mussies, "Some Astrological Presuppositions of Matthew 2: Oriental, Classical and Rabbinical Parallels," in *Aspects of Religious Contact and Conflict in the Ancient World*, ed. Pieter Willem van der Horst (Utrecht: University of Utrecht, 1995), 25–44.

CHAPTER EIGHT

CHILD IN DANGER, CHILD OF WONDER

> Let fiction written for pleasure be close to the truth so that
> your fable not demand belief for just anything it desires.
> —*Horace*[1]

After telling the story of the star, the author of Matthew lifts the curtain on a new scene. King Herod, duped by the Magi, is red-faced in fury. This king, according to Matthew, is not the rightful ruler of the Jews but an illegitimate upstart. The upstart then tries to kill his infant rival. From the Magi, Herod knows the time frame of the Messiah's birth; from the Jewish scribes, he learns the place: Bethlehem. To Bethlehem, Herod launches a battalion to slaughter its infants. Thankfully, Joseph had already been warned in a dream to flee to Egypt. Such is the presentation of the political "facts."

At the end of the story, Matthew reveals that his "historiography" of Jesus is based on a mythic model: Israel's flight to and from Egypt. It was Joseph in Hebrew mythology who first came to Egypt, sold as a slave by his brothers. Joseph's entrance into Egypt paved the way for the holy family of Israel to escape there. In Egypt, Israel grew from a family of seventy into a body of two million souls. The people would return, a mature nation, to its homeland in the days of Moses.

This is what the prophet referred to: "Out of Egypt I called my son" (Matt. 2:15, quoting Hos. 11:1). All Israel is God's son, but the author of Matthew found in this text a different meaning. For him the special son of God was the Messiah, Jesus. It was fitting for the Messiah to recapitulate the mythology of Israel: first the holy seed goes into Egypt for protection and growth, then it is delivered out of it.

Jesus's life thus recapitulates the mythic history of Israel. This recapitulation is the product not of empirical historiography but of the evangelist's deliberate design. No other early evangelist refers to Jesus's flight into or out of Egypt. The gospel of Luke contradicts it. According to this text, Jesus's birth in Bethlehem was followed by a visit to Jerusalem and a quiet return to Nazareth. No maniacal king killed the babies in Bethlehem. If such a chilling event had occurred, other historians (not to mention the other evangelists) would have paraded it as an example of Herod's cruelty and the divine protection of Jesus.[2]

Perseus

Yet Jesus was not the first child to be put in danger from a fearful king. According to Greek lore, Perseus was the son of the high God Zeus and the mortal Danae. Perseus's grandfather, King Acrisius, learns from the oracle at Delphi that his grandson (Perseus) will one day kill him.[3] In an effort to prevent the pregnancy, Acrisius hides away his daughter in an underground vault. But the will of Zeus is not blocked. Danae miraculously becomes pregnant after being soaked with golden rain.

Away in hiding, Danae gives birth without her father's knowledge. But it is hard to hide a crying baby—especially in a brazen echo chamber. The king finds out. Thinking that Danae has been deflowered by some suitor, Acrisius orders a small ark (or coffin-shaped box) to be constructed. This done, he sees to it that baby Perseus and his mother are sealed into it and dumped into the Aegean Sea. But lo and behold, the coffin bobs over the waves, floats off, and is eventually caught in the net of a fisherman. The fisherman brings both mother and child to an island, where Perseus is raised in safety.

Augustus

Modern readers classify Perseus's fantastic birth story as myth. Yet a similar account appears in a work of ancient historiography. The historian in this case is the Syrian-born author Julius Marathus; and its transmitter is the learned biographer Suetonius.

Suetonius's biography of the emperor Augustus (sole rule 31 BCE–14 CE) is known for its thorough research, detail, and abundance of documentation. Suetonius had read Augustus's private correspondence, his autobiography, his will, and many other records reported in archives and by other historians. One of these was Julius Marathus, the freed slave of Augustus and his recordkeeper. As the former slave of Augustus, Marathus had detailed knowledge of his master, such as his exact height.[4]

According to Marathus, there was a public portent that appeared months before the birth of Augustus. Suetonius did not transmit its content. It could have been a shooting star, a shower of blood, a lamb born with a pig's head, and so on. Whatever it was, the portent was formally reported to the Senate, and the interpreters of portents (or *haruspices*) were asked to offer their interpretation. These interpreters proclaimed that "Nature" was about to bear a king for the Roman people.

This was shocking news. Hundreds of years prior to this, the Romans had driven out their kings. Roman aristocrats, who hated royalty, reconstituted the government as a republic. In this republic, the Senate ruled and chose two of its own members to serve as annual leaders. The system worked for centuries. But if "Nature" was now providing a king, this prized system of government would be overturned.

The terrified Senate thus took extreme measures. It issued a decree that forbade the rearing of any male child for an entire year. The effects of this decree would have been as tragic as Herod's slaughter of the infants. Parents throughout Italy would have been forced to kill their own children or let them starve.

Nevertheless, a group of senators whose wives were expecting babies blocked the decree by a simple measure. They saw to it that the decree was never filed at the Treasury building. This intentional oversight prevented the measure from becoming law. In this way, Augustus—deliverer and future king of Rome—was saved.[5]

Julius Marathus (and Suetonius) told this story with the apparent intention that it be understood as describing real events. There is nothing in it that is strictly speaking impossible from a modern point of view. Even if one detects some obvious propaganda for the Julian family, the ancient reader would have classified this story as a historical report.

Romulus and Remus

Yet this very story of Augustus is probably based on a mythic model, that of Romulus and Remus, twin founders of Rome. The mother of these twins was a woman by the name of Rhea Silvia. As in the myth of Perseus, Rhea Silvia had been impregnated by a divine being—in this case, the war god Mars. The father of Rhea Silvia was Numitor. Numitor had been deprived of his kingdom by his brother Amulius. Amulius then tried to ensure that no heir of Numitor could take the throne.

Thus when Rhea Silvia bore twins, the wicked Amulius ordered them to be exposed in some desolate place. They were left in a basket by a swollen river, which soon picked them up and carried them to a safer shore. There the boys were fed by a she-wolf's teats and a woodpecker that brought morsels of food in its beak. Some writers historicized the myth by saying that the "she-wolf" was actually a loose woman called Acca Larentia. It was Acca Larentia and her woodland husband, named Woodpecker, who supposedly raised the child.[6]

Moses

Matthew's myth of the infant Jesus in danger appeals to a specifically Jewish model: the infant Moses's escape from the hands of Pharaoh. The myth is told in the biblical book of Exodus. Yet Josephus, the Jewish historian, adapted Moses's myth at roughly the same time that the author of Matthew wrote. Josephus was attempting to package the Hebrew *mythos* for a Greek and Roman audience. In so doing, he not only added additional Jewish traditions but made sure that the whole story was imbued with a realism fit for historical discourse.

According to Josephus, a sacred scribe of Egypt announced to Pharaoh that a boy (Moses) would be born who would "abase the sovereignty of the Egyptians."[7] Josephus did not explain how the sacred scribe made his prophecy, but the historian Diodorus notes that Egyptian royal personnel often prophesied using astrology.[8] In later rabbinic tradition, the prophets who advise Pharaoh about the child to be born are explicitly said to be astrologers (recall the Magi in chapter 7).[9]

Josephus's Pharaoh is not amused. Since he cannot identify the baby who will be the savior, he decrees that all Israelite male babies be sunk into the Nile River. The decree causes obvious panic and despair among the Hebrews. The father of Moses, a man by the name of Amram, is petrified because his wife is pregnant. Broken with grief, he prays to Israel's deity for help.

That night, Amram has a dream. The Hebrew god reveals to him the exalted destiny of his child. Moses will earn three accolades: he will exceed all other people in virtue, deliver Israel from the tyrant, and be remembered for all time.

Given the assurances of this dream, Amram feeds and protects the child who is born. Yet after three months, Amram decides to entrust him to the Lord's care. He sends baby Moses out into the Nile bobbing in a bulrush crib. Providentially, the child is picked up and adopted by Pharaoh's own daughter, here called Thermouthis.

Thermouthis, after making arrangements for a wet nurse (Moses's own mother), decides to adopt the baby as her own. Some months later, she brings baby Moses to Pharaoh, proud that she now can provide him with an heir. Pharaoh gives the child a tender hug and—to please his daughter—puts his cloth diadem on the child's head. Yet as toddlers sometimes do, the young Moses acts up: he removes the crown, lets it fall to the ground, and treads on it.

At that moment, there is a heard a scream. Its author is the sacred scribe who once predicted the appearance of a Hebrew deliverer. He now shouts that the deliverer is here, being dandled on the knees of Pharaoh himself. The scribe urges the immediate execution of the child, who is quickly scooped up and protected by Thermouthis.

In this story, Pharaoh is a tyrant but is more benign than Herod. The real enemy is Pharaoh's sacred scribe, who plays a more assertive role than the Jewish priests and scribes who advise Herod. These officials know the truth about the Messiah, though they fail to worship him. They are guilty of neglect, not murder. Josephus's sacred scribe uses his own prophetic powers to recognize Moses and comes near to murdering the child himself.

Despite the dissimilarity, basic structural parallels recur in the stories of Moses and Jesus. There is a prophecy about a royal child, a wicked king, priestly (and prophetic) personnel, an attempt to kill the child (sometimes involving the deaths of other children), a father's prophetic dream (only in Josephus and Matthew), a divinely engineered escape, and the child's return to fulfill prophecy.

Beyond these overlaps in content is the form of the story according to Josephus and the Matthean evangelist: these authors both desired their accounts to sound historically plausible. Josephus explicitly used the tropes of historical discourse to rewrite biblical mythology. The author of Matthew was admittedly less refined. At the same time, if we use Josephus's story of Moses as a gauge for what would be considered historically plausible in the late first century, nothing that the evangelist wrote about his infant Christ is intrinsically incredible. After all, credibility is established by coherence with other similar beliefs that are culturally and historically defined.

Does ancient historical credibility translate into modern historical believability? Not usually; but it partially depends on whether the interpreter is a believer or a scholar. Those who are both sometimes try to find a middle way. Raymond Brown, for instance, was a famous twentieth-century Roman Catholic commentator on the infancy narratives. He remarked that the "simplest explanation" for Matthew's story about the child in danger is that it records "factual history."[10]

As a scholar, however, Brown asserted that there are "serious reasons for thinking that the flight to Egypt and the massacre at Bethlehem may not be historical."[11] He concluded, as a kind of compromise, that "Matthew did not draw upon an account of historical events but rewrote a pre-Matthean narrative associating the birth of Jesus, son of Joseph, with the patriarch Joseph and the birth of Moses."[12]

Importantly, Brown recognized that Matthew's story has the virtue of verisimilitude. Herod was recognized, especially at the end of his life, as a power-hungry tyrant who killed his own sons in cold blood. Josephus reported that Herod, in order to receive mourning at his funeral, instructed his soldiers to kill noble political prisoners immediately after he died. This act would ensure that many a tear would fall at Herod's funeral—even if not for Herod himself.[13] Thus an ancient reader could imagine Herod killing innocent people for political purposes.

Egypt, moreover, was a standard place of refuge for people fleeing the tyranny of kings in Palestine. In Jewish lore, Jeroboam fled to Egypt to escape Solomon (1 Kings 11:40). Uriah fled before King Jehoiakim (Jer. 26:21). The Jewish high priest Onias IV fled to Egypt to escape King Antiochus Epiphanes.[14] Josephus incorporated all these flights to Egypt into his lengthy history called *Jewish Antiquities*.

The flight of Jeroboam is especially significant as Matthew's mythistorical model. To translate the Septuagintal version of 1 Kings 11:40, "And Solomon sought to execute Jeroboam. Thus he arose and fled to Egypt . . . and was there in Egypt until Solomon died." There are fairly strong verbal overlaps with Matthew 2:13–15: "[An angel speaks:] 'Herod is going to search for the child to destroy it.' He [Joseph] got up, took the child and its mother . . . and took refuge in Egypt. He was there until the death of Herod." Once again, the language of biblical historiography fosters the historical feel of the account.

In short, fantastical stories could be written and rewritten as historiography in the late first century CE. The historical cast of the *mythoi* helped to validate them. If Jewish authors did not attempt to present their stories as historical fact, they could be dismissed by a typical educated reader. Admittedly, a Gentile reader unfamiliar with Jewish historiography might still dismiss or think lightly of fantastic elements in the stories there discussed. But many of these same fantastic elements—and some even more fantastic—appeared in Greco-Roman historiography.

The message of the story, validated in part by its historiographical form, is a message about the Jewish deity and his providence. Despite initial danger to Yahweh's son, he is divinely protected. The prophecies given by human and divine messengers prove true. The destiny of the child, despite terrible opposition, is fulfilled: he returns to his kingdom. The child's initial triumph over his political enemies foreshadows still greater victories to come.

Childhood Precocity

Once the heroic child survives the wrath of the king, he has a chance to prove his precocity. Jesus is no exception to this rule. According to the gospel of Luke, the twelve-year-old Jesus astounds the elders and priests at the temple with his wisdom and knowledge of Jewish Law. The scene is set at a festival. Jesus's parents had taken him up to Jerusalem. On the journey back, they thought he was in the caravan. But they were wrong. Rushing back to Jerusalem, his parents anxiously searched for him in the crowded city. Jesus was lost for three days without family and presumably without food.

Where did his parents finally find him? Exactly where they would have found him as an adult. He was in the temple "sitting among the teachers, listening to them and asking them questions." In this scene, Jesus the questioner quickly morphs into Jesus the teacher, answering the inquiries of men who spent their lives studying Jewish Law. "And all who heard him were amazed at his understanding and his answers" (Luke 2:46–47). The precocity of this child is presented as historiography, but virtually all the elements of the story grow out of type scenes familiar in mythic historiography.

Cyrus

At the age of twelve, Cyrus the Persian displayed his wisdom at court. He was to be the greatest Persian conqueror and king. Thus it was logical for him to reveal his royal nature when young. He learned faster than his peers and performed his duties like a grown man. In terms of the Greek heroic ideal, a conqueror does not waste his time on luxuries. Thus Cyrus chastised his grandfather Astyages for eating dainties and getting drunk with his courtiers. A king administers justice. Cyrus was such a model of righteousness that he judged lawsuits even as a young boy.

A king is also judged by his wisdom and native intelligence. Cyrus's "rich love of learning was such that he always inquired from every one he met the explanation of things. He himself was asked questions by others on account of his intelligence, and he answered with alacrity." In being such a "know-it-all," the boy did not act arrogantly. Rather, he was simple and warmhearted to those with whom he conversed.[15]

Thus we have Cyrus at the same age as Jesus, admonishing his elders, asking them questions, and responding to theirs. He is not arrogant but humble; and his show of curiosity veils a great intelligence within. The author of Cyrus's childhood saga is no poet or playwright but the famous Greek historian Xenophon (about 430–354 BCE).[16]

Alexander the Great

Plutarch tells a similar story about the Macedonian prince Alexander the Great. On one occasion, Persian envoys came on a visit to the Macedonian court. Alexander's father, King Philip, was away on a mission. Accordingly Alexander, a boy no older than twelve, entertained the envoys himself. Although there was bad blood between Greece and Persia (Persia had invaded Greece a century before), the young Alexander became familiar with the Persians and treated them as friends.

Yet the boy was shrewd. Instead of asking the envoys trivial questions about the famous golden vine of Persia, the hanging gardens, and the king's royal robes, Alexander was already thinking about strategy. He inquired precisely about the details of their journey, the best road to the capital of Persia, and the Persian king's ability to make war. Not more than ten years later, Alexander would burst into Asia, putting to flight the Persian king and taking over his magnificent capital. In the story, however, the Persian envoys could not have known this. Instead of being offended, they were tickled with astonishment, admiring the boy's eagerness and thirst to accomplish great things.[17]

Augustus

As a young boy, the future emperor Augustus impressed his elders by delivering a funeral oration for his grandmother Julia.[18] It occurred at the rostra, the speakers' platform in the heart of Rome. The crowds that heard the oration were astonished by Augustus's abilities, and the public memory of the speech lasted for over a century.[19] Suetonius said that Augustus gave the speech at age twelve. Writing during the lifetime of Augustus, Nicolaus of Damascus (64–4 BCE) reported that Augustus spoke the oration around age nine. At this tender age, Nicolaus wrote, "Augustus produced no small astonishment among the Romans by manifesting the superiority of his nature."[20]

When Augustus was around fourteen, another sign of future greatness happened at the Latin festival. By custom, the magistrates of the city spent the holiday at the Alban Mount offering a special sacrifice. Therefore the priests of the city took it upon themselves to administer justice. A year or so prior to this occasion, Augustus had been made a priest of the Roman gods. In this capacity, or possibly as temporary governor of the city, Augustus took his seat in the massive judge's chair, which the Greeks called the *bēma*. It was a perfect picture of Augustus's future role as supreme judge. Dozens of people came up to him to receive judgment in their individual cases. Some people, however, had no case to offer. They arrived simply for the chance of viewing the wondrous boy make judgments in all his splendor. The likelihood of this report is minimal by modern standards. It may have been exaggerated from real events. Yet the important point is that Nicolaus presented it as any other event in the life of Augustus.

Nicolaus also wove a short story that illustrated Augustus's special relationship with his mother. The great-uncle of Augustus, Julius Caesar, had just successfully campaigned in Europe and Egypt. He was now setting forth for North Africa, where opposing generals had gathered in civil war. As a lad around fifteen, the future Augustus was eager to accompany Caesar in order to learn the rules and strategies of war. Yet when he perceived that his mother, Atia, was against it, the future emperor obediently held his peace and remained behind.[21]

This story is worth comparing with the little vignette describing Jesus and his mother. After she discovers him sitting in the temple, Mary asks in exasperation, "Child, why have you treated us like this? Look, your father and I have been searching for you in great anxiety." The boy Jesus responds with honest surprise. He says to them, "Why were you searching for me? Did you not know that I must be in my father's house?" Jesus's parents did not fully grasp that he was calling the Jewish deity his father. The divine child was not attempting to be rebellious. He followed his parents to Nazareth "and was obedient to them." Like Augustus, Jesus was no problem child but a dutiful son.

Jewish Examples

The myth of childhood precocity was something of a biographical trope. It is no surprise, then, that Jewish heroes begin to conform to the pattern. Josephus asserted that Samuel, the last of the Judges in Hebrew mythology, started prophesying at age twelve.[22] The Septuagint indicates that Solomon ascended his throne when he was twelve years of age (3 Kingdoms 2:12). Philo of Alexandria (first century CE) wrote that the young Moses excelled his teachers, devising and propounding problems not easily solved. What Moses learned was mostly self-taught or at least self-motivated, and the learning resulted in the perfection of his soul.[23] Josephus remarked that Moses's growth in understanding outstripped his physical maturation. Even in childhood games, Moses displayed his moral and intellectual superiority. Like Cyrus, Moses gave promise of greater deeds to come.[24]

The wonder-child convention was so widespread that Josephus applied it to himself. "While still a mere boy, about fourteen years old," he wrote, "I won universal applause for my love of letters; insomuch that the chief priests and the leading men of the city used constantly to come to me for precise information on some particular point in our [Jewish] ordinances."[25] With regard to local color, Josephus's story of self-praise strongly resembles Luke's account of the boy Jesus in the temple. That even the chief priests needed to consult an adolescent on points of Jewish Law might indicate either the surprising ignorance of these priests or the unsurprising vaunt of Josephus. What it really indicates is Josephus's use of a type scene, the child sage, depicted as a historical event.

Conclusion

What is the point of the wonder-child template? Perhaps one point is that heroes are great not so much by nurture as by nature. They begin as wise and virtuous and gain superhuman knowledge often with no imposed education required. The child's natural talent is a sign, in many cases, of his or her superhuman status.

As is typical in hero myths, the child grows at an incredible pace. Jesus matures so quickly, in fact, that his entire adolescence was summed up in a single sentence. "And Jesus increased in wisdom and in years, and in divine and human favor" (Luke 2:52). This sentence is an adaptation of one in the Hebrew Bible: "Now the boy Samuel continued to grow both in stature and in favor with Yahweh and with the people" (1 Sam. 2:26). Jesus's increase in wisdom may be influenced by the Greek biographical tradition. Wisdom is the characteristic attribute of the mythic Solomon, yet it is only in Greek literature that Solomon's wisdom blossoms at a young age (Wisdom 7:1–22).

The wisdom of the wonder child is such that it never needs to grow. Within the child is hidden the mind of a grown-up. Even as an adolescent, the hero is a mini-adult fully formed in character, ready to fulfill the prophecies spoken at birth. Yet even though the wonder child is certainly fantastic, none of the stories recounted here fall outside the bounds of ancient historiography.

Further Reading

Bradley S. Billings, "'At the Age of 12': The Boy Jesus in the Temple (Luke 2:41–52), the Emperor Augustus, and the Social Setting of the Third Gospel," *Journal of Theological Studies* 60 (2009): 70–89.

John Dominic Crossan, "The Infancy and Youth of the Messiah," in *The Search for Jesus,* ed. Hershel Shanks (Washington, DC: Biblical Archaeology Society, 1994), 59–81.

Henk J. de Jonge, "Sonship, Worship, Infancy: Luke II.41–51a," *New Testament Studies* 24 (1978): 317–54.

R. T. France, "Herod and the Children of Bethlehem," *Novum Testamentum* 21 (1979): 98–120.

John J. Kilgallen, "Luke 2:41–52: Foreshadowing of Jesus, Teacher," *Biblica* 66 (1985): 553–59.

Robert Miller, *Born Divine: The Births of Jesus and Other Sons of God* (Santa Rosa, CA: Polebridge, 2003).

CHAPTER NINE

THE RIGHTEOUS LAWGIVER

History is very close to poets and is rather like a poem in prose.
— *Quintilian*[1]

The gospel of Matthew's narrative of the adult Jesus is complex, combining aspects of Jewish kingship mythology, the lives of prophets and martyrs, and portraits of famous lawgivers. To manage the material, I focus on the author's portrayal of Jesus as a righteous lawgiver.

When Matthew's gospel was written, there were in fact many lawgivers revered throughout the Mediterranean world. Solon of Athens comes to mind, as well as Lycurgus of Sparta and Numa, Rome's second king. Some Greeks would have included Zoroaster from Persia and Minos of Crete, together with Charondas and Zaleucus from southern Italy.[2]

These lawgivers (several of whom were also kings and priests) are all fictional to some degree. (Even in the ancient world it was doubted whether Zaleucus ever existed.)[3] All of them, at any rate, follow distinct mythic patterns. Most of them are of noble blood. That is, they are outfitted with good genealogies (see chapter 4). They grow up in a state riddled with conflict. Going abroad for their education, they become disciples of the greatest teachers. By means of their native excellence, they come to power, hand down laws inspired by a deity, and restore social order. Often the lawgiver undergoes the ungrateful backlash of the people; sometimes he is banished or goes into voluntary exile. In the end—usually after the lawgiver's death—he receives vindication and, frequently, divine honors as a founder figure.

The life of Jesus in Matthew both conforms to and diverges from this mythic template. As we saw, this evangelist supplies Jesus with the best of genealogies. Yet Jesus's education is completely passed over. Jesus certainly does not go abroad (Jesus is only an infant in Egypt), and none of his teachers is ever mentioned. Probably the author of Matthew was trying to underscore the divine character of his hero, who transcended human needs for training. Jesus's laws were not a matter of human learning; they were the authoritative words of a deity.

Let us dwell for a moment on the theme of divine inspiration. It is customary for the heroic lawgiver to receive his legislation from a deity. According to Diodorus of Sicily, the Egyptian lawgiver Mneves claimed to have received his laws from the god Hermes (equated with the Egyptian Thoth). Minos received his laws from Zeus, Zaleucus from Athena, Zoroaster from the Good Spirit (or Agathos Daimon), Zalmoxis from Hestia (goddess of the hearth), Moses from Iao (the Greek form of Yahweh), and Lycurgus from Apollo.[4] It is said that Minos received his laws from the high deity on a certain mountain. Minos disappeared into a cave in this mountain throughout the course of nine years.[5] His story resembles that of Moses, who vanished into the clouds above Mount Sinai. Forty days later, Moses came back bearing tablets written with the divine finger.

Lycurgus's laws were inspired in a different way. According to Herodotus, Lycurgus entered the temple of Apollo at Delphi. There he was greeted by the Pythia (the priestess of Apollo) as "beloved of Zeus." Speaking under Apollo's inspiration, the Pythia asked Lycurgus whether he should be addressed as a man or a god. Apollo himself considered Lycurgus to be a deity and through prophecies paved the way for his postmortem worship.[6]

Sometimes the divinity of the lawgiver is emphasized to such an extent that he can administer laws in his own person. Zalmoxis, for instance, is said to have lived as a man among the Getae (a Thracian tribe living in what is now northern Bulgaria) and later to have been elevated to divine status.[7] As a divine being in his own right, Zalmoxis proffered sacred laws to his people.

Possibly the author of Matthew wanted his readers to intuit that Jesus was this sort of being. The people are amazed that Jesus has such wisdom and that he speaks with such authority (Matt. 13:54). One of Jesus's most famous sayings is, "You have heard it was said [by Yahweh through Moses] . . . but I say to you" (Matt. 5:22, 28, 32). Here it would seem that Jesus is speaking as a deity himself. Apart from this assumption, it is difficult to understand how Jesus can so easily correct the confessedly eternal legislation of Moses (Matt. 5:18).

Moses is indeed Matthew's most direct model for the lawgiving Jesus. According to Josephus, Moses came from a prominent Levite family (the family of Jewish priests). He was then adopted by Pharaoh's daughter— giving him the highest possible pedigree. He grew up when his own people were oppressed by their Egyptian overlords. After killing an Egyptian taskmaster, Moses went into exile to Arabia. He returned to deliver his people from slavery and to create a new society centered on a deity of desert and mountain. Despite these bold deeds, the Israelites muttered against Moses. Yet the lawgiver was vindicated by abundant miracles and died duly lamented. In short, the biographical tradition of Moses as it was told in the first century CE conforms to well-known mythic patterns.[8]

By no means does the author of Matthew slavishly adhere to the Mosaic or any other pattern to depict Jesus as a lawgiver. Like any good artist, the gospel writer picks and chooses what suits him from his models. To be sure, the author was strongly motivated to depict Jesus as fulfilling Messianic prophecy. One of these prophecies indicated that the Messiah would be a prophet like Moses (Deut. 18:15). The evangelist was systematically motivated to conform his character to the model of the Hebrew lawgiver—if only to surpass him.

Today, historians are unsure whether Moses, like many other famous lawgivers, ever lived. Outside the Bible and sources dependent on it, Moses never appears prior to the Hellenistic period (starting in 323 BCE). The writings ascribed to him (the first five books of the Bible) do not actually claim to be written by Moses. And since the last of these books contains a report of Moses's death in the past tense, he would have had to be resurrected to write it. Since the nineteenth century, all five "books of Moses" have been pulled into different sources and assigned to periods hundreds of years after Moses was thought to have lived.

If famous lawgivers such as Moses, Lycurgus, and Numa were mythic figures, their lives were historicized in Roman imperial times. Eventually, their biographies came to serve as political foundation myths. The biography of Moses, for instance, is inextricably bound up with the founding *mythos* of Israel. Much the same can be said of the Spartan Lycurgus and the Roman Numa. The laws attributed to these men functioned as the "constitutions" for the societies that claimed them. Those who set up the constitutions were thought to found or refound the state. Those who founded the state were often considered heroes—divine or semidivine beings who were worshiped by their respective nations.

Matthew's story of Moses was already to some degree Hellenized (that is to say, fitted to the modes and codes of Greek thought). The Alexandrian writer Philo is a good witness of this process. He wrote his *Life of Moses* some fifty years before the gospel of Matthew. Naturally, Philo's primary source was the Pentateuch in the Septuagint. But Philo transformed the story. He affirmed, for instance, that Moses had a good Greek education in which he learned music, math, and astronomy. This material does not derive from Exodus, where Moses himself implies that he received none of the rhetorical training so important to the Greeks (Exod. 4:10). It is, moreover, deeply anachronistic—for presumably Moses lived long before Greek education was invented. The point is that Philo presented Moses as a distinctively Greek hero. To emphasize that Moses received the best (Greek) education, Philo was (at least here) willing to be heedless of chronology.

We observe similar chronological squirming in Plutarch, who suggested a link between the traditions of Numa (commonly assigned to the eighth century BCE) and one of the fountainheads of Greek wisdom, Pythagoras (late sixth century BCE).[9] Other historians were prepared to say outright that Numa was a disciple of Pythagoras.[10]

Although the men were two centuries apart, there were certain political motivations for allowing their acquaintance to stand. At least one Roman family (the Aemilii) took pride in descending from a son of Pythagoras.[11] At the beginning of the third century BCE, a bronze statue of Pythagoras was set up in the most prominent place of the Roman Forum.[12] One of the most famous Latin poems of the era, the *Annales* of Ennius, began with reference to transmigration—a staple Pythagorean doctrine.[13] In short, Romans took pride in Pythagoreanism and to some degree considered it to be their native (Italic) philosophy.[14] This point of pride was all the more confirmed if Numa was Pythagorean or foreshadowed Pythagorean principles.

When it comes to depicting the lawgiver's character, moreover, the strategies of Plutarch and Philo were close. Philo celebrated Moses's self-control, rejection of luxury, and aptitude for philosophy. Plutarch's Numa had precisely these traits.[15] There were other ways in which Moses was Hellenized. One Jewish author living in Egypt presented Moses as the Greek deity Hermes—or rather the culture hero who would later be deified as the god Hermes (the Egyptian Thoth).[16]

The point is that what served as Matthew's model for Jesus was not strictly Jewish as we conceive of Judaism today. He was Hellenized; and this Hellenized Moses was adapted and historicized to resemble other Greco-Roman lawgivers as they were conceived centuries prior to Jesus.

Yet Moses was not the only model. When Jesus fails to resemble Moses, he sometimes appears like a Greek or Roman lawgiver. For example, Jesus differs from Moses on the issue of writing. Moses inscribed his laws on stone, whereas Jesus wrote nothing. (The "commands" that Jesus spoke were all written by later authors.)

In this respect, Jesus resembles the Spartan lawgiver Lycurgus. Lycurgus himself wrote no laws. Instead, he gave the Spartans what was called the "Great *Rhētra*," or the Great Oral Commandment. Lycurgus brought the Great *Rhētra* back to Sparta as the word of the god Apollo. Only later were Spartan laws collected and written down by those who inherited the mantle of Lycurgus.

Due to the way the gospels were recorded, it will always remain disputed what exactly Jesus said. Yet the development of certain core sayings into long discourses—such as we find in Matthew's Sermon on the Mount—is a general pattern we see among biographers. Sayings of the lawgivers were collected, expanded, and organized to make up a coherent "constitution" for a developing community. From Exodus to Numbers, for instance, Moses's speeches are fairly short and to the point. But almost the entire book of Deuteronomy (over thirty chapters) is depicted as a long speech of Moses spoken on the eve of his death. Iamblichus collected a whole series of Pythagorean teachings and presented them as introductory speeches given to different sectors of the population (namely, men, boys, and women).[17]

Still, if Moses was not the only model, he was the evangelist's main model for the mythistorical Jesus. We have already seen Matthew's imitation of Moses in the infancy narratives. As a baby, Jesus is saved from the hands of a wicked king, just as the infant Moses is spared from Pharaoh. Both Moses and Jesus go into exile. They do not return until the murderous king dies. The report of the king's death comes wondrously in both cases. Moses gets word through a burning bush. Jesus's father is informed in a dream. As a result, both Moses and Jesus are divinely recalled from their exile.

There is more. Before Jesus's ministry begins, he undergoes a time of testing in the desert. The period specified is forty days, analogous to the forty years Moses spent in the desert, a time of testing for the Israelite nation. Moreover, the calling of both Moses and Jesus involves a symbolic vision of the divine. Moses sees the Hebrew deity (or his angelic instantiation) in flame. Jesus sees a dove alight on his head. Both visions are accompanied by a disembodied divine voice. During Jesus's commission, he becomes God's son; Moses is appointed "a god" to Pharaoh (Exod. 7:1; Matt. 3:17).

Moses chose twelve tribal leaders (Num. 1:4–17), while Jesus chose twelve disciples (Matt. 10:1–4). The tribal leaders are specifically named individuals, as are Jesus's disciples. Moses sent the twelve leaders into the land of Israel to survey and to spy on it (Deut. 1:22–23). Jesus sent out twelve disciples to tell the good news specifically to Israel (Matt. 10:5–7). The twelve tribal leaders were rulers who governed their tribes. Jesus promised his disciples that they would sit on twelve thrones, ruling the twelve tribes of Israel (Matt. 19:28).

The historian Diodorus observed that Moses chose the number twelve because it equaled the number of months in the year. Philo said something similar: "Twelve is the perfect number, . . . the paths of the sun attest to this. For it completes its circuit in twelve months."[18] Already in the fourth century BCE, Plato had mandated that his ideal legislator apportion both the land and the people of his ideal state into twelve parts.[19] The number twelve was a symbolic figure that appealed to both Greek and Jewish authors. These authors do not typically suppose that the symbolic number indicates the mythic nature of the account. Rather, they assume that their "historical" hero knew the symbolic number and used it to good effect.

The author of Matthew presents Jesus delivering a sermon on a mountain in imitation of Moses delivering the Law from Mount Sinai. The mountain setting is unique to Matthew; in the gospel of Luke, Jesus speaks a similar sermon on a plain (Luke 6:17). Moses fasts for forty days before he receives the Law on the mountain. Jesus fasts for forty days before he speaks the Sermon on the Mount. Notice the precision of the imitation. Jesus is said to sit on the mountain (Matt. 5:1), just as Moses sits on Mount Sinai (*yāšab;* Deut. 9:9). Yet there is also emulation: Moses must receive his law from God on a mountain; Jesus delivers the law as if he were God (or a god).

Even after a superficial reading, Jesus's sermon strongly resembles the long, admonishing discourses that Moses speaks in Deuteronomy. At the same time, Matthew's Jesus regularly takes the opportunity to correct Moses (or the contemporary interpretation of Moses's teachings). Moses, for instance, instituted the rule of an eye for an eye and a tooth for a tooth (Exod. 21:24). Matthew's Jesus recommends that if your attacker throws the first punch, let him strike twice (Matt. 5:39).

A story of Lycurgus the Spartan is worth comparing here. When a mob attacked him in the marketplace, Lycurgus sprinted toward a place of refuge. Nearing safety, he whirled round only to have his eye knocked out by the staff of a young pursuer. When Lycurgus appeared before the people half blind and streaming with blood, they delivered the offender into his hands. Instead of exacting punishment, however, Lycurgus invited the reckless youth into his house and taught him the way of virtue.

Here we see a highly respected lawgiver who quite literally refused to take an eye for an eye. One might speculate that the author of Matthew knew this story about Lycurgus.[20] Yet even if had never heard of the Spartan hero, he would have known what laws sounded most virtuous and humane to the people of his time. All this was in the interests of making Jesus and his law code seem more credible and applicable.[21] Jesus was fitted to the times of a new historical era in which ancient barbaric punishments were no longer culturally acceptable.

Conclusion

Jesus the lawgiver closely follows mythic templates. The templates were both Greek and Jewish, though the Jewish templates were typically Hellenized. During the time of Matthew, Jewish, Greek, and Roman historians competed with each other to depict the most plausible (i.e., historical) law-giver and founder. Plutarch wrote on Numa and Lycurgus, Aristoxenus and Apollonius wrote on Pythagoras, while Philo and Josephus wrote on Moses. The author of Matthew, in turn, wrote about his hero, Jesus. In each case, historians and biographers used mythic templates and seem-ingly historical details to make their works both memorable and plausible. In our terms, these authors wrote mythical historiographies. And they were not just rhetorical exercises. These documents proved both useful and beneficial for those who looked back to divine lawgivers as real per-sons who founded their communities and their whole way of life.

Further Reading

Dale Allison, *The New Moses: A Matthean Typology* (Minneapolis: Fortress, 1993).

J. C. Edmondson, Steve Mason, and J. B. Rives, *Flavius Josephus and Flavian Rome* (Oxford: Oxford University Press, 2005).

Gerard B. Lavery, "Training, Trade, and Trickery: Three Lawgivers in Plutarch," *Classical World* 67 (1974): 369–81.

Thomas Römer, "Moses, the Royal Lawgiver," in *Remembering Biblical Figures in the Late Persian and Early Hellenistic Periods: Social Memory and Imagination*, ed. Diana V. Edelman and Ehud Ben Zvi (Oxford: Oxford University Press, 2013), 81–94.

Andrew Szegedy-Maszak, "Legends of the Greek Lawgivers," *Greek, Roman and Byzantine Studies* 19 (1978): 199–209.

CHAPTER TEN

MIRACLES

> Something extraordinary, therefore, does not occur contrary to
> nature, but contrary to what is known in nature.
> —*Augustine*[1]

For most modern readers, a miracle is by definition mythic (something wondrous and fantastical). It has no secure place in historiography, because in modern historiography, gods and superhuman agents cannot normally break into the chain of human events. Yet not everyone lives in so disenchanted a universe—and certainly not the peoples of the ancient Mediterranean world. Miracles are wonders, to be sure, but wonders do happen—or at least people so believe. Wonders are not impossible "by nature"—for "nature," too, is a construct governed by the structures of current knowledge and plausibility.

Miracles are better defined by their inexplicability. Aristotle observed that what is inexplicable (*to alogon*) is the peculiar means of conveying the wondrous (*to thaumaston*).[2] Valerius Maximus, a first-century CE Roman author, said something similar: "Since it is hard to discern where [strange events] started to circulate or for what reason, they are rightly called 'wonders' [*miracula*]."[3] Stefan Alkier formulates a modern version of this notion: "The miraculous represents a break in the binary logic of the everyday experience. It is an aspect of reality that resists all the worldly explanations that cannot think something really new, truly contingent, creatively creative."[4]

There are plausible and implausible ways of relating miracles. Swimming out of a flash flood can qualify as a "miracle" in colloquial English. Yet if someone relates that an angel came and picked a person out of the flood, the account typically breaches historiographical discourse. In the ancient world, plausible miracles could parade as historical; implausible ones were often labeled "mythical" (*mythōdes*).

Some miracles were too fabulous to believe, such as the huge snake that impregnated Alexander the Great's mother. The story that the Pamphylian Sea receded before Alexander's army, however, was apparently credited. According to historical report, Alexander's entire army in all their heavy equipment passed through a sea channel that would have normally drowned them. This account was first told by Callisthenes of Olynthus, official historian of Alexander's campaign and an apparent eyewitness of the event. Callisthenes assimilated Alexander to Poseidon by writing that the Pamphylian Sea "did not fail to recognize its lord, so that arching itself and bowing, it seemed to do obeisance [to Alexander]."[5]

Josephus mentioned the Pamphylian Sea miracle to make plausible his historiographical account of Moses parting the Red Sea.[6] He knew that qualified and respected historians presented Alexander's sea miracle as historiography.[7] He even remarked that "all" historians agreed that the sea made a path for Alexander's army.[8] Thus Josephus felt justified in presenting his own (Jewish) sea miracle as an actual event in the past.

There was another important development that affected the registers of plausibility. To a certain degree, Christians pushed back against the Palaephatean principle of uniformity (see the introduction). The principle of uniformity states, most basically, that all events must have happened as events do today. Not everyone has a doctorate in physics, but we know how things normally occur. A cat might learn to swim but not fly. One can take the unexpected only so far before if falls outside the bounds of believability and the mind cries "foul!" Therefore, if a historian was going to describe an event that is abnormal or fantastic, there had to be a good reason.

The historian Diodorus offered such a reason in his *Library of History*. He lamented that the magnitude of Heracles's deeds made them unbelievable to most readers of his day. Yet judging the deeds of Heracles by the works done "in our times" (*en tois kath' hēmas chronois*) was to use, Diodorus urged, an unfair standard (*ou dikaiai . . . krisei*). Heracles lived in an age before the Trojan War and was the greatest of heroes. Consequently, he was stronger than men are today, and the greatness of his deeds should not be diminished by people's incredulity.[9]

It was a historical judgment that in the so-called heroic age, men were bigger, faster, and stronger than people are today. They were also more pious, which earned them the right of dining with deities and even (as in the case of Heracles) being changed into them. Today one can label the heroic age a "mythic" one, but for the Greeks it was a real time in the past that gradually melted into our own time with its known dates and calendars.[10]

Christians too advertised their own mythic age. This age was not one in the distant past but one recently dawned. Christians called it the "Kingdom of God"; and modern scholars typically refer to it as "the eschatological age" or simply "the eschaton." The eschaton is no less a mythic age than the age of heroes. The difference is that Christians thought that they lived in the eschaton and invited other people to imagine—and live—the same reality. In this final age, miracles gained a kind of acceptability since they were signs that the new time of the Kingdom had arrived. This notion modified what early Christians were willing to believe about reported wonders.

At the same time, the gospel narration of miracles did not veer into utter fancy. Jesus walks over the sea; he does not fly over it with a cape. He heals people by word, not by magic formulas and mind melds. The daimons that fly into pigs remain invisible, without horns, pointy beards, or pitchforks. The characters in the miracle story remain lifelike, and miracles are represented as responses to real human needs. By depicting the lamentable infirmities that demand the miracle, the stories remained anchored in a reality that corresponds to the unpredictability of "normal" human experience. The point of the miracle story, one might say, is to bring readers out of the gritty normality of their own space and time into the new "reality" of mythic time. Yet to accomplish this transition, the gospel writers still had to represent "real life," in which tragedies and disappointments were expected and nature ran its course. The evangelists, in short, still sought to authenticate their miracle stories by narrating them in the larger context of "real" (quotidian) human events.[11]

Walking on Water

A good example of a miracle framed by realistic narration is Jesus's walking on water. At the time the gospels were written, superhuman water travelers were well known in Greek lore. The Greek god Hermes, outfitted with super-sandals, was said to whizz over water like a seabird. The Homeric poet describes him: "At once he [Hermes] bound beneath his feet his beautiful sandals, immortal, golden, which bore him over the waters of the sea and over the boundless land swift as the blasts of the wind. . . . On to Pieria [in northeastern Greece] he stepped from the upper air, and swooped down upon the sea, and then sped over the waves like a bird, the cormorant, which in quest of fish over the frightening gulfs of the unresting sea wets its thick plumage in the salt water. In such fashion did Hermes convey himself over the multitudinous waves."[12]

Other gods, including the Jewish deity Yahweh, rode over the sea in huge chariots (Habakkuk 3:15). Yahweh's chariot was pulled by water-stomping horses. The chariots of Poseidon and Triton (Greek sea deities) were pulled by massive sea-horses (horse legs in front, fish tails in back).

Still other heroes and demigods such as Atalanta and Camilla could run so swiftly that they did not sink as they ran over water.[13] Similarly swift was the Argonaut Euphemus (son of the sea god Poseidon), who "was wont to skim the swell of the gray sea, and wetted not his swift feet, but just dipping the tips of his toes was borne on the watery path."[14] The giant hunter Orion, another son of Poseidon, was not known for speed. Still, he was given the gift of "striding upon the waves as upon the ground."[15] The text is clear that Orion (as a giant) did not simply move his feet along the sea floor but actually walked over the waves.[16] The same is true of Abaris, whom we met in chapter 3, since he also walked on the surface of water (*eph' hydatos badizonta*).[17]

These heroes, giants, and demigods would still have been widely viewed as historical persons even if they lived in ancient times. What is strange about Jesus is not so much that he walked on water but that he performed this feat so recently! The earliest known version of the wonder I translate here:

> When evening came, the boat [of the disciples] was out on the sea, and he [Jesus] was alone on the land. When he saw that they were straining at

the oars against an adverse wind, he came towards them early in the fourth watch of the night, walking on the sea. He intended to pass them by. But when they saw him walking on the sea, they thought it was a ghost and cried out; for they all saw him and were terrified. But immediately he spoke to them and said, "Take heart, it is I; do not be afraid." Then he got into the boat with them and the wind ceased—and they were utterly astounded. (Mark 6:47–51)

The feat is impressive; yet amid the whipping wind and mist-like shadows, a sense of realism remains. Jesus is not a giant whose legs stretch to the bottom of the sea. He has no super-sandals or chariot. He does not run like the wind. In fact, he seems to walk over the water rather slowly, with an air of divine authority. His feet appear to float on the water. Or perhaps the reader is meant to assume that Jesus hovered slightly over the surf. This might explain, at any rate, why the disciples thought that he was a ghost.[18]

Jesus's water-walking also occurs at a precise time (the fourth watch of the night)—as if it were based on historical memory.[19] Yet the seeming memory is probably motivated by a previous *mythos*. The fourth watch—or very early morning—is also when Yahweh acted against the Egyptians at the Red Sea (Exod. 14:24). In this episode, Yahweh demonstrated his dominance over the sea by splitting it and letting it crash back down on the Egyptians.

In ancient Hebrew myth, the sea was personified as an enemy. The ancient Phoenicians (Semitic neighbors to the north of Israel) called the sea "Prince Yam."[20] In Job 9:8, Yahweh strides over the sea; yet the text can also be understood to mean that he tread on the back of Yam, the deity called "Sea." In Job 38:8–11, Yahweh defeats "Sea" in battle and wraps him in a cloud like an infant in diapers.

Note the contrast in Mark. The author granted Jesus the water-surmounting powers of Yahweh. Yet the openly mythological images are played down. Sea is not personified. Jesus does not split the sea or trample it like a dragon or dash over it with a chariot. He walks on it like a human would walk on dry land. Despite the wonder of water travel itself, the realism is consistent. Jesus has a motive for crossing the sea, and he does so nonchalantly, without pageantry. The author of Mark evidently wanted the sea miracle to be read as a historical event, on par with Jesus talking and climbing into the boat.[21]

Additional cues of historiographical discourse are evident. The evangelist twice mentioned that Jesus's disciples saw Jesus walking on water and emphasized that all (*pantes*) of them saw him (Mark 6:49–50). The writer of Matthew, for his part, included an episode in which Peter walked out on the water toward Jesus (Matt. 14:27–31). By adding this tale, Matthew put the spotlight on an eyewitness who could vividly remember the details of the event. The author of John suppressed the Markan detail that Jesus was a ghost. He evidently wanted the story to seem even more real not as a vision of terrified sailors subject to night visions. The fourth gospel also includes the particular distance that the boat traveled (twenty-five or thirty stades, which is about three miles; John 6:16–21). The precise detail gives the impression that the story occurred in measurable space.[22]

Water-Walking Heracles

For a contemporary example of historicization, we turn to the Latin writer Seneca. Seneca was a philosopher and playwright who flourished shortly before the gospels were written. He was privileged to have the finest education anyone could desire in the ancient world and was recognized as a gifted writer even in his own day. Seneca wrote his play *Hercules Gone Mad* (*Hercules Furens*) in partial imitation of a similar play written by the famous Greek playwright Euripides.[23] As a Stoic philosopher, Seneca was trained to rationalize myths, and the myth of Heracles was no exception.

According to traditional accounts, when Heracles was on his way to take the cattle of Geryon (or, alternatively, to pick the golden apples of the Hesperides), he had to cross the sea. Crossing the straits of the Mediterranean put the hero into desperate straits. In Heracles's time, boat travel had only just been invented. The first boat (the *Argo*) had set sail but recently. In fact, Heracles had been a sailor on the *Argo* but was forced to abandon the voyage early in order to search for his lost friend. Now on the other side of the Mediterranean, Heracles had to take another voyage across the sea—but without a vessel.

In earlier versions of the story, it seems, Heracles fought Helios (the Sun) and won from him a gigantic golden cup or *kylix*.[24] By riding in this gigantic chalice, Heracles crossed the sea. Hence in Greek artwork one sometimes sees Heracles bobbing on the sea in a shiny yellow bowl. By the first century BCE, this fabulous story had already been rationalized. Diodorus of Sicily presented Heracles as traveling by fleet.[25] Servius, a fourth-century commentator, says that the "bronze pot" in which Heracles sailed was actually a sturdy ship fortified with bronze (*navem fortem et aere munitam*).[26] Seneca has Heracles ply his path by regular ship.

Yet if Heracles had simply sailed by boat, the tale would hardly have been worth telling. But Seneca says more. On Heracles's voyage to Africa, tragedy struck. His boat became stuck in the Syrtes. The Syrtes was a famous stretch of shifting, hidden sand banks north of the African coastline. These shallows were dangerous due to an unusually high tide that left many boats stranded when the waters ebbed. Stuck fast in these shallows, Heracles could no longer navigate his vessel. Therefore the hero left the boat behind and walked on the shoals the rest of the way to Africa.[27]

Now some readers might suppose that Heracles merely treaded on the sandbanks.[28] And one must admit that the Syrtes was imagined as a hopelessly confused mixture of sand and sea. The poet Lucan called it "sea fractured by shoals, earth broken up by the deep."[29] Nevertheless, Seneca explicitly says that at least at some stages in his journey, Heracles walked on the "seas" (*maria*). The miracle was not that Heracles ran over the sea at a speed to prevent sinking. Nothing in Seneca's play suggests that Heracles went faster than walking pace. Nor did Heracles glide over the sea with magical footgear. He clearly "went over it on foot" (*maria superavit pedes*) just as Jesus walked "over the sea" (*epi tēs thalassēs*; Mark 6:48–49). Seneca is even clearer than Mark that Heracles performed his feat by using his feet (*pedes*) as opposed to levitating slightly over the waters.

The concept of buoyant feet was apparently common enough for the satirist Lucian to poke fun at it. In the second century CE, he concocted a tale of men running over the sea with feet made of cork. This race of men is duly called "Phellopod," or "Corkfeet." Their unusual anatomy allowed them to skid across the sea as if on surfboards, waving to ship-bound sailors who stood agape in awe.[30]

In the context of Seneca's play, the example of the water-walking Heracles is cited to prove that Heracles can free himself from impossible situations. Heracles's wife, Megara, was under attack from a wicked king, and Heracles could not help because he had entered Hades, the Greek underworld. Fearing for her life, Megara asks her father-in-law, Amphitryon, how Heracles will manage to climb up out of Hades. She assumes, as did most everyone else in the ancient Mediterranean world, that coming back from the land of the dead is impossible for a human being. To encourage Megara, Amphitryon responds that Heracles had already performed the impossible—he had crossed the seas on foot.[31] If he had merely walked on the sandbanks, Amphitryon's response would not make sense in context. Heracles needs to be superhuman to find a path out of Hades. There is nothing superhuman about walking on loose sand (though it is admittedly a difficult task). Only if Heracles could walk on the seas could he climb out of hell itself. He could perform the impossible only if he had already done it sometime in the past.[32]

The ancients knew that normal people could not walk on water. But gods and divine men played by different rules. They had "super bodies" not subject to normal human limitations. What moderns call "the laws of physics" did not apply to divine bodies, especially the bodies of sea gods (or sons of sea gods). Jesus and Heracles were more than just sea gods. They were children of the high deity, whether he be called Zeus or Iao. Thus the main point of Mark's story accords well with Greco-Roman conceptions. Jesus is a divine being. His stunning appearance on the waters constitutes an epiphany, the manifestation of a god. He has powers that only a deity could perform.

It might seem surprising to modern readers that ancient writers such as Seneca historicized myths but left what moderns call "fictions" floating in the story. That Heracles crossed the sea in a golden goblet is a miracle, but that he walked on the shoals is an even greater miracle—at least to readers today. Yet here again we deal with the shifting sands of plausibility. Most modern people would deny that any person could walk on water at any time. Yet some ancients could apparently believe that Heracles, son of god, was an exception. Thus Seneca (or a character in his drama) could still describe Heracles walking on water as if it really happened years ago off the coast of Africa.[33] When such wonders were further contextualized in otherwise-realistic situations, additional credibility was garnered. It was because these seemingly impossible events really happened in the past that further wonders could be believed. In fact, Jesus and Heracles would both perform the impossible by climbing out of Hades.

Stilling Storms

Related to the water-travel episode is another sea miracle: the stilling of the storm. This story is told with slight variations in the Synoptic gospels (Mark 4:35–41; Matt. 8:23–27; Luke 8:22–25). In all three variants, quieting the stormy sea is Jesus's first nature miracle. Perhaps it is even more miraculous, however, that Jesus can sleep in the boat as it comes near to sinking (Mark 4:38). He must be awoken by his friends, who kindly inform him that they are drowning.[34]

Several other Mediterranean deities were known for controlling chaotic seas. Perhaps the best-known storm-stillers were the Dioscuri, the twin sons of Zeus who saved many a storm-tossed sailor. In a Homeric hymn, the Dioscuri are called

Deliverers of men on earth and of swift-going ships
When storm gales rage over the ruthless sea.

Immediately afterward, we encounter a little vignette illustrating their salvific activity:

The strong wind and the waves of the sea lay the ship under water,
Until suddenly these two are seen darting through the air on tawny
  wings.
Forthwith they allay the blasts of the cruel winds and
Still the waves upon the surface of the white sea.
. . . .
And when shipmen see them they are glad
And have rest from their pain and labor.[35]

By comparison, one can see how the evangelists shaped Jesus's sea-stilling miracle to better approximate historiographical discourse. Jesus, although he is a son of a deity, does not fly down to the ship "on tawny wings." He does not have wings. He is not even quick. In fact, he is asleep. By sleeping, Jesus seems supremely human. When he awakes, however, he performs the work of a god.

More historicized sea-stilling miracles were developed in the era of the gospels. Diodorus, for instance, retells the myth of the Argonauts. According to this historian, a terrible storm threatened the ship *Argo*. Blasted by the waves, the leading sailors give up all hope of being saved. But Orpheus, the famous singer, prays to the Dioscuri (identified with the Great Gods of Samothrace). Immediately the wind dies down. The Dioscuri do not themselves rush on the wings of the wind. Only their stars appear twinkling in the sky above.[36]

We know that Diodorus is historicizing, because in other versions of the tale, Orpheus does not need to pray. He can still the winds by his voice— meaning his singing voice.[37] "By his mother's art," the poet Horace wrote, "Orpheus checks the rapid flow of rivers and swift winds."[38] Orpheus's mother was the Muse Calliope ("Beautiful Voice"), who passed on her musical talent. By Orpheus's song, he made "smooth the rough seas."[39]

Mastering winds by words is not without parallel in biography. It was recorded that Pythagoras calmed storms on both rivers and seas for the safety of his friends. Porphyry wrote, "Ten thousand wondrous and divine deeds are uniformly narrated about this man [Pythagoras] and with common consent: . . . his infallible predictions of earthquakes, speedy deterrents of plagues and violent winds, reductions of hail showers, and the pacifications of waves on rivers and seas for the easy passage of his companions."[40]

Likewise, Jesus's sea-stilling miracle is stated in the matter-of-fact tone of historiography: "Jesus got up, rebuked the wind and said to the sea: 'Shut up, be muzzled!' Then the wind died down and there was a great calm" (Mark 4:39).[41] In fact, Jesus seems rather grumpy after being awoken— another peculiarly human trait. His sea-stilling is fabulous, to be sure, but within the range of possibility for the "son of God" (Mark 3:11). Wind and sea are rebuked, but they are not personified. The timing is precise: Jesus calms the storm in the evening after a long day of weaving parables. The route can be traced on a map: Jesus sails across the Sea of Galilee to the region of the Gerasenes (Mark 5:1). It does not matter that Gerasa (modern Jerash) is thirty-seven miles southeast of the Sea of Galilee (no one but scholars seem to notice); what is important is that the geographical marker is there. The temporal and chronological markers generate a historical frame, a frame that soothes the turbulence of the miracle and fosters the calm of astounded belief.

Fishing Miracle

As readers of the gospels know, Jesus made an excellent fishing partner. Despite his reputation, however, there is only one main fishing miracle in the gospels, told in two different ways. The author of Luke placed the fishing miracle at the beginning of Jesus's ministry, and the author of John set it at the end (after the resurrection). Both versions of the story are creative, though I will focus on the Lukan variant.

In Luke, the miracle is narrativized as the call of the first disciples.[42] It is thus woven into the chronology of Jesus's life and given a seemingly historical setting. There is also significant character development in the interaction between the protagonists, Jesus and Peter. Peter is presented realistically as a frustrated and fallible fisherman. The realism of the characters contributes to the sense that the narrative is presented as an account of actual events.

Jesus orders Peter to push off from the shore and let down the nets. Peter protests that he and his team had spent all night hauling their dragnet without a single fish to show for it. Yet when Peter reluctantly obeys, virtually all the fish in the Sea of Galilee spring into the net, threatening to snap its fibers and flood the boat. Later on the beach, Peter sinks to his knees before Jesus; but instead of making Jesus his fishing partner, Peter joins Jesus's company and starts fishing for people (Luke 5:1–11).

A comparable miracle is related about Pythagoras. Porphyry lists several miracles of Pythagoras in which he communicated with animals. The final one describes the salvation of over a hundred fish.[43] Like the author of Luke, Iamblichus places Pythagoras's fish miracle at the beginning of his ministry.[44]

The setting is the southern Italian shoreline. A pensive Pythagoras stops to watch men drag a full net of fish out of the deep. He casually tells them the number of fish in the nets. The fishermen are surprised but keep to their task. Then Pythagoras makes a kind of bet. If, when the fish are counted, he is correct about their number, the fish must be released for a fair price. The fishermen agree. While they start to count, the fish breathe on land as if in the sea—as long as Pythagoras stands over them. When Pythagoras's number is proved right, he pays the fishermen, and the fish are freed. The miracle is a prelude for Pythagoras's great catch of disciples in the city of Croton.

Pythagoras's ability to divine the number of the fish recalls the Johannine variant of the fishing miracle. In this telling, exactly 153 fish are counted (John 21:11). It is the triangular number of seventeen, or the sum of the addition of each number from one to seventeen. Interpreters have struggled over the significance of this number in John, yet it may well be a subtle allusion to Pythagoras. Pythagoras was well-known for theorizing about triangles (think of the Pythagorean Theorem) and—as we have seen—for counting fish.

Yet the Lukan variant of the myth shows more striking parallels with Iamblichus's account. The major points of similarity are three. The fish miracle begins Pythagoras's ministry, it puts Pythagoras in dialogue with reluctant fishermen, and it results in his gaining disciples and admirers. One might attribute these parallels to emulation, but there is no evidence that Iamblichus knew or read the gospel of Luke.

In addition, the fishing miracles are different in their details. The Lukan writer is interested in portraying Jesus as lord of all, including the animal kingdom. Pythagoras is interested in saving the lives of fish. In the ancient world, Pythagoras is perhaps best known for prohibiting animal slaughter (what we might call "the gospel of vegetarianism"). "Our partnership with animals is genetic," he taught, "for on account of our common life, elements, and their composition, we are linked by a kind of brotherhood."[45] Thus when Luke's Jesus says that humans "are worth more than many sparrows" (Luke 12:7), Pythagoras would have shuddered. In a comparable episode, Jesus casts two thousand daimons into pigs. When the pigs commit suicide by hurling themselves off a cliff, their owners duly complain about their massive loss of property (Mark 5:11–14). Jesus, however, shows no concern about the loss of property or animal life.

Contrast Pythagoras, who, in the words of Plutarch, "was not uncaring to fish as beings of another race or hostile, but paid a ransom for them as for friends and kin who had been captured."[46] According to Plutarch, Pythagoras was trying to "accustom people to refrain from savagery and rapacity" with regard to animals. Thus he would try to dissuade birdcatchers from practicing their art; he would buy catches of fish, ordering them to be let go; he also forbade the slaughter of any domesticated animal.[47] If there is a basic ethical message of Pythagoras, it is "preserve life!"

Pythagoras is a divine being (as we saw in chapter 3). He proves his divine identity by keeping the fish alive on the shore. Yet he does not expect, receive, or accept worship from the fishermen or anyone else. The story in the gospel of Luke, however, culminates with Peter's humble adoration of Jesus, who says nothing to prevent this act of public worship (Luke 5:8–10).

For modern readers there is something fishy about both tales. Fish simply do not act in the way that they are portrayed in these stories. They do not survive on land, and they do not spontaneously jump en masse into dragnets. Yet both stories appear in ancient biographies marked by the conventions of plain reports. Even if the accounts are proved significantly different in content, they still appear similar in their (historiographical) form. Both the Lukan evangelist and Iamblichus were attempting to present a miracle as if it happened in time and space. Both used historiographical discourse to authenticate the miracle and the master who performed it. Both were writing biographies that presented divine heroes as genuine human beings. And both were trying to win converts to what they perceived to be a universal religion. In short, both used historiographical discourse as an apologetic tool to "catch" converts in Mediterranean culture.

Casting Out Daimons

Philostratus's biography of Apollonius is helpful for comparing miracles of exorcism. On two occasions, Philostratus showed how eastern sages of the late first century cast out daimons. One of the exorcists is a man called Iarbas the Indian; the other is Apollonius himself.[48]

In the gospel of Mark, Jesus's ability to cast out daimons is his main claim to fame. The emphasis is striking because it appears to have no model in native Jewish mythology. That is to say, no hero in the Hebrew Bible casts out daimons. The idea that daimons possess people and take over their consciousness was not native to Hebrew culture. Yahweh could send a spirit to torment King Saul (1 Sam. 16:14). Yet this spirit was part of Yahweh's retinue. It was not part of a separate army of superhuman beings led by a chief daimon roaming the lower heavens. These ideas seem to have filtered into Judaism from Persian mythology (the Jews were ruled by the Persians from 538 to 331 BCE); hence they appear in later Jewish texts such as Tobit and the Testament of Solomon.

By the late first century CE, the idea of daimon possession was prevalent in eastern Mediterranean culture and appears in a number of historical works. With a touch of pride, Josephus indicated that Jewish wonder-workers had gained a great reputation as exorcists. One even performed before the emperor himself, as Josephus recorded:

> I have inquired about a certain Eleazar, a fellow countryman who, when the emperor Vespasian was present with his sons, tribunes, and a host of other soldiers, freed men possessed by daimons. This was the manner of the cure: Eleazar put to the nostrils of the possessed man his ring, which had under its seal one of the roots prescribed by Solomon. Then, as the man smelled it, Eleazar drew out the little daimon through his nostrils. When the man immediately collapsed, Eleazar adjured the daimon never to come back into him, mentioning Solomon and adding the incantations Solomon had composed. Eleazar, wanting to convince the bystanders and prove to them that he had this power, placed a small chalice or foot basin full of water a little way off and ordered the daimon, as it left the man, to overturn the basin and make himself known to the spectators.[49]

Not only is this exorcism presented as historical, but it is "verified" by Josephus's own research and possible observation.[50]

Here we compare an exorcism of Jesus with a similar one by Apollonius. When Apollonius was sojourning in Athens, he was in the habit of offering public lectures on the correct worship of the gods. One day, he began to discourse on the subject of libations (that is, how to pour drink offerings to the gods). As he was explaining a fine point about pouring the liquid over the handle of the cup, he was interrupted by a loud guffaw. Apollonius looked up to see a young man dressed in a cape acting utterly bizarre.

For a long time, in fact, the young man had been troubled. For no reason at all, he would burst out in wild laughter or suddenly start to sob. He also regularly talked to himself and even sang loudly in public. In general, he gave the impression of being drunk or simply crazy.

Apollonius diagnosed the young man's problem immediately. "It is not you," he told him, "who commit this outrage but the daimon who drives you." Suddenly the youth stopped laughing. As Apollonius stared at him, the youth began to utter fearful whines and angry snorts such as people do when being burned alive or tortured. Recognizing the power and nature of Apollonius, the daimon inhabiting the young man quickly promised to leave him and never return.

Apollonius rebuked the daimon and commanded him to provide a concrete sign of his departure. The daimon replied that he would knock down a statue in the neighboring portico as he departed. Sure enough, the crowd looked in that direction just in time to see a statue totter, slowly lean, and crash to the ground. The people buzzed with amazement. Then they fixed their gaze back on the young man, who, after rubbing his eyes, sheepishly wondered why everyone was gawking at him. From that day forth, the man put aside his capes and luxurious ways. He donned the cloak of a philosopher and—in imitation of Apollonius—lived a life of self-discipline.[51]

In the case of Jesus, the very first miracle that he performs in Mark is an exorcism. On a Sabbath day, he enters the synagogue at Capernaum (a town on the shore of Lake Galilee). He lectures for some time, and the crowds are astounded by his teachings. Suddenly a man in the synagogue lets loose a scream. In a maniacal voice, he shouts, "What is your truck with us, Jesus of Nazareth?! Have you come here to destroy us? I know who you are—the holy one of God!" (Mark 1:24).

Jesus immediately intuits that the man is possessed. With an angry growl, Jesus rebukes the daimon. He commands him to be silent and to come out of the man. As if in protest, the daimon throws the man into convulsions and shouts as if in agony. Then, quite suddenly, all is still. The man is picked up, now in his right mind. The people of the synagogue explode with excitement. Jesus not only speaks with authority but demonstrates his power by his control over superhuman agents. The daimons recognize the true (divine) nature of Jesus, and Jesus demonstrates his divinity (Mark 1:21–28). As we have already seen, the author of Mark later tells a story in which daimons who exit a man make known their departure by entering a herd of pigs. These pigs then hurl themselves off a cliff as proof that they have left (Mark 5:13).

Both Jesus and Apollonius seem to work from their own power. They do not pray to other deities before they exorcise daimons. Instead, they show by their power to perceive and exorcize daimons that they are divine beings. Their words alone drive out the daimons, and these words are not the seeming gibberish of magicians and quacks.

Literarily speaking, the stories of Jesus and Apollonius are probably unconnected. Philostratus, even if he knew about Jesus, did not cherish—and probably did not read—the Christian gospels. Still, the stories follow a similar pattern. The holy man impresses the crowds by his religious teaching. He is interrupted by a daimoniac who recognizes the higher nature of the teacher. The hero rebukes the daimon and expels him. There is a sign of the daimon's exit. The possessed man recovers his senses, and the crowds are filled with wonder. When put in this schematic form, a mythic template is revealed. The template is not confined to Jewish literature. It can be found in other texts written in antiquity.

Important for our purposes is that the template occurs in two biographies. These biographies, though they contain some fantastic elements (certainly to modern sensibilities), strove to conform to historiographical discourse. Whether or not the events happened, Philostratus and the Synoptic writers wrote their tales as if they occurred in space and time. Indeed, Philostratus provides a helpful measure of what could and could not count as historical discourse by educated readers. By ancient standards at least, an exorcism was an event that could have occurred not just at the margins of Palestine but in the center of Greece.

Healings

According to the gospels, Jesus healed both the blind and the lame merely by touching them. Such were the signs, according to the evangelists, of the Messiah. When John the Baptist's disciples ask Jesus if he is the Messiah, he responds, "Go and tell John what you have seen and heard: the blind receive their sight, the lame walk, the lepers are cleansed, the deaf hear, the dead are raised!" (Luke 7:22).

In performing these miracles, however, Jesus was not alone. Three different historians report that the emperor Vespasian healed both a blind and a lame man while he sojourned in Alexandria.[52] Two of the historians (Tacitus and Suetonius) were well-educated Roman aristocrats who wrote shortly after the evangelists. None of the historians who report the miracle show any knowledge of the gospels.

According to the historians' accounts, Vespasian arrived in Alexandria late in 69 CE. There he was proclaimed emperor even before his armies had defeated the incumbent in Italy. Vespasian entered the city as the favorite of Serapis, the state deity of Alexandria. It was at the prompting of Serapis that a blind man, a commoner well-known in the city, approached Vespasian and begged that the emperor spit in his eyes. Another man, afflicted with a withered hand, asked the emperor to tread on his hand. By these strange means, the god Serapis had indicated that they would be healed.

Vespasian was incredulous. He was known to be a hard-headed, practical man who would joke about his own divinity. Yet both his advisers and local doctors urged him to perform the deed. Vespasian looked around and noticed that the crowds were on tippy-toes with expectation. So it was that the nascent emperor, with smiling countenance (like the benign Serapis), deigned to spit in one man's eye and place his heel on the other man's hand.[53] Both were cured instantly before many witnesses.

Vespasian, by using his foot to heal, assimilated himself to Serapis. The foot of Serapis was well-known for its healing properties.[54] By showing the same abilities, Vespasian proved to the Alexandrians that he participated in the power and divinity of Serapis. On what seems to be a contemporary papyrus fragment, Vespasian is even addressed as "Serapis, Son of Ammon [the Egyptian high deity], Savior and Benefactor."[55] Heaven was smiling on Vespasian, who now seemed more than human and thus fit to be emperor. Tacitus even notes that, some thirty-five years after the event, eyewitnesses still confirmed both healings at a time when deceit would have brought them no reward.

Modern readers who have no investment in the divinity of Roman emperors remain skeptical. Commenting on this episode, one scholar remarks, "a false witness would not be less obstinate than an honest one, and the history of any religious movement knows of hallucinations and delusions that were taken for reality."[56] Another scholar proposes priestly collusion: "It seems almost certain that these wonders were the work of the priests of Serapis, who wished to gain credit for the cult, but it is also likely that they were prompted by some of Vespasian's adherents, with or without the knowledge of the emperor himself."[57]

Such modern incredulity demonstrates an important point. There is a certain investment required to believe in the historicity of *mythoi*. For the Romans, the worship of the deified emperor was a sacred institution. The imperial cult was a religious institution funded by the Roman state and flourishing all over the empire. Stories confirming the divinity of an emperor could be recorded as historiography, and they were apparently believed on some level even by the well-educated elite.

Thus when we read a story of Jesus spitting in the eyes of a blind man or using spittle to heal, one should not think that these stories fell outside the boundaries of ancient historiography. In Mark 8:23, for instance, Jesus spits directly into the eyes of a blind man. This act initially opens the man's eyes, allowing him to see people that look like trees. A second touch of Jesus makes his vision clear. The circumstantial details of the double touch and the tree people increase the reality effect of the story. In John 9:6, Jesus spits on the ground, makes mud with his saliva, and applies it to a blind man's eyes. After a quick wash in a nearby pool, the man—said to be born blind—comes back seeing.[58]

Furthermore, all three Synoptic gospels speak of Jesus healing a man with a withered hand. The miracle is set in a scene of Sabbath controversy. Jesus's enemies wait to see if he will heal on the Jewish day of rest. Jesus clearly views healing as an act of goodness fully approved by the Jewish deity. Yet Jesus does not actually seek Yahweh's approval. He merely asks the man—in a packed synagogue—to stretch forth his hand. When he does so, the hand is instantly healed (Mark 3:1–6; Matt. 12:10–14; Luke 6:6–11).

After Jesus heals the withered hand, there is increased opposition. The Pharisees join forces with the Herodians to kill Jesus in secret (Mark 3:6). The miracles of the divine man are evidently not accepted by all. In the case of Vespasian, the historian Dio Cassius noted that the emperor too received opposition in the wake of his wonders. "Even though Divinity sanctified him [Vespasian], the Alexandrians did not rejoice. Rather, they were irked so as not only privately but also publicly to mock and revile him."[59]

In both cases the opposing party is depicted as foolish and wrong. The miracles were clear to all and performed in public. They were situated in space and time and told as if they were historical events. One even has the impression that, at the time the reports were written, eyewitnesses could still be adduced to confirm the wonders.

Resuscitations

Perhaps the greatest miracle is resuscitating people from the dead. Jesus's resuscitation of Jairus's daughter is told in the Synoptics (Mark 5:21–43; Matt. 9:18–26; Luke 8:40–56). Yet only the author of Luke tells the story of Jesus raising a widow's son from the dead. In telling this tale, he (or his source) creatively adapts a story from Jewish mythic historiography.

In 1 Kings 17, Elijah meets a widow by a gate. He is taken into the house by this woman, who, we later find out, has an only son. During Elijah's stay, the son unexpectedly dies. Elijah thrice stretches himself over the corpse and, after several fits and starts, makes the boy live. When risen from the dead, the boy cries aloud. Elijah hands the boy back to his mother. Ecstatic, the widow cries out that Elijah is a prophet.

In the Lukan adaptation, Jesus passes by the gate of a town. He sees a widow walking in the funeral procession of her only son. Jesus touches the casket, causing the son to rise up and immediately start a conversation. Gracefully, Jesus hands the boy back to his mother. The people respond, "A great prophet has arisen among us!" (Luke 7:12–15). Enough of the material is familiar to give it a sense of credibility. Enough of the material is changed to impress readers with awe.

As expected, the new material portrays Jesus as superior to Elijah. Unlike the ancient prophet, Jesus takes the initiative to resuscitate a person confirmed dead for a longer period. The resuscitation is instant, and there is an additional acclamation: "god has visited his people!" (Luke 7:16). (Here the "god" may in fact be Jesus himself.)

A story of Philostratus in his biography of Apollonius resembles this account in Luke.[60] Like the evangelist, Philostratus tells his story as if it happened in real time and space. In Rome, Apollonius stumbles upon the funeral procession of a young girl. This time, it is her fiancé who mournfully follows the casket. Suddenly Apollonius orders the men carrying the funeral bier to set it down. When he asks her name, the people think that he will deliver a tear-jerking eulogy. Yet Apollonius merely touches the girl and whispers something over her. Immediately the girl awakes, speaks, and is led home.

To increase the historical plausibility of the myth, Philostratus added his own rationalization. Perhaps the girl really was dead. Yet perhaps, he speculates, Apollonius saw a little steam rise from the girl's nostrils in the light rain and so realized that a spark of life still burned within her.[61]

One might argue that Luke's stories of resuscitation influenced that of Philostratus. In the raising of Jairus's daughter, for instance, Jesus whispers a word over the girl before she awakes (Luke 8:54). In Mark, what he whispers is a foreign phrase with a magical ring to it: "Talitha cum!" (Mark 5:41). Philostratus might have adapted this old sorcerer's trick for his own divine hero. Yet the motif of using a powerful word is common, and both the Lukan author and Philostratus are eager to avoid portraying their heroes as magicians.

In short, both Philostratus and the third evangelist present their resuscitation miracles as if they were historical events that took place before real people in known locations. This is a historicizing technique that they independently adapted from a shared literary culture to increase the plausibility of their accounts.

Conclusion

The way that the evangelists reported miracles conforms in part to Pascal Boyer's understanding of religious representations in general. For Boyer, everyone learns a set of basic ontological expectations—beliefs about what can and cannot happen. Most miracle stories stay within the horizon of ontological expectations or, one might say, the discourse of "normal" historical events. Yet in the story, there is one memorable violation of expectations—the miracle itself.[62]

The miracle is a counterintuitive element, to be sure, but the counterintuitiveness is kept to a minimum. The miracle might have been considered mythic; but fixed in a textual world of other normal human events, it gained the hook of credibility. Sometimes the characters in the story, who putatively share the ontological expectations of the reader, are depicted as surprised by the miracle but in the end compelled to believe it. For willing but cautious readers, this literary technique also encourages belief.

The chief element of wonder is the inexplicable, yet what is inexplicable can still be believed. The believability of a miracle story depends on both the way it is told and the investment of the person who hears it. In the case of Jesus, many Christian believers today still affirm that Jesus's miracles happened. Sometimes the miracles are rationalized, as if Jesus were an expert in healing psychosomatic disorders. The modern need to believe reflects the ancient cultural expectations as well. To be sure, if we were to resurrect Philostratus or Tacitus or Suetonius and ask him if Jesus's miracles occurred, he might discount them as drivel fit for superstitious and gullible people. Yet those historians themselves, if somewhat guardedly, reported wonders of a similar stripe, all the while expecting to be believed—at least on some level. So the wheel of mythic historiography grinds on; and the miracle stories themselves—though increasingly hard to credit—have lost none of their wonder.

Further Reading

Wendy Cotter, "Cosmology and the Jesus Miracles," in *Whose Historical Jesus? Studies in Christianity and Judaism*, ed. Michael Desjardins and William E. Arnal (Waterloo, ON: Wilfrid Laurier University Press, 1996), 118–31.

Wendy Cotter, *Miracles in Greco-Roman Antiquity: A Sourcebook for the Study of New Testament Miracles* (London: Routledge, 1999).

Howard Clark Kee, *Medicine, Miracle and Magic in New Testament Times* (Cambridge: Cambridge University Press, 1986), 67–94.

Hartmut Leppin, "Imperial Miracles and Elitist Discourses," in *Miracles Revisited: New Testament Miracle Stories and Their Concepts of Reality*, ed. Stefan Alkier and Annette Weisenrieder (Berlin: de Gruyter, 2013), 233–48.

Trevor S. Luke, "A Healing Touch for Empire: Vespasian's Wonders in Domitianic Rome," *Greece & Rome* 57 (2010): 77–106.

Harold Remus, *Pagan-Christian Conflict over Miracle in the Second Century* (Cambridge, MA: Philadelphia Patristic Foundation, 1983).

Ulrike Riemer, "Miracle Stories and Their Narrative Intent in the Context of the Ruler Cult of Classical Antiquity," in *Wonders Never Cease: The Purpose of Narrating Miracle Stories in the New Testament and its Religious Environment*, ed. Michael Labahn and Bert Jan Lietaert Peerbolte (London: T&T Clark, 2006), 32–47.

J. A. Romeo, "Gematria and John 21:11: The Children of God," *Journal of Biblical Literature* 97 (1978): 263–64.

Gerd Theissen, *The Miracle Stories of the Early Christian Tradition*, ed. John Riches, trans. Francis McDonagh (Philadelphia: Fortress, 1983).

CHAPTER ELEVEN

THE *PHARMAKOS*

A *mythos* that is made up, if it carries conviction,
always enthralls its audience.
—*Alexander Romance 2.15.5*[1]

There appears in ancient Mediterranean mythography a sacred figure named the *pharmakos*. *Pharmakos* is a Greek word often translated as "scapegoat." It designates a human being expelled or killed in order to heal the community. The human being is often the most virtuous and noble person, but he or she is treated like scum and the worst criminal.

In Greek antiquity, there were rituals in which *pharmakoi* (the plural of *pharmakos*) were mistreated and expelled by their respective cities. These *pharmakoi* tended to be marginal persons—slaves, beggars, the deformed, and so on. In mythography, by contrast, *pharmakoi* were often portrayed as royal or of noble blood. Despite their pedigree, however, *pharmakoi* sometimes appeared in the guise of beggars or slaves.

We see the template play out in the account of Codrus, king of Athens. His story was already popular in the fourth century BCE and can be summarized as follows. When enemy troops invade the lands surrounding Athens, the people of the city ask Apollo of Delphi whether the invaders will capture their city. The god responds that they will do so unless the

Athenian king is killed. Knowing this, Codrus secretly decides to sacrifice himself. To do so, he must change his form; he must go from the one highest in honor to the lowest. So the king dresses himself in the rags of slaves. He heaves on his shoulders a load of wood and walks outside the city. When enemy troops accost him, he pulls a weapon and is slaughtered in the ensuing brawl. When the invaders recognize the king's corpse, they immediately break camp and march off.

Ambiguity plays a key part in this tale: the *pharmakos* is both the best and the worst member of society. Only the best ought to be sacrificed; only the worst is fit for slaughter. To modern readers, Codrus's story is a myth; but ancient Athenians understood it as part of their history. To prove it, they could point to a local sanctuary of Codrus erected in honor.[2]

The Theban prince Menoeceus was another widely known example of a *pharmakos*. When his city (Thebes in central Greece) is about to fall in battle, the aged priest Tiresias makes a prophecy. He prophesies that if a person of royal blood is offered as an atoning sacrifice, the city will be saved. Menoeceus was part of the royal family and son of the future king. In his own mind, he readily recognizes the will of Apollo: he must die on behalf of his people.

Twice the poet Statius (a contemporary of the evangelists) called Menoeceus a "sacrificial animal," led "like a silent sheep from the flock." Yet the hero's heart is possessed by heavenly power. Before he sacrifices himself, he prays, "O gods above . . . and you who grant me to die by so great a death, Apollo, give constant joy to Thebes. This joy I have covenanted to give and lavishly bought with the price of all my blood." When Menoeceus plummets to his death, his spirit rises before the high deity. In the city, the hero is worshiped with altars and temples.[3]

In the gospels, there is no more valuable and noble sacrifice than the anointed king and son of Yahweh, Christ. Jesus prays passionately before his sacrificial death, "Father, for you all things are possible; remove this cup from me; yet, not what I want, but what you want" (Mark 14:36). Here the historiographical Jesus conforms to an ancient mythic pattern. According to this template, the *pharmakos* dies both willingly and by force. The death occurs by force in that the *pharmakos* is condemned and executed. The death occurs willingly in the sense that the *pharmakos* chooses his or her fate beforehand and does not refuse the sentence of death.

The *pharmakos* is often convicted of what moderns would call a religious crime. He or she is accused of robbing a temple or somehow damaging it. Alternatively, the *pharmakos* may criticize how temple rituals are carried out and so incur the charge of blasphemy (hostile speech against a god). The perceived crime leads to a violent response on the part of the temple staff and city officials. They attempt to capture the *pharmakos* by deceit. When they capture him, they often beat him, parade him around the city, try him in a kangaroo court, and murder him. The willing *pharmakos* dies sacrificially to safeguard the community. Yet the unjust death of the *pharmakos* incites divine punishment against the civic leaders—a plague, famine, or invasion.

In this chapter I explore how the *pharmakos* pattern was historicized in the biographies of two figures: Jesus and Aesop. Jesus is generally considered to have lived in the early first century CE. The existence of Aesop in the sixth century BCE is doubted by many researchers today. The ancients, however, never questioned the historicity of either figure. Regardless of what one thinks of their historicity, their stories follow mythic patterns (specifically, the *pharmakos* pattern). By the first century CE, when the biographies of Jesus and Aesop were written, this mythic pattern was adapted to historical discourse.

We begin with Jesus. In the so-called passion narratives of the Synoptic gospels, Jesus visits the Jewish temple. Instead of being welcomed as a deity, Jesus is conspired against by the chief priests and scribes. The gospel hero responds by flipping over the tables of the money changers, a prophetic sign that the temple itself will be overturned.

In the wake of Jesus's temple tantrum, he locks horns with the chief priests, scribes and elders. They question him about the source of his authority. The hero coyly finds a way to avoid providing a direct answer. Since the scribes and elders do not provide a straight answer to his question, Jesus does not directly answer theirs (Mark 11:27–33).

Jesus does, however, provide an indirect answer in the form of a parable. A landowner (representing the Jewish deity) leases his vineyard (a common symbol of Israel) to some tenants (the Jewish leaders) expecting to receive a portion of its harvest. But when the owner sends representatives (the prophets) to collect his share, the tenants repeatedly beat and kill them. The tenants want to inherit the land for themselves. Thus when the owner sends his own son (Jesus), the tenants murder him in cold blood. The owner of the vineyard then launches a military force (the Romans) and slaughters the tenants (Mark 12:1–11).

To the audience both without and within the text, the parable cuts like a sword. The Jewish leaders, to whom God "leased" the land and heritage of Israel, had killed the prophets sent to them. Now they are on the verge of killing God's son, for which they will soon be slaughtered themselves. The author of Matthew presents Jesus himself as revealing the consequence: "Therefore I tell you, the kingdom of God will be taken away from you [Jewish leaders] and given to a people that produces the fruits of the kingdom" (Matt. 21:43).

The parable is powerful but problematic. By telling this tale, Jesus is outright inflammatory. He accuses the Jewish leaders of wanting to kill him in order to usurp the inheritance of God. He prophesies that they will be slaughtered by God, who will send the Roman army. The Jewish leaders are no fools. They immediately catch his meaning but play exactly the role foretold in the parable. "When they realized that he had told this parable against them, they wanted to arrest him" (Mark 12:12). Although too cowardly to drag him from the temple precincts, the priests succeed in arresting Jesus in the dead of night.

The parable is designed by the evangelists to convict their own antagonists (Jews who rejected Jesus as the Messiah). In the world of the story, the hero has already been rejected. The Jewish leaders will never accept him, and so he turns the tables. He convicts them not in an elaborate trial but in a simple story that serves virtually as a self-fulfilling prophecy. Before they condemn the hero to death, the opponents know in their hearts that they are the ones convicted of deceit and murder. The hero is the unwanted moral mirror of the community. By doing away with him, the community strives to erase its guilt but ironically magnifies it.

A similar pattern of events unfolds in the *Life of Aesop*. This biographical work exists in two main versions, a fuller version called "G" and an abbreviated version (with some unique passages) called "W." The texts are anonymous, like the gospels. The *Life of Aesop* is close to the gospels in its vocabulary and style. The prose is unpretentious, the narratives episodic, and the minor characters unidimensional. The *Life of Aesop* incorporates many more comic elements than the gospels, though both include aspects of tragedy.[4]

Despite the novelistic traits of the *Life of Aesop,* it is more than what moderns call fiction. Like the poet Homer, Aesop was widely considered to have been a real person. The historian Ister (late third century BCE) thought that Aesop flourished around 570 BCE.[5] In antiquity, his fables were universally known. Thus it made sense to record the life of this famous man. Generally speaking, Aesop's biography does not relate physically impossible or fantastical events (at least not any more than the gospels do). In the narrative itself, there is considerable realism—notably in the depiction of how slaves are bought, treated, and whipped.[6]

As noted, Aesop was (and is) best known for his fables (such as "The Tortoise and the Hare"), which were known already in the fifth century BCE. By this time, Herodotus knew and briefly related the plot of Aesop's demise.[7] Today, most scholars question whether there was actually a man behind the fables. Yet such doubts do not undercut the widespread ancient perception that Aesop once lived. At least one educated writer in the first century CE attempted to put Aesop's life into historical form, and several editions of the biography indicate considerable interest in the era of the gospels.

According to the *Life of Aesop,* the hero was originally a slave who by his sharp wits and acid tongue became free and famous but eventually fell into disaster. The content of Aesop's life is different from that of Jesus, as any reader of the biographies will see. Materially speaking, however, Aesop resembles Jesus in rising from a humble station, upsetting societal norms, attaining fame, perishing by the plot of his enemies, being vindicated after death, and earning worship. Almost all these elements are common to the *pharmakos* template.

Yet there is one similarity that is rather uncommon: both Aesop and Jesus tell inflammatory parables. Aesop's parables are usually called "fables," which call to mind talking animals and moralistic epigrams. In Greek, however, myth and fable represent the same word (*mythos*), and Aesop's *mythoi* cover a range of etiological tales involving gods, personified abstractions, and human beings.[8] The Aesop scholar Ben Edwin Perry offered a definition of fable that overlaps with the gospel parable: (1) a deliberately fictitious story that (2) purports to be an utterance that took place once in past time through the agency of a particular character, (3) told not for its own sake but to make a personal or moral point.[9] For simplicity, we can categorize both parables and fables as short figurative stories with deeper (sociopolitical) meanings. These stories had a common function: they offered what initially seems like a harmless analogy that caused the hearers to see themselves and their situations in a new light.

As in the case of Jesus, Aesop's incendiary parables occur toward the end of his life. At the height of his fame as a political adviser, Aesop visits the city of Delphi in central Greece. Delphi was the city sacred to Aesop's own personal deity, Apollo. Apollo was known as the god of prophecy, and Delphi was the site of Greece's most famous oracle. Twelve days out of the year, rich individuals and representatives of Greek states lined up to ask Apollo questions about important state and personal affairs.

While in Delphi, Aesop is treated much as Jesus is in the holy city of Jerusalem. At first, the people enjoy hearing him, but they offer him no gifts of hospitality, show a flighty temperament, and eventually turn against him. Stung by their inhospitality, Aesop enters attack mode. He tells several insulting parables against the priests of Delphi. The parables convict them of greed, accuse them of injustice, and prophesy future judgment.

Initially, Aesop likens the Delphians to driftwood. From a distance, it appears to be something valuable bobbing above the waves. Yet on closer inspection, it is discovered to be worthless. In his own case, Aesop had heard of the Delphians' reputation as far away as Babylon (in modern Iraq). He supposed them to be rich and generous at heart. Now he accuses them of being inferior to other peoples and unworthy of their ancestors.[10]

When Aesop is later arrested, he relates a longer, more insidious parable:

> A farmer who had grown old in the country and had never seen the city begged his children to let him go and see the city before he died. They hitched the donkeys to the wagon themselves and told him, "Just drive them, and they'll take you to the city." On the way, a storm came up, it got dark, the donkeys lost their way and came to a place surrounded by cliffs. Seeing the danger he was in, he said, "Oh Zeus, what wrong have I done that I should die this way, without even horses, but only these miserable donkeys, to blame it on?"

After relating the parable, Aesop makes clear that the "miserable donkeys" are the priests of Delphi and Aesop will be the one to fall from a cliff.[11] But Aesop hardly needs to interpret the parable for them. They instantly understand its meaning and fly into a rage.

Yet Aesop does not stop. He aims his arrow-like tongue and pierces them with another parable:

> When animals spoke the same language, a mouse befriended by a frog invited the frog to dinner. He led him into a very rich storeroom, in which there was bread, meat, cheese, olives, and figs, and said, "Eat!" Having been richly treated, the frog said, "Now I invite you to come to my house for dinner, and I will repay the favor."
>
> He took the mouse to his pond and said, "Dive in!" The mouse said, "Swimming is not my forte." The frog said, "I'll teach you," and tying the mouse's foot to his own with a string, jumped into the pond and dragged the mouse along with him. As the mouse was drowning, he said, "Although I am dead, I will have my revenge on you who live." When he had said this, the frog dove down and suffocated the mouse. But as the dead mouse lay floating on the water, a raven seized it with the frog still attached by the string. The bird devoured the mouse, then skewered the frog as well.
>
> Thus the mouse got his revenge on the frog. In the same way, men of Delphi, though I die, I shall be your doom. For indeed, Lydians, Babylonians, and practically all of Greece will reap the fruits of my death.[12]

When Aesop tells these parables of judgment, his fate had already been decided. The priests had already arranged for Aesop's arrest on the charge of blasphemy. Yet the real reason for his arrest was more personal. Aesop had accused the Delphic priests of greed and had insulted their reputation. Thus the rulers convened a council. "Seeing how abusive he was, they reason to themselves, 'If we let him go away, he'll go around to other cities and damage our reputation.' So they plotted to kill him by a trick."[13]

This council looks very much like the one portrayed in Mark's gospel. After Jesus tells his insulting parable, "The chief priests and the scribes were looking for a way to arrest Jesus by stealth and kill him; for they said, 'Not during the festival, or there may be a riot among the people'" (Mark 14:1–2; compare the council scene in John 11:50). The priests were upset about being humiliated by Jesus's wisdom (Mark 12:13–40). They also resented the fact that Jesus caused a commotion in the temple, calling it a "den of thieves" (Mark 11:17).

According to one version of Aesop's biography, he criticized a specific sacrificial custom of the priests. According to this rite, the one offering an animal sacrifice was not able to partake of it because the priests of Delphi claimed all the fine cutlets for themselves.[14] Normally the one who offered an animal shared in the meat. But not at Delphi. An Old Comic poet once joked that, "If you sacrifice at Delphi, you'll have to buy your dinner." There was even a custom that the knife used in the sacrifice also "earned" a share of the meat (though this portion probably went to the cook). Thus there arose a proverbial saying, "the Delphic knife," which came to designate people who were greedy and inclined to take a share of something from everyone.[15]

Aesop's criticisms, much like those of Jesus, condemned a corrupt priestly institution. As in the case of Jesus, the priests running the institution were furious at being denounced. As the narrative unfolds, both the priests of Jerusalem and Delphi deceitfully engineer the hero's death. In the case of Jesus, the priests pay one of his disciples to betray his lord under cover of darkness. In the case of Aesop, the priests (or their lackeys) plant an ornate golden chalice from Apollo's temple in Aesop's luggage. Aesop is allowed to leave the city, but he is quickly pursued, bound, and hauled back. There, the arresting party rifles through his bags. Aesop precipitously declares his innocence on pain of death. When the chalice is discovered, Aesop is summarily accused of temple robbery, a form of blasphemy. Aesop is then paraded through the city and jeered at before being thrown into jail.[16]

In this way, the priests of Delphi condemn the fabulist on trumped-up charges. The condemnation is swift and without due process of law. Though Aesop tries, he is not allowed to defend himself. By vote of the citizens, he is sentenced to a frightful execution: he will be hurled from a cliff.[17]

In this way, Aesop's earlier observation about the tongue is proved correct: "Through the tongue come hostilities, conspiracies, ambushes, fights, jealousies, dissensions, and wars."[18] During Aesop's stay in prison, his friend informs him that he should have kept his mouth shut. Yet Aesop, realizing Apollo's will, accepts his fate: "How can I, a mortal man, escape what is to be?"[19] Earlier, Aesop had saved others; now he cannot save himself. Jesus's enemies mockingly declare that the same is true for him (Mark 15:31).

The day of execution arrives. On the way to the cliff, Aesop suddenly breaks free and takes refuge in Apollo's temple. Thus the fabulist seeks the defense of his god. By necessity, then, the Delphians must commit sacrilege against their own deity to murder Aesop. They drag him out of the temple to the top of the cliff. Inching toward the edge, Aesop warns them of coming doom.

These prophecies adapt a mythographical template that one might call clairvoyance before death.[20] In Homer's *Iliad*, for instance, the Trojan hero Hector spears Patroclus in the gut. Dying, Patroclus looks up to his killer and prophesies,

> Boast while you still can, Hector. Your triumph was given
> by Zeus and Apollo. They were the ones who really
> brought me down. . . .
> And one thing more: You too will die before long,
> for at this moment your irresistible fate
> is approaching, and you will be killed by Achilles' hands.[21]

The pattern is repeated later when Achilles slays Hector. It will not be long, the dying Hector gasps, before Achilles himself is laid low by Paris's arrow and the hand of Apollo.[22]

Similarly, when the people of Delphi are preparing to push Aesop off a cliff, he cries, "If I die, I will be your doom!" The armies of Lydia, Babylon, and practically all of Greece will soon take vengeance on the Delphians.[23] These final prophecies are more than desperate attempts at psychological compensation. The prophesied judgment is real. The dying hero is innocent; the killers are ruthless and, as is typical, pay no heed.

Even though Luke's Jesus prays for the forgiveness of his enemies, he also foretells their destruction. Historically speaking, the death of Jesus at the hands of the Romans and the Roman sack of Jerusalem (70 CE) had no direct historical connection. Yet Lukan historiography created a new reality: because the Jews murdered Jesus, the Romans will punish them for destroying Jerusalem and burning the temple.

How did the author portray this? He gave Jesus his own prophecy before death. The scene is set as Jesus stumbles through the streets of Jerusalem one final time. The author of Luke, in accordance with his tendency to portray Jesus's death as noble, omits from Mark's passion narrative the taunting of the onlookers (Mark 15:29–30). Instead, he even makes some bystanders burst into tears.

Suddenly the spotlight beams on the "daughters of Jerusalem." These women wail as Jesus heaves the cross through narrow lanes. Bearing a heavy beam and driven ruthlessly by Roman soldiers, Jesus finds time to turn round and deliver a thoughtful speech: "Daughters of Jerusalem, do not weep for me, but weep for yourselves and for your children. For the days are surely coming when they will say, 'Blessed are the barren, and the wombs that never bore, and the breasts that never nursed.' Then they will begin to say to the mountains, 'Fall on us!'; and to the hills, 'Cover us!'" (Luke 23:28–30).

In short, Jesus prophesies the destruction of Jerusalem, poetically depicting the extreme pain of its citizens who will see their children murdered. The prophecy, from the Lukan vantage point, described events that had already occurred. In 70 CE, Jerusalem underwent a terrible siege (accurately described in Luke 19:42–44, 21:20). During the siege, people trapped in the city starved en masse.

Reference to a historical event boosted the plausibility of the Lukan narrative. Luke's audience would have known about the siege and destruction of Jerusalem. Educated readers (and the author of Luke himself) could have read about the horrors as they were recounted by the Jewish historian Josephus.[24] Yet Jesus's eloquent prophecy spoken immediately before death is doubted by modern historians. The author of Luke was almost certainly adapting a mythic template (the *pharmakos*), presenting it as historiography. As we see by comparing the *Life of Aesop,* the Christian author was not alone.

To be sure, neither Jesus nor Aesop fit the *pharmakos* pattern in every detail. Yet both conform in ways that strikingly converge. Both Aesop and Jesus suffer from the inhospitality of a famous temple city. Both are the victims of deceit and murder. Both undergo a sham trial followed by a speedy death. On Aesop's way to execution, he is marched throughout the city before he is thrown out of it. Jesus, similarly, is paraded through the city of Jerusalem (on the so-called Via Dolorosa, or Route of Pain) before being nailed up outside the gate.

The killing of both Jesus and Aesop leads to the community's guilt and punishment. Hostile armies arrive at the gates of Delphi. An oracle tells the Delphians how they wronged Aesop and how they can right that wrong. They are instructed to recognize Aesop as a god and institute his worship.

In the gospel of John, there is an analogous oracle, but it is told before Jesus's death. The oracle is given by the high priest, who responds to the genuine fear that "the Romans will come and remove our temple and our people." The high priest then unwittingly prophesies, "it is better . . . to have one man die for the people than to have the whole nation destroyed" (John 11:48–50). The *pharmakos*, like Codrus and Menoeceus, is a substitute for the nation.

Jesus died on behalf of his people, the nation. Possibly this prophecy represents an early Christian viewpoint in which Christ died to atone for the Jews. In what became normative Christian thought, however, the expiation provided by Christ's death covered only the sins of those (mainly Gentiles) who came to believe in him. The Jewish nation and its leaders, increasingly blamed for killing Jesus, were not (or no longer) viewed as beneficiaries of Jesus's death. Their destiny was destruction at the hands of Roman armies.

In *pharmakos* mythology, an oracle sometimes commands that the victim be deified in some way and thus receive worship by members of the community.[25] The worship of the *pharmakos* has its analogy in gospel mythology. In one way or another, Matthew, Luke, and John depict the postcrucified Jesus as receiving adoration worthy of a deity. People prostrate themselves before him, even calling him "Lord" and "God" (for instance, by Thomas in John 20:28). The gospels are themselves products of the worship of Jesus, so the narrated veneration is unsurprising.

In the case of Aesop, there was an altar commemorating him at Delphi at the place where his body was supposedly found. Some form of sacrifice was performed on this altar, indicating Aesop's divine status. Version W of the *Life* even says that the Delphians dedicated a temple to Aesop. In the case of Jesus, Christians today still visit his holy sepulcher in Jerusalem— or its re-creations.

The final vindication of Jesus is expressed by resurrection. Oddly enough, there is also a long-standing tradition in which Aesop is said to have returned to life. This is not a common element of *pharmakos* mythology, but it is worth exploring. In a fragment of the comic poet Plato (flourished about 400 BCE), two dialogue partners speak. The first says, "Swear to me that the body does not die." His interlocutor answers, "I swear." Then the first man says, "Swear also that the soul returns to the body." The second responds, "Just as the soul of Aesop once returned to his body."[26] When a soul returns to its body, the body is reanimated. Apparently a standard case of reanimation was Aesop.

In the early second century CE, two other authors attest to the resurrection of Aesop. One of them, the innovative historian Ptolemy Chennus ("the Quail"), says that Aesop came back to life and even fought with the Greeks in the battle of Thermopylae (480 BCE).[27] Are we to think of bodily resurrection? Perhaps not. But Aesop could not pick up sword and shield without being physically present in some way.

Around the same time, Zenobius the rhetorician wrote, "For Aesop was so dear to the gods that the story is told of him that he was resurrected like Tyndareus, Heracles, and Glaucus."[28] Although Christian influence is not impossible, Zenobius is probably too early to have imitated Christian stories. The figures that Zenobius compares (Tyndareus, Heracles, and Glaucus) are all Greek heroes whose narratives long predate the gospels. Aesop's resurrection was, in short, both well-known and confirmed by better-known Greek precedents.[29]

Conclusion

The "passion narratives" of Aesop and Jesus are similar, to a certain degree, because they follow a common mythic template: the *pharmakos*. Both figures tell inflammatory parables, are arrested on trumped-up charges of blasphemy, and are sentenced to horrific deaths. In both cases, the *pharmakos* pattern has been adapted to historical discourse. It is applied to persons, that is, who are presented as historical and who are the subjects of biography.

It is probably safe to say that Aesop's passion and death—along with Aesop himself—is a *mythos* with no basis in historical fact. Yet his story (contemporary with the gospels) is presented as if it really occurred in sixth-century BCE Delphi. The Delphic local color and the realistic description of priestly excess add to the aura of verisimilitude.

In the case of the gospels, we have reason to doubt that the details of the passion narratives, which strongly misrepresent the Jewish leaders, relate the past as it actually happened. It is evident, however, that they are presented as historical reports and use the tropes of historical narration and causation. Jesus dies because he provokes the Jewish leaders. He provokes them, like Aesop, by telling an inflammatory parable that helps to secure (one might even say *engineer*) his death. The parables are taken to be allegories of a sort, but the stories in which they are framed are biographies. The biographical form of the lives of both Jesus and Aesop shows that there was a tendency in the first century CE to historicize the lives of heroes even if the plot of their lives was adapted from a mythic pattern.

Further Reading

Francisco R. Adrados, "The 'Life of Aesop' and the Origins of the Novel in Antiquity," *Quaderni Urbinati di Cultura Classica*, n.s. 1 (1979): 93–112.

Mario Andreassi, "The *Life of Aesop* and the Gospels: Literary Motifs and Narrative Mechanisms," in *Holy Men and Charlatans in the Ancient Novel*, ed. Stelios Panayotakis, Gareth Schmeling, and Michael Paschalis (Gröningen: Barkhuis, 2015), 151–66.

Jan Bremmer, "The Scapegoat between Northern Syria, Hittites, Israelites, Greeks and Early Christians," in *Greek Religion and Culture, the Bible and the Ancient Near East*, Jerusalem Studies in Religion and Culture 8 (Leiden: Brill, 2008), 169–214.

Todd M. Compton, "The Trial of the Satirist: Poetic Vitae (Aesop, Archilochus, Homer) as Background for Plato's Apology," *American Journal of Philology* 111 (1990): 330–47.

Todd M. Compton, *Victim of the Muses: Poet as Scapegoat, Warrior and Hero in Greco-Roman and Indo-European Myth and Historiography* (Washington, DC: Center for Hellenic Studies, 2006).

Albert Henrichs, "Human Sacrifice in Greek Religion: Three Case Studies," in *Le sacrifice dans l'antiquité*, ed. Jean Rudhardt and Olivier Reverdin, Entretiens sur la Antiquité Classique 27 (Geneva: Fondation Hardt, 1981), 195–242.

Mary R. Lefkowitz, *The Lives of Greek Poets*, 2d ed. (Baltimore: Johns Hopkins University Press, 2012).

Richard Pervo, "A Nihilist Fabula: Introducing the Life of Aesop," in *Ancient Fiction and Early Christian Narrative*, ed. Ronald F. Hock, J. Bradley Chance, Judith Perkins (Atlanta: Scholars, 1998), 77–120.

Jan Willem van Henten, *Martyrdom and Noble Death: Selected Texts from Greco-Roman, Jewish, and Christian Antiquity* (London: Routledge, 2002).

Lawrence M. Wills, *The Quest of the Historical Gospel: Mark, John, and the Origins of the Gospel Genre* (London: Routledge, 1997).

CHAPTER TWELVE

EMPTY TOMBS AND TRANSLATION

It is the myth that gives life. . . . The heart of Christianity is a
myth which is also a fact. . . . By becoming a fact it does not
cease to be myth; that is the miracle.
—*C. S. Lewis*[1]

The gospel of Mark ends with women discovering Jesus's empty tomb.
At first light, three women bring perfumed ointment to the grave in order to anoint Jesus's corpse. They proceed to the tomb without anyone
able to help them roll away the huge stone blocking the entrance. Luckily
the boulder has been mysteriously removed, and a young man dressed in
white is waiting in the tomb to announce the great reversal: "He is not
here!" (Mark 16:1–8).[2]

The youth reports that Jesus will dutifully appear in Galilee. But this testimony does not answer the question smoldering in the back of the reader's
mind: What happened to Jesus's body? Did it simply wake up and walk out
of the tomb? Did an angel whisk it away to Galilee? Did it mysteriously dissolve and reappear amid the stars above? What appears to be assumed, at
least originally, is that Jesus's body has been taken to heaven. From heaven
his body can appear on earth in virtually any location that Jesus pleases—
including his old haunts in Galilee.[3]

In Greek mythology, many heroes, such as the Trojan prince Ganymede, were also translated to a heavenly location or paradise. In Homer's *Odyssey*, Proteus, the Old Man of the Sea, reveals to the Spartan hero Menelaus,

> You shall not die in Argos [in Greece]; instead, the immortals
> will carry you to the Elysian Fields, at the end of the earth,
> to the land where Rhadamanthus is king
> and where life flows by without effort for humankind.[4]

The translation of Menelaus involved both a permanent change of residence (the Elysian Fields) and the immortalization of his body (fit for the eternal enjoyment of Ocean's breezes).

This kind of mythology, which a recent writer calls the "translation fable," was widely historicized during the era of the Roman Empire.[5] Philostratus, for instance, described how Apollonius of Tyana disappeared in a temple on the island of Crete. The elderly sage, Philostratus says, ran into the temple of Dictynna (a Cretan goddess). The doors shut automatically behind him. Bystanders then heard an uncanny song, as if sung by a chorus of maidens: "Proceed from the earth! Proceed to heaven. Proceed!" Those who inspected the temple later found that Apollonius had vanished.[6]

Achilles

Menelaus and Apollonius were translated before their physical deaths. The Greek hero Achilles, however, was different. Achilles was a demigod, son the mortal Peleus and the sea goddess Thetis. Like Jesus, Achilles actually dies. He is killed in battle by the lethal arrow of Paris, prince of Troy. Afterward, his body is recovered, hauled into the Greek camp, and prepared for burial. Dirges are sung. A funeral mound is built. All begin to cry. In the words of the poet Pindar,

> But when he [Achilles], died, songs did not forsake him,
> but the Heliconian Maidens [the Muses] stood by his
>   pyre and his funeral mound,
> pouring forth their polyphonic dirge.[7]

Achilles's own mother, Thetis, joins the Muses in mourning. Like depictions of Mary at the foot of the cross, Thetis is portrayed as utterly distraught upon seeing her dead son. According to a later epic, the god Poseidon consoles her:

> Refrain from endless mourning for thy son.
> Not with the dead shall he abide, but dwell
> With Gods, as doth the might of Heracles,
> And Dionysus ever fair. Not him
> Dread doom shall prison in darkness evermore,
> Nor Hades keep him. To the light of Zeus
> Soon shall he rise; and I will give to him
> A holy island for my gift: it lies
> Within the Euxine Sea: there evermore
> A God thy son shall be. The tribes that dwell
> Around shall as mine own self honor him
> With incense and with steam of sacrifice.[8]

Achilles will reappear far to the north, on an island in the Euxine (that is, the Black Sea, north of Turkey). In the meantime, his body is gently laid on a large pile of wood. An attendant proceeds to ignite the fire. Before Achilles's body is engulfed by the flames, however, Thetis herself snatches it away. In accordance with the prophecy, she deposits the body—now alive and immortalized—on White Island in the Black Sea.[9]

This bright, luminous island may originally have been one of the Islands of the Blessed familiar in Greek mythology.[10] Yet the Greeks also knew White Island as a real place in the Black Sea. It was located thirty miles southeast of the mouth of the River Danube and is probably identical to what is now called Snake Island.[11] On this island, Achilles's body was vivified so that the hero—or rather god—could appear to many witnesses.

Knowing these other stories allows one to better grasp how the first readers of Mark understood Jesus's disappearance from the tomb and reappearance elsewhere. Like Achilles, Jesus actually died, and his corpse vanished. His corpse was then enlivened, immortalized, and transferred to a different location. Jesus did not remain on earth but went to heaven. Though existing in heaven, Jesus could appear in different places on earth. Although Mark did not narrate the event, presumably Jesus appeared in Galilee to his disciples. Later evangelists, such as the authors of Matthew and John, filled in the gaps by describing (and quite possibly inventing) Jesus's various Galilean manifestations.

Similar appearance stories recur in the mythistorical reports of Achilles. Some who sailed to White Island reported that they saw Achilles on the beaches darting about in golden armor. Others said that they heard him singing or galloping on a horse in the open fields.[12] Sometimes Achilles instructed sailors exactly where to land and anchor their ships near the island. Achilles was no mere phantom haunting a single place. He appeared to wide-awake sailors on the sails of their ships or the tips of their prows.[13]

According to one story, Achilles physically ripped apart a young girl on the island since she was a descendant of his enemy Hector. In another tale, a squadron of warriors—identified with Amazons—invaded the island. Yet Achilles quickly repulsed them from his shores.[14] All these activities are physical, which suggests that Achilles had some kind of material body. The appearances themselves are strange, since in Greek tradition, a hero normally manifested himself only near his grave. Achilles's burial mound was in Troy, far away from White Island. The ancients would have realized that Achilles was more than a hero. He was not actually buried. He had assumed the powers of a god.

Achilles was duly worshiped as a deity. According to Pausanias, a Greek travel writer of the second century CE, Achilles had altars, a temple, and a statue on White Island. The same writer reveals that Achilles healed those who worshiped him there.[15] Yet Achilles's worship was not limited to White Island. His cult has been documented to exist all over the Mediterranean world, including Astypalaea in the Aegean Sea, Sparta, Elis, and Thessaly in Greece, as well as Tarentum, Locri, and Croton in southern Italy.[16] Citizens of Olbia, a city not far from White Island, worshiped Achilles as one of their most important deities.[17]

Remnants of Achilles's worship survive to this day. The oldest stone dedication to Achilles comes from the 400s BCE. It reads, "Glaucus, child of Posides, set me up for Achilles, lord of White Island." Later inscriptions give thanks to Achilles for deliverance from shipwreck, a safe journey home, and victory at athletic games held in his honor.[18] We know that in the time of Hadrian (Roman emperor from 117 to 138 CE), Achilles was worshiped under the name "Ruler of the Sea" (*Pontarchēs*). The worship of Achilles seems to have lasted up until the fourth century CE.

Such worship grew out of the recognition that the resurrected Achilles was more than a hero. He had become a deity. Although the nature of his body was left unclear, Achilles existed in a physical place and could perform palpably physical activities. And it was not only mythographers and poets who spoke of Achilles's postmortem life. His story appears in the work of orators (Maximus of Tyre), historians (Arrian, *Voyage Round the Euxine*), and writers who imitated historical—supposedly "eyewitness"—reports (Philostratus, *Heroicus*).

The evangelists who reported the reappearances of Jesus were apparently aiming at the same kind of historiographical discourse. The earliest narrative gospel (Mark) would not allow Jesus's body to appear except in Galilee. Later evangelists permitted him to appear in and around Jerusalem. In these later renditions, it becomes increasingly clear that Jesus's body took on a physical form, even if it had special properties (such as the ability to disappear and walk through walls).

True, there are some elements that an educated ancient reader would have found incredible in the gospels, such as the young man who becomes an angel (or angels) in later gospels. (They resemble Poseidon in Greek myth, who announces that Achilles will reappear on White Island.) Overall, however, the gospel accounts of Jesus's translation and reappearances have the form of a historical report that mentions real places in apparently real time. If in a general way the gospel writers were influenced by Greek mythography, then they were specifically imitating those who put it into historical form.

The Empty Tomb

The author of Mark presented the body of Jesus as placed in a tomb, but the Matthean evangelist depicted the tomb as carefully sealed. The act of sealing guaranteed that the tomb could not be opened without the express permission of the Roman authorities. According to Matthew's gospel, the Jews even ensured that a Roman guard was posted at the tomb to ward off robbers.

A similar act of sealing occurs in another historiographical report. Numa Pompilius, second king of Rome, was upon death sealed in his coffin. The coffin was made of stone, eight feet in length, and sealed with molten lead. It was then buried beneath the Janiculum Hill in Rome. When by accident the tomb was unearthed by plowmen, it evoked wonder. The discovery was precisely dated by the Roman consuls (or heads of state) at the time. In modern chronology, the date was 181 BCE.

The Romans in this story wasted no time in cracking open the coffin—but to everyone's surprise, the body had disappeared. To be sure, the decay of the flesh was expected after several centuries, but the absence of bones in a sealed coffin was impossible to explain. There were also no grave goods such as royal jewelry or remnants of clothing. Complete dissolution seemed an unlikely hypothesis since in a companion coffin, Numa's books—made of organic materials—survived with virtually no damage.[19]

The historians who record these events are ineloquent about what happened to Numa's body (they are more interested in Numa's books). The assumption, however, seems to have been that Numa's body had been transported to some other (probably heavenly) location. Numa had become a *numen*, a kind of Roman divinity.[20] This interpretation could emerge even if the coffins were fake and the books forgeries. Indeed, the translation of Numa would only add to the perceived authority of the books. The king who wrote them had been immortalized.

There was never any doubt as to who was supposed to occupy the coffin. It was carefully labeled with an inscription to this effect: "Numa Pompilius son of Pompon, king of the Romans, lies buried within." Buried as a man, he was raised as a god.[21] No one doubted, moreover, that Numa's books had been found. The fact that they were burned by the Roman Senate was considered a well-known historical event.

In Matthew's gospel, Jesus's body also disappears from his tomb without much explanation. Glorious angels open the tomb so that the female witnesses can see that it is empty. According to Mark, these women run from the tomb in terror. Such uncertainty proved intolerable to later evangelists. Accordingly, the author of Matthew presented the resurrected Jesus as immediately greeting the women outside the tomb (Matt. 28:1–10).

Despite the added story of Jesus's appearance, reports of fraud arose. The disciples were rumored to have stolen the body (Matt. 28:13). In Matthew, this report is implicitly belittled since the disciples would have needed to subdue the well-trained and heavily armed Roman guard.

The rumor of theft and double-dealing has an interesting parallel in the mythic historiography of Romulus. Romulus was the first king of Rome, and his death (or departure) story was widely known in the first century

CE. The Roman historian Livy (late first century BCE) provides the basic account. When Romulus was reviewing his troops outside of Rome, a storm suddenly arose with great peals of thunder. A miraculous eclipse of the sun, together with a thick cloud, hid the king from the sight of his soldiers. The people fled in terror. When the darkness dissipated, King Romulus was no longer sitting on his throne. The senators informed the people that Romulus had bodily ascended to heaven.[22] There arose a persistent rumor, however, that the senators had seized their king during the confusion and had torn his body into pieces.[23]

In the gospel of Matthew, similar signs accompany Jesus's death and resurrection: preternatural darkness, the rending of the temple veil, and a powerful earthquake (Matt. 27:45, 51; 28:2). These seem like incredible events but no more incredible than those reported about Romulus. Although there are doubts today, the Romans considered their first king to be an undisputedly historical figure.

Like the people in Romulus's story, the women flee in terror (Matt. 28:8). There is, moreover, a double report of Jesus's fate. Jesus's disciples come to believe his resurrection; but the Jewish leaders tell the Roman guards to report the body's theft (Matt. 28:11–15). By virtue of this report, the author of Matthew attempted to explain the reason why, even in his time, the story of the stolen body lingered on.

In providing this alternative tradition, the Matthean evangelist used the language of historical causation. The conniving Jewish leaders *created* the theft story; hence it continues to persist. Although this evangelist preferred to explain the missing body by narrating resurrection appearances, the fact that he offered an alternative report is significant. Providing such a report was a common historiographical technique. Offering the reader a choice between the reports gave the (albeit fleeting) impression of objectivity.[24]

The alternative-report trope is reminiscent of Plutarch, who narrated the tradition that Romulus rose bodily to heaven. Plutarch himself would not accept this report on philosophical grounds: physical bodies cannot rise to heaven. Yet Plutarch conceded that Romulus's *soul* had ascended to become a deity. This is a rationalizing tradition that would have made better sense to readers versed in Platonic philosophy.

Livy, as previously mentioned, also reported alternative traditions concerning Romulus's last earthly moments. Romulus was either dismembered by the senators during the storm or taken to heaven and deified. With regard to historiographical rhetoric, Livy appears more objective than Matthew, since he did not try to debunk the alternative (dismemberment) tradition. To a Roman, however, affirming the deification rather than the dismemberment of Romulus was both more appealing and more pious, given that Romulus was worshiped in Rome as a state deity (called Quirinus).[25]

Tomb Tokens

The gospel of John presents Peter and the so-called Beloved Disciple running to inspect Jesus's tomb. It had already been declared empty by Mary Magdalene, a close female disciple of Jesus. A woman's testimony was apparently not enough, however, so the fourth evangelist portrayed two chief apostles confirming the report. Contrary to the suspicion of modern skeptics, they do not go to the wrong tomb. They recognize the right tomb by the presence of Jesus's personal items, namely, the linen wrappings that formerly covered his body and a neatly folded cloth that covered his face (John 20:5–7). These details undercut the supposition that the body was stolen, since robbers would presumably not have taken the time to carefully fold Jesus's face cloth.

What the author of John did, then, is present the reader with a tomb token: a sign that guides the interpretation of what happened to the body. The fourth evangelist even introduced a model interpreter into his story. When the Beloved Disciple sees the tomb tokens, he internally recognizes (or chooses to believe) in Jesus's resurrection (John 20:8).

Such scenes of recognition via tomb tokens appear in other mythic historiographies of the time. Plutarch relates the story of Alcmene (mother of Heracles), who was buried in Haliartus of Greece. According to one version of the story, Alcmene's dead body disappeared from her funeral couch. In place of her body, a life-size stone was left behind.[26] According to another version, Alcmene's body was placed in her tomb. Much later, the tomb was cracked opened at the command of Agesilaus, king of Sparta (ruled from 398 to 360 BCE). Agesilaus had intended to move her remains to Sparta, but Alcmene's body was never found. The excavators discovered only a stone (as in the previous version), together with some personal effects of the woman: a bronze bracelet and two clay urns.[27]

Just as Jesus's body wrappings and head covering indicated that he was once present, Alcmene's stone and bracelet showed that her body was at one time extant in the tomb. At some point, however, Alcmene was transported away and immortalized—or so Agesilaus and his ministers believed. The sight of Jesus's tokens provoked a similar response in the so-called Beloved Disciple. When he entered the tomb, "he saw and believed" (John 20:8).

Conclusion

In these stories we observe special figures who appear on an apparently historical stage. Yet underlying the narration is a template that is well recognized from mythography: the translation and immortalization of famous heroes. The presence of the mythic template indicates that the stories do not describe what happened in space and time. All the same, the *mythoi* have been modified to fit the frame of historiography. Tropes have been added to make the stories seem more historical: alternative reports, tomb tokens, staged skepticism, and so on.

Readers can speculate about the so-called historical core of these stories. Yet the truth is that one can never firmly separate mythic elements from historiographical report since there is no independent confirmation of what happened, and templates from more ancient mythography informed how events were remembered and composed. It is better, then, to accept these stories as instances of mythic historiography—stories that moderns might take as myth but were presented as ancient historical writing.

Further Reading

Stephen J. Bedard, "A Nation of Heroes: From Apotheosis to Resurrection," in *Resurrection of the Dead: Biblical Traditions in Dialogue,* ed. Geert van Oyen and Tom Shepherd (Leuven, Belgium: Peeters, 2012), 453–60.

Jonathan S. Burgess, *The Death and Afterlife of Achilles* (Baltimore: Johns Hopkins University Press, 2009), 98–130.

Adela Yarbro Collins, "Ancient Notions of Transferal and Apotheosis in Relation to the Empty Tomb Story in Mark," in *Metamorphoses Resurrection, Body, and Transformative Practices in Early Christianity,* ed. Turid Karlsen Seim and Jorunn Økland (Berlin: de Gruyter, 2009), 41–58.

Dag Øistein Endsjø, *Greek Resurrection Beliefs and the Success of Christianity* (New York: Palgrave Macmillan, 2009), 54–64.

Guy Hedreen, "The Cult of Achilles in the Euxine," *Hesperia* 60 (1991): 313–30.

J. T. Hooker, "The Cults of Achilles," *Rheinische Museum für Philologie* 131 (1988): 1–7.

M. David Litwa, *Iesus Deus: The Early Christian Depiction of Jesus as a Mediterranean God* (Minneapolis: Fortress, 2014), 141–80.

Andy Reimer, "A Biography of a Motif: The Empty Tomb," in *Ancient Fiction: The Matrix of Early Christian and Jewish Narrative*, ed. Jo-Ann Brant (Atlanta: Society of Biblical Literature, 2005), 297–316.

H. A. Shapiro, "Hêrôs Theos: The Death and Apotheosis of Heracles," *Classical World* 77 (1983): 7–18.

Charles Talbert, "The Concept of the Immortals in Mediterranean Antiquity," *Journal of Biblical Literature* 94 (1975): 419–36.

Jean-Pierre Vernant, *Mortals and Immortals* (Princeton, NJ: Princeton University Press, 1991).

CHAPTER THIRTEEN

DISAPPEARANCE AND RECOGNITION

Already patently false and fabricated accounts about new
and recent events have gained credibility.
—*Plutarch*[1]

The author of Luke is the only evangelist to record Jesus's disappearance and sudden reappearance several miles away. The event occurs in the "Emmaus Road" episode. Emmaus seems to have designated a real place, but modern scholars—despite great efforts—have yet to precisely identify it on the map. It was sufficient for the third evangelist that Emmaus seemed to be a real town, some seven miles distant from Jerusalem (Luke 24:13).

Walking toward this town, the resurrected Jesus suddenly approaches two of his disciples. The fact that these disciples have never before been mentioned is surprising. Yet at least one of them is given a name, which seems to vouch for his reality (Luke 24:18, cf. 8:1–3, 24:10). More surprising is that these disciples are traveling away from Jerusalem, where they have just heard the report of Jesus's resurrection. Surely they would have stayed in the city to see if the report was confirmed? They even imply that virtually everyone in Jerusalem knows the recent events surrounding Jesus (Luke 24:18)—a common technique of objectifying discourse.

Yet the greatest mystery of all is that these disciples fail to recognize Jesus. The author of Luke tries to explain this point by saying that their eyes were "restrained"—evidently by divine will. However the restraint occurred, the lack of recognition is necessary for the story to unfold.

The unknown Jesus strikes up a conversation along the road. The conversation soon becomes Jesus's monologue attempting to prove that his suffering and death were prophesied in Jewish scripture. When the travelers reach Emmaus, the disciples invite Jesus to a meal. His initial resistance is polite, but he eventually comes to the table. The meal seems to proceed normally until, all of the sudden, it becomes a repetition of the Last Supper. Jesus picks up bread, breaks it—and in that instant the disciples recognize him. Then, in the blink of an eye, Jesus disappears. He later reappears miles away in Jerusalem with a body able to pass through walls (Luke 24:13–36, cf. 9:16, 22:19).

This kind of story, with regard to its action sequence, resembles several Greek *mythoi* in which a disguised god is recognized in a meal setting. The Roman poet Ovid, for instance, tells the tale of two travelers—the disguised Zeus and Hermes—coming to visit the elderly couple Philemon and Baucis.[2] They are the only persons in their whole town who grant the gods room and board and are duly rewarded.

To give a lesser-known example: in olden days, when wine was still undiscovered, a man named Falernus offered hospitality to the disguised Bacchus (otherwise known as Dionysus). Falernus did not recognize the god but invited him to dinner. With kindly zeal, Falernus served Dionysus the finest foods of his humble pantry. Gratified, Bacchus made wine well up from the wooden cups—as well as every other pitcher and bucket in the house. Falernus was thunderstruck. He whirled round to see the god in his true form, decked with ivy and rubbing a wine glass.[3]

Recognizing the gods in these stories is not automatic but a gift. According to Homer's *Iliad,* a mist naturally covers the eyes of mortals, preventing them from seeing the gods. Homer's Odysseus once asked, "Who with his eyes could behold a god if the god did not will?"[4] When Athena reveals herself to Odysseus but not to his son, the narrator explains, "It is by no means to everyone that gods grant a clear sight of themselves."[5] Elsewhere in Lukan myth, the eyes of Paul can see Christ (or the light surrounding him), while his traveling companions only hear a voice (Acts 9:7). (In a later retelling, the companions do not even hear a voice; Acts 22:9.) In Luke's gospel, the eyes of the Emmaus disciples need to be divinely opened before they can recognize the resurrected god (Luke 24:31).

Gods typically allow themselves to be recognized by certain tokens. Aphrodite, veiled behind the form of an old wool-carding woman, is recognized by her beautiful neck, lovely breasts, and flashing eyes.[6] Achilles recognizes Athena by the terrible gleam in her eye.[7] Odysseus recognizes Hermes by his golden wand.[8] Jesus is recognized by a characteristic action in the meal—the breaking of bread (Luke 24:35).

Finally, the fact that Jesus's body can pass through walls would not have surprised anyone familiar with Greek *mythoi*. The god Hermes was able to pass into a room through the keyhole "like mist on the breath of autumn."[9] The playwright Euripides provided a more realistic example. In his play the *Bacchae*, Dionysus is arrested but easily escapes from prison. His warden, king Pentheus of Thebes, is enraged by this strange turn of events. Huffing and puffing, he shouts, "How can it be that you have come outside and shown yourself at the door of my palace?" Spiraling into a frenzy, Pentheus orders his soldiers, "Shut all the towered gates all the way round the city!" Dionysus scoffs, "What? Do not gods pass over walls?"[10] The question is rhetorical. Whether Dionysus goes overtop the wall or through it, he demonstrates a point well-known in Greek mythology: a god cannot be contained.

What concerns us here, however, are mythic elements presented as history. Hermes passing through the keyhole is not very realistic. Euripides wrote a play with certain realistic effects. The author of Luke, however, wrote a biography that he apparently intended to be taken as historiography. To be sure, there are certain events in this biography that would seem to stretch the limits of credibility. After all, people do not normally rise from the dead. They do not, moreover, come back to talk to people and disappear into thin air. Nonetheless, these tales were not outside the bounds of ancient historical narration, as is shown by comparison.

Aristeas of Proconnesus

The father of history, Herodotus, related his own resurrection and vanishing act. According to his report, a man called Aristeas dies at the ancient equivalent of a Laundromat. In response, the owner of the establishment locks up shop and hurries to tell the man's relatives. The family is on its way to retrieve the body when they meet a man from another town. The man claims that he has just seen Aristeas on the road moments before.[11] The two travelers conversed as they journeyed along. This report causes immediate consternation. When the family finally reaches the Laundromat, they unlock the shop but find no body.[12] Seven years later, Aristeas reappears and—before vanishing once again—leaves behind a long poem called the *Arimaspea*.[13]

That Aristeas was no con man but was truly immortalized is indicated by his appearance 240 years later. Hundreds of miles away in southern Italy, Aristeas appears and orders the local inhabitants to set up an altar to Apollo. Alongside the altar, Aristeas urges that they erect a statue bearing his own name. That is to say, Aristeas institutes his own worship (later confirmed by the oracle of Apollo at Delphi)—and rightly so, since by virtue of his teleportation and extremely long life, Aristeas proves himself to be a divinity worthy of worship.[14]

This story features all the trappings of a *mythos,* yet it appears on the pages of historiography. The narrative is presented in a known place with temporal and spatial markers. The events of the story are fantastical, to be sure, but they are presented with the soberness of historical narration. It is this matter-of-fact mode of Herodotus's presentation that parallels the Emmaus story.

There are material parallels as well: the disappearance, the conversation on the road, the death and resurrection, the presence of witnesses, the worship of the resurrected one. For the author of Luke, the Last Supper was already an act of Christian worship in which Jesus manifested himself as Lord. In the narrative, he made clear that the disciples, after Jesus's vanishing act, worshiped him as a deity (Luke 24:52).[15]

We know that many Christians (still today) read the Emmaus story as a historical report. Christians are invested in the story, which has, in the meantime, become scripture. The account appears in historiographical form, and so Christians tend to credit its historicity—or at least do not openly question it.

Not every ancient person would have been invested in the Aristeas story. Thus not everyone—not even Herodotus himself—was inclined to believe it. Yet on this score Iamblichus made an interesting comment in his biography of Pythagoras. He wrote, "All the Pythagoreans are disposed to believe the stories told about Aristeas of Proconnesus. . . . They believe all such things were done and themselves attempt many of them, and keep in memory the stories that seem mythical [*dokountōn mythikōn*], not disbelieving anything that might lead to the divine."[16]

Iamblichus spoke like a true insider and revealed an important principle. Plausibility exists on a scale determined in large part by prior investment. Certain fantastic or fabulous events in historical narration might, for the average listener, push it outside the bounds of belief. Yet if readers of the tale were theologically invested, they would presumably give it the benefit of the doubt. The insider would not apparently deny the historicity of an event if its historicity was perceived to be connected to the moral and spiritual value of the story. Pythagoreans would have taken a special interest in the postmortem teleportation of Aristeas. He appeared in Metapontum, a key site of Pythagoras's ministry, and was closely associated with the god that Pythagoras incarnated, Apollo (see chapter 3).

Jesus's act of teleportation from Emmaus to Jerusalem, though it pushes the limits of historical narration, still fits within its frame. Pythagoras performed a similar feat, though it is unclear whether he teleported or was the subject of bilocation. At the same hour on the same day, he was seen talking publicly in both Italy and Sicily.[17] "Almost everyone is sure of this," Iamblichus insisted, "though there are many miles of land and sea between, which cannot be crossed even in very many days."[18] Later, after predicting the outbreak of civil strife, Pythagoras disappeared and reappeared in another city without anyone seeing him travel.[19]

These miracles were imitated by a later Pythagorean, Apollonius of Tyana. According to Philostratus, Apollonius was seen in the cities of Smyrna and Ephesus at the same time. Apollonius was later arrested and put on trial in Rome. In his trial, Apollonius electrified bystanders by disappearing from the courtroom and reappearing to his followers several miles outside the city.[20]

This very story of Apollonius mirrors a tale in Luke. After the Emmaus episode, Jesus appears inside a room and challenges his disciples, "Touch me and see, because a spirit [*pneuma*] does not have flesh and bones as you see that I have" (Luke 24:39). In this story, the author is concerned to prove that the hero is not a ghost, despite the ironic fact that he has just walked through a wall.

In a similar fashion, Apollonius suddenly materializes before his dejected followers outside Rome. Stunned at the sight of their master, they cannot believe their eyes. In response, Apollonius stretches out his hands and says, "Grasp me, and if I escape you, I am a ghost [*eidōlon*] come back. . . . But if I remain when grasped, . . . believe that I am alive and have not lost my body [*to sōma*]."[21] In both biographies the firm substance of the body is analogous to the evidentiary language of historical discourse. Both biographers aimed to present a disappearing hero who reappeared substantially.

In the gospel of Luke, Jesus is so eager to prove his materiality that he samples some broiled fish. (There may have been some lingering doubt, since in Emmaus he only broke bread and did not consume it.) Other "historical" accounts present figures eating with the dead who come back to life. Six months after the death of a maiden named Philinnion, she visited a lover over the course of three nights. She dined and drank with him—and even had sex with him (leaving her bra behind). Sex would seem to be the ultimate proof of one's fleshly nature—even if Philinnion's resurrection was short-lived.[22]

Herodotus reported a similar story. Astrabacus, a dead but reanimated hero, had sexual intercourse with a maiden. He even fathered a son called Demaratus. His paramour described Astrabacus as being a *phasma* or "apparition" in the form of her dead husband, Ariston. Despite being an apparition, Astrabacus was apparently not ethereal. In order for him to have sired a child, at least one part of him must have been substantial.[23]

To highlight Jesus's materiality, John's gospel presents the disciple Thomas as touching—indeed, penetrating—Jesus with his fingers.[24] Thomas had declared, "Unless I see the nail wound in his hands, thrust my finger into the nail wound, and thrust my hand into his side, I will not believe." A week later, Thomas was staying in a locked room when Jesus walked through the walls. Admittedly, this was not a good way to prove Jesus's materiality. Still, the hero approached Thomas and said, "Thomas, place your finger here; observe my hands, then bring your hand and thrust it into my side" (John 20:25–27). Thomas instantly realizes that Jesus is not a ghost but a god (John 20:28).

Even ghosts were said to bear the wounds they received in life. After Clytemnestra is stabbed to death by her son Orestes, for example, she upbraids the Furies (daimonic avengers of matricide) for not taking revenge, directing them, "look at these wounds in my heart!" (the bloody stab marks in her chest). By her poignant display, Clytemnestra galvanizes the Furies into action.[25]

Aeschylus, who gave us this image of Clytemnestra, used poetic license. Philostratus, however, presented another wounded hero as part of an eyewitness report. In Homeric tradition, Protesilaus was the first Greek soldier to die on Trojan soil. He was speared in the upper thigh. His dead body was washed and buried. When Protesilaus was resurrected, his scar remained. Worshipers of the embodied hero, according to Philostratus, saw the scar with their own eyes. This immortalized hero was more than a mere ghost. His devotees could see and interact with him in physical form. One devotee even attested, "He [Protesilaus] likes being embraced, and he allows me to kiss him and have my fill of his neck."[26]

Conclusion

Today, the stories discussed here would probably, if heard for the first time, be classified as fictions. Several of them, nevertheless, gesture toward historiography in the ancient sense. Instead of gods being the actors, divine humans take center stage. The flexible humanity of these figures allowed them to be the subjects of seemingly historical reports. Aristeas, Apollonius, Jesus, and Pythagoras were all venerated figures thought to have lived in antiquity. Some people considered them to be divine beings worthy of worship. The way to honor them was in part to present their stories in the most believable (that is, historical) way.

Ancient historiographical discourse allowed a blip to occur in the normality of the narrative world (such as the disappearance of the hero) while still leaving the realism of the discourse intact. Historiographcal discourse thus gave the impression that the textual and empirical worlds were one. The generally realistic representation urged invested readers to become, to some degree, a kind of Don Quixote who could not or did not wish to distinguish fully between textual and external worlds. Readers were led to believe that what could happen in the textual world—despite occasional oddity—could also happen in an external, lived world, perhaps in part because that lived world belonged to a now inaccessible (and sacred) past.

Further Reading

Wendy Cotter, "Greco-Roman Apotheosis Traditions and the Resurrection Appearances in Matthew," in *The Gospel of Matthew in Current Study: Studies in Memory of William G. Thompson, S.J.*, ed. David Aune (Grand Rapids, MI: Eerdmans, 2001), 127–53.

April D. DeConick and Grant Adamson, eds., *Histories of the Hidden God: Concealment and Revelation in Western Gnostic, Esoteric, and Mystical Traditions* (London: Acumen, 2013).

Kasper Bro Larsen, *Recognizing the Stranger: Recognition Scenes in the Gospel of John* (Leiden: Brill, 2012).

Deborah Thompson Prince, "The 'Ghost' of Jesus: Luke 24 in Light of Ancient Narratives of Post-Mortem Apparitions," *Journal for the Study of the New Testament* 29:3 (2007): 287–301.

Marie-Laure Ryan, *Narrative as Virtual Reality: Immersion and Interactivity in Literature and Electronic Media* (Baltimore: Johns Hopkins University Press, 2003).

Daniel Turkeltaub, "Perceiving Iliadic Gods," *Harvard Studies in Classical Philology* 103 (2007): 51–81.

Sjef van Tilborg and Patrick Chatelion Counet, *Jesus' Appearances and Disappearances in Luke 24* (Leiden: Brill, 2000), 193–234.

CHAPTER FOURTEEN

ASCENT

> What is likely [*eikota*] though impossible should be preferred
> to what is possible and unconvincing [*apithana*].
> —*Aristotle*[1]

Ascent to heaven is a common narrative in ancient Mediterranean heroic mythography. Heracles soared to heaven in a chariot, Asclepius rose
within a lightning bolt, and Romulus was lifted in the midst of a thunderstorm. We learn of these reports not only from poets but also from prose
writers, biographers, and historians who assumed that they were relating
past, if wondrous, events.

The early Christian Justin Martyr even used these *mythoi* as a measur-
ing rod of historical plausibility: "When we [Christians] say also that the
Logos [i.e., Christ] . . . was crucified and died and rose again and ascended
into heaven [*anelēluthenai eis ton ouranon*], we propound nothing new [*ou . . .
kainon ti*] beyond [what you believe] concerning those whom you call sons
of Zeus."[2] Justin's argument only works if the Greeks and Romans understood their ascent *mythoi* as records of real events.

Typically, the immortalizations of ancient heroes occurred simultaneously with their ascents. In this respect, Jesus proves no exception. The

authors of Mark and Matthew did not record Jesus's ascent to heaven, apparently because they felt no need. Resurrection and ascent were two sides of the same coin.[3] From heaven, Jesus could appear in his immortalized body anywhere on earth—in Galilee, Jerusalem, outside Damascus— wherever it was required.

The author of Luke is the only gospel writer to depict Jesus's ascent to heaven as a separate event.[4] At the end of his earthly career, Jesus takes his disciples to the Mount of Olives. He promises them that they will receive power when a sacred spirit comes upon them. Jesus then levitates and is gradually removed from the sight of his disciples by an intervening cloud (Acts 1:7–9).

The author of Luke employs in this description a cumulonimbus means of conveyance. The motif of a cloud-borne ascent to heaven was so widespread in Greco-Roman culture that no one author could claim ownership of it. Heracles ascended to heaven by means of a billowing cloud.[5] The patriarch Enoch soared to heaven on moving clouds.[6] Josephus said that Moses was raptured to heaven on a cloud.[7] At the end of Romulus's life, he was "encompassed with a cloud and taken up to heaven."[8] The cloud, one might say, was the Cadillac of deified heroes.

To modern people, such ascents do not seem historically plausible. It is simply too fantastic to believe that a body can levitate on a condensed mass of water vapor. It breaks the laws of physics, defies gravity, and misunderstands the nature of cloud formations. To be sure, the modern hero Superman has no problem soaring through the sky, but no one would call him a historical figure. Our cosmology has changed radically since ancient times. The immortal gods no longer live in heaven. What the ancients called "heaven" is the upper stratosphere and, beyond it, the vast reaches of outer space. Aliens may reside on other planets, but gods no longer have a home in the universe.

When the Lukan evangelist is considered in his own time, however, he did not transgress the limits of historical narration. Roman historians, for instance, recorded the bodily ascent of Romulus.[9] Cicero, one of the most educated Romans of the first century BCE, upheld the tradition: "When the sun was darkened, he [Romulus] was no longer manifest. So it was supposed that that he was added to the number of the gods."[10]

Such a fantastic story, Cicero urged, could not have been believed apart from Romulus's reputation for extreme virtue. It is the hero's virtue, not any archival information, that demands belief in Romulus's ascent. Yet to establish the plausibility of his myth, Cicero also relied on what he considered to be historical facts. He wrote, "Other people said to have been transformed from humans into gods lived in ages when people were less learned, when reason was inclined to make-believe, and naive people were easily seduced into believing. Yet we know by research that the age of Romulus was less than six hundred years ago, when literature and education were well established and the ancient blunders that grew out of uncultivated human life had been removed."[11]

The earliest Romans had a reputation for being barbarians—but this view, Cicero believed, is itself a fable. Rome was founded in the year 751 BCE (using the current dating system but Cicero's calculation). This was the seventh Olympiad, according to the common Greek calendar used at the time. Olympiads were four-year periods measured by the occurrence of the Olympic Games. The first Olympiad began in 776 BCE. Prior to this (essentially arbitrary) date, things might have been recorded in a looser way. Yet 776, or thereabouts, began the "historical" period in which "events" (*res gestae*) were recorded "in truthful history books" (*in veris historiis*).[12]

Within the "historical" period, dates could become precise. For instance, Plutarch, following the Roman author Varro, calculated the conception of Romulus to June 24, 772 BCE—the beginning of the second Olympiad.[13] For Cicero, this was not an age of barbarism but a time when learned poets and musicians thrived. During this time, Cicero observed, "slight credence [*minor fides*] was given to fables [*fabulis*], unless they were about ancient events [such as the Trojan War]." When Romulus lived, "there were educated people, and the times themselves were learned. There was hardly any place for make-believe [*ad fingendum*]. Antiquity accepted made-up tales [*fabulas fictas*]—sometimes even crude ones. But the age of Romulus was one of high culture. It mocked and rejected everything that could not have happened."[14]

Cicero thereby retrojected the ideas and attitudes of his own times into the era of Romulus. Still, it is the time of Cicero with which we are concerned—the time of the early Roman Empire (established de facto during the final days of Julius Caesar, or 48–44 BCE). During this era, the Romans were beginning to take pride in their own intellectual cultivation. In accordance with such cultivation, Cicero proposed the basic rule, widely assumed by Greek intellectuals: an event that could not have happened could not be believed. Yet bodily ascent, apparently, was not considered impossible, even for someone as sophisticated as Cicero.

True, the way Romulus departed earth was slightly embarrassing to the Roman orator. Cicero lived in an age in which men were deified, not one in which they actually floated into the sky. But Cicero did not for that reason reject a literal reading of Romulus's ascent. Instead, he did his best to defend its historicity by appealing to the concrete accomplishments of Romulus and to the sophistication of Romulus's time. It was not some bygone age of primitive stupidity. It was an age in which learned men believed in wonders because the deeds of their hero compelled them.

Greeks such as Plutarch with different philosophical commitments rationalized Romulus's story. For Plutarch, it was impossible for a human body to rise to heaven. Thus he could not accept a literal reading of Romulus's ascent. Nevertheless, Plutarch—who addressed himself partly to Roman readers—did not reject the ascent outright. Instead, he found another way to make it intellectually acceptable. It was not Romulus's body that rose, explained Plutarch, but his virtuous soul.[15] Only the soul, for a Platonist, can be deified. Plutarch has no problem with the ascent and immortalization of Romulus in itself. He merely modifies the *understanding* of it—that it was not bodily. Plutarch made this modification even though he agreed that Romulus's body had disappeared.

As it turns out, Plutarch's rejection of bodily ascent was the exception, not the rule. Other educated writers invested in their own cultural lore could, like Cicero, accept the reality of bodily ascent. A good example is the Jewish historian Josephus. Josephus's hero was Moses, whose life he described at length in book 4 of his *Jewish Antiquities*. According to Josephus, Moses experienced a literal ascent at the end of his life: a "cloud of a sudden descended upon him [Moses] and he disappeared in a ravine."[16] Moses, instead of dying, mysteriously disappeared. On the basis of this account, people supposed that he had "returned to divinity." Thus Moses was forced to compose an alternative account establishing his actual death.

The parallel to Romulus's end is palpable (in its dual versions), as is the attempt to portray it as reputable historiography.

More in the vein of Plutarch, Philo rejected the bodily ascent of Moses and replaced it with the ascent of Moses's mind (*nous*). Moses's "migration" from this world, said Philo, was an "exaltation," in which Moses "noticed that he was gradually being disengaged from the [bodily] elements with which he had been mixed."[17] When Moses shed his mortal encasing, God resolved Moses's body and soul into a single unity, "transforming [him] wholly and entirely into most sun-like mind."[18] Again, the strategy was not to deny the *mythos* of Moses's ascent or his bodily disappearance but to reinterpret them so that they became (philosophically) plausible.[19]

The author of Luke did not have the philosophical commitments of Philo or Plutarch. More in tune with Cicero and Josephus, he was inclined to present the ascent of Jesus as a literal and bodily one. A story of bodily ascent has many mythical analogues. Yet there were ways in which the evangelist molded the account to appear like historiography.

The premier trope of historiography is objectivity: the presentation of an event as perceptible to normal human senses. The ascents of other Greco-Roman heroes tended to be conflicted and fuzzy. The truth surrounding Romulus's disappearance, for instance, was never actually discerned. He disappeared in the darkness of a storm. A single witness, Proculus Julius, swore to the Roman Senate that he had seen Romulus ascend to heaven. Both Livy and Plutarch express amazement that so much faith was placed in the testimony of one man.[20]

The translation and ascent of Jesus in Mark presents a similar problem. No human actually saw Jesus disappear and ascend, so no one could confirm that the event really happened. By contrast, the Lukan author provided more than a dozen witnesses to Jesus's ascension, all of whom saw Jesus rise in broad daylight (according to Acts 1:9). In the space of three verses (Acts 1:9–11), the author repeats four times that these disciples physically saw Jesus rise to heaven.[21]

The author of Matthew noted that some of Jesus's eleven disciples doubted the resurrection even when they saw him physically present (Matt. 28:17). Similar doubts are noted in Luke 24:41. Although such doubts are not upheld as the proper response, they do indicate that the disciples were not easily fooled by a fake resurrection. Literary doubt is another factor that actually increases plausibility for the later reader, who needs to trust the "eyewitnesses" who first saw and believed.

Conclusion

For the author of Luke and other Greco-Roman writers, a story of ascent on a cloud could still be presented as historical fact. Modern people might reject the account as physically impossible. Yet most ancient readers, including the most sophisticated, admitted the possibility of bodily ascent, especially when there was prior investment in the hero's divinity.

There was also a recognition that the gods, when they entered the pages of historiography, had a special license. It is one thing for the poet Pindar to say, "Wonders, if gods accomplish them, never seem unbelievable to me."[22] Yet Arrian, the most meticulous of the surviving historians of Alexander the Great, vouched for a similar point. In speaking about the campaign of Dionysus, son of Zeus, against India, Arrian encountered a host of mythical tales. Instead of rejecting the reports, however, the historian wrote, "One must not be an overly strict examiner. . . . For what seems unbelievable according to probability is not entirely unbelievable when divine power [*to theion*] is added to the story."[23] Philo, for his part, when he came to explain whether there was a talking snake in the garden of Eden, accepted the literal and historical meaning of the story on this basis: "when some miraculous deed is prepared, God changes the inner nature."[24] In short, the normal strictures of historical probability could on occasion be loosened due to theological commitments.

There is an interesting example of this phenomenon in Plutarch's *Life of Coriolanus*. In this text, the biographer reported about a statue that supposedly spoke twice before many witnesses. Rationally, Plutarch could not bring himself to believe that a stone could speak, since it had no vocal chords. Yet he commented, "For those affected by their goodwill and love for the divine, and unable to set aside or disown anything of this kind, the biggest factor for belief is the wonderful and superhuman nature of the divine power. For divinity is in no way like the human in nature, movement, skill, or strength; nor is it irrational if it does what we cannot do or contrives what we cannot contrive. Rather, it is entirely other in everything and especially unlike and superior to us in its works."[25] Piety, for Plutarch, plays an important part even in historiography. The gods can make the impossible possible.

We observe the culmination of this sentiment in Iamblichus. According to him, Pythagoreans deny, in opposition to the sophists, that "some things are possible for God and others impossible. . . . Rather," Iamblichus insisted, "all things are possible."[26] He then quoted what he took to be a Pythagorean poem:

> We must expect all things, since nothing is beyond expectation.
> All things are easy for God to fulfill, and nothing is impossible of
>   fulfillment.[27]

In context, this is not a point about the writing of historiography, but it can be applied to it; and it seems to lie in the background of Christian historiography as well. The author of Luke, speaking through the angel Gabriel, made the point more simply: "Nothing," he said, "shall be impossible with God" (Luke 1:37).

Further Reading

Peter Borgen, "Heavenly Ascent in Philo: An Examination of Selected Passages," in *The Pseudepigrapha and Early Biblical Interpretation,* ed. James H. Charlesworth and Craig A. Evans (Sheffield, UK: Sheffield University Press, 1993), 246–68.

Adela Yarbro Collins, "Traveling Up and Away: Journeys to the Upper and Outer Regions of the World," in *Greco-Roman Culture and the New Testament: Studies Commemorating the Centennial of the Pontifical Biblical Institute,* ed. David Aune and Frederick Brenk (Leiden: Brill, 2012), 135–66.

Catherine Playoust, "Lifted Up from the Earth: The Ascension of Jesus and the Heavenly Ascents of Early Christians" (Ph.D. diss., Harvard University, 2006).

Alan Segal, "Heavenly Ascent in Hellenistic Judaism, Early Christianity and Their Environment," in *Aufstieg und Niedergang der Römischen Welt,* 2.23.2, ed. Hildegard Temporini and Wolfgang Haase (Berlin: de Gruyter, 1980), 1333–94.

Morton Smith, "Ascent to the Heavens and the Beginning of Christianity," *Eranos* 50 (1981): 403–29.

James Tabor, "'Returning to the Divinity': Josephus's Portrayal of the Disappearances of Enoch, Elijah, and Moses," *Journal of Biblical Literature* 108 (1989): 225–38.

CHAPTER FIFTEEN

EYEWITNESSES

My dear Titus, those "some people" of yours are naive in demanding
the truth . . . not as from a poet but as from a witness.
— *Cicero*[1]

Generally speaking, the impression of objectivity is warranted by empirical evidence. Yet this evidence is not often accessible for events that
happened in the past. Nevertheless, an ancient historian could introduce
a character who was able to serve as an ideal observer. To believe the
account, the reader would only then need to trust this ideal eyewitness.[2]
Through the eyes of the literary eyewitness, a subjective and spiritual event
could be represented as real and verifiable. The represented act of seeing
could appear to link the world of the narrative to the "real" world of events
in space and time.

Fictive or not, eyewitnesses were greatly valued in ancient Mediterranean culture. In Homer's *Odyssey*, the hero Odysseus praises the singer
Demodocus for relating the events of the Trojan War "as if you were present yourself, or heard it from one who was."[3] Demodocus was definitely
not present, a point that Odysseus well knows. Still, by means of his vivid
presentation, Demodocus could make it *seem* as if he were an eyewitness or

had heard from one who was. Homer knew that if one was not an eyewitness, skillful literary art could produce an eyewitness effect.

Historiographers also appealed to eyewitnesses to generate a sense of trust. In doing so, they were tapping into general cultural assumptions. The historian Polybius approved a well-known saying: "The eyes are truer and more accurate witnesses than the ears."[4] The historian Philo (early second century CE) began his historiography with the words, "The ears are less faithful than the eyes, so I am writing what I have seen, not what I have heard."[5]

In the ancient world, people listened to books read aloud. But mere bookish learning, Polybius observed, did not qualify one to write historiography. A true historian would go to the site of an event and interview eyewitnesses with critical judgment (since not all eyewitnesses told or remembered the truth for psychological, personal, and political reasons).[6]

Preferably the writer of historiography also ought to be an eyewitness. The historian Ephorus insisted, "If it were possible for us to be present at all events, this would be much the best means of gaining information."[7] In the mid-second century CE, Lucian offered this advice: "The historian must exercise judgment about events, especially as a present observer. But if not, he should pay attention to the most impartial informants and those whom one can surmise to be least likely through favor or hostility to subtract or add to what happened."[8]

Historians who lived through the events they described took pains to claim their eyewitness status. Thucydides, who wrote the history of the Peloponnesian War (431–404 BCE), claimed to have lived through the entire (thirty-year) conflict. When the war began, Thucydides insisted, he was already a mature man. Initially, he was a general in the war until, after failing to defend a city from capture, he was exiled for twenty years. Exile, if personally arduous, proved beneficial for the historian, since he gained the leisure to gather information precisely. As a noncombatant, Thucydides was also able to interview witnesses from both sides of the conflict to develop a more balanced perspective.[9]

Josephus (contemporaneous with the evangelists) made even more forceful claims to being an eyewitness. The subject of his first history was the Jewish War that raged from 66 to 73 CE. In the early phase of the war,

Josephus was appointed general in an effort to defend the region of Galilee. Needless to say, the Romans made short work of Josephus's Galilean defense force. After losing all his men, Josephus himself was captured and imprisoned. Yet his detainment proved advantageous for his later vocation as a historian. With the war in full swing, Josephus could observe it from the opposing side. Traveling around with the Roman army, he became an eyewitness of events he would otherwise have missed. Based on his eyewitness status, Josephus promoted his credibility and launched attacks on his critics.[10]

The gospels were probably not written by eyewitnesses. If they were, the authors would have named themselves and explicitly claimed to have seen the events that they narrated. If they based their accounts on eyewitness reports, they would have named those eyewitnesses specifically and related their differing accounts. Real eyewitnesses would not have left firsthand experience open to doubt. They would have boasted, like Josephus, of their eyewitness status and used it to confirm their authority.

To be sure, the author of Luke mentions receiving traditions from eyewitnesses (1:2). The fact that none of these witnesses is ever named and none of their reports is ever distinguished in the narrative, however, raises many questions. In fact, the author of Luke seems content to hide the nature of his sources. He clearly used the gospel of Mark, though he never once gives any impression that he did so. The details of his other sources, both oral and written, are never supplied.[11]

The Beloved Disciple

Despite the unlikelihood of the evangelists being eyewitnesses, at least one of them indicates that he based his material directly on an identifiable eyewitness who appears as a character in his story. Late in the fourth evangelist's account, he introduces an unnamed figure whom he refers to as "the disciple whom Jesus loved." This disciple, who appears nowhere else in gospel literature, is portrayed as one of Jesus's most intimate companions. At the Last Supper, the Beloved Disciple rests his head on Jesus's breast (John 13:21–25). This posture represents a privileged, intimate relationship mirroring Jesus's own relationship with his Father, in whose bosom he abides (John 1:18).

The personal intimacy shared between Jesus and the Beloved Disciple deepens as the story rises to its climax. When Jesus is dying on the cross, he touchingly entrusts the Beloved Disciple with the care of his mother (John 19:25–27). The Beloved Disciple is the first male disciple to reach the empty tomb, the first to believe in the resurrection, and the first to recognize the resurrected Jesus in Galilee (John 20:8, 21:7). As the story completes its course, the reader is meant to think that this figure, who acts as Jesus's kin, is the most spiritually mature, insightful, and trustworthy of Jesus's disciples.

Depicting the trustworthiness of this character is vital, for this disciple is also presented as a key source for the fourth gospel itself and therefore an authority for its distinctive presentation of Jesus's identity. In the penultimate sentence of John, the Beloved Disciple is described by the main narrator: "This is the disciple who is testifying to these things and has written them, and we know that his testimony is true" (John 21:24). In the crucifixion scene, apparently the same kind of literary aside occurs: "He who saw this has testified so that you also may believe. His testimony is true, and he knows that he tells the truth" (John 19:35). Regardless of the wonders about which this disciple testifies (in this case, that blood and water flowed out separately from Jesus's pierced side), the disciple's trustworthiness, accrued throughout the narrative, is gradually felt to confirm his testimony.[12] We do not need to speculate about the identity of the Beloved Disciple to realize his function: to validate the fourth gospel's vivid and alternative presentation of Jesus.

Literary Eyewitnesses

To understand the Beloved Disciple as eyewitness in the gospel of John, we turn to compare other eyewitness claims in contemporaneous literature. This literature indicates that the appeal to an eyewitness was a well-known historiographical convention helping to make a story appear believable.

The truth or falsity of an eyewitness claim is not always clear. Lucian complained against many historians who falsely declared that they had seen the events they described.[13] In his *True History*, he exposed the device in the historian Ctesias, "who wrote a history of the land of India and its characteristics, which [despite his eyewitness claim] he had neither seen himself nor heard from anyone else who was telling the truth."[14] The eye-witness authenticating device was centuries old (Ctesias lived in the fifth century BCE) and prevalent as a convention—as Lucian attests—not long after John was written. Yet we do not need to lean wholly on Lucian. There are surviving "historical" narratives claiming to be written by eye-witnesses roughly contemporary with John.

Dictys of Crete

The first narrative I will explore is ascribed to Dictys of Crete. Dictys putatively wrote a historical work called the *Diary of the Trojan War*. In it, he presented himself as both a historian and an eyewitness of Greece's most famous campaign.

Dictys reports that he went to Troy in the train of the most renowned generals of Crete (namely, Idomeneus and Meriones). He went for the express purpose of compiling a historiography of the war. Throughout the work, Dictys presents himself as a model historian. He refers to his own credibility as an eyewitness and claims to have questioned other eyewit-nesses. At the beginning of his work, he attests, "In their company [namely, of Idomeneus and Meriones] I recorded with great care the prior events that took place at Troy, which were known by Odysseus. The remaining events, which took place afterward, I was present for myself [*ipse interfui*] and will expound them as truthfully [*verissime*] as I can."[15]

The goal of strict accuracy via autopsy is associated with the Thucydidean tradition of historiography.[16] Thucydides wrote about his historiographical endeavors, "[They rest] partly on what I saw myself, partly on what others saw for me, the accuracy of the report being always tried by the most se-vere and detailed tests possible."[17] Dictys, in short, presents himself as the strictest kind of historian (though he technically lived long before the genre of historiography was invented).

Dictys's work is written almost entirely in the third person. Yet toward the end of the text, the writer breaks into the first person: "I, Dictys of Knossos, companion of Idomeneus, have inscribed these matters in that idiom that I could best follow and understand among the very different types of speech. . . . I have handed on with full knowledge [*cuncta sciens*] and for the most part from memory gained by experience [*perpessusque magna ex parte memoriae*] what happened in the war between Greeks and barbarians."[18] To bolster his appeal to memory, Dictys frequently refers to "us," "our men," or "our commander," to give a sense that he participated in the events.[19] He uses the rhetoric and methods of historical narration to distinguish between versions of a story and to provide the most reliable account. He strives to present himself as an impartial witness who faithfully records what other eyewitnesses were saying.

Upon returning home, Dictys (as he says) completed his historiography. When he died and was buried, wooden tablets inscribed with his text were laid in his tomb. Hundreds of years later, these tablets were rediscovered when, according to report, Dictys's grave was opened in the thirteenth year of the Roman emperor Nero (about 67 CE). Shepherds unearthed a sealed tin box that they thought contained hidden treasure. They hurriedly opened it but were disappointed to find only tablets inscribed with a strange script. They then turned the tablets over to a local ruler, who brought the work to the attention of the emperor. Nero commissioned a Greek translation of the text and lodged it in his library.

Dictys's *Diary* circulated widely in antiquity, was translated into Latin, and was cited by several Greek historians. For instance, the Christian chronographer John Malalas in the sixth century CE called the author "the most astute Dictys, who . . . recorded all of the . . . events of the Greeks who warred against Troy." In the eleventh century, George Cedrenus in his *Historical Compendium* invoked Dictys as "a noteworthy and sagacious man . . . who truthfully described the entire succession of events, beginning to end, and sketched the warriors' characters, since he had observed them all."[20]

By virtue of Dictys's reputation as an eyewitness, he secured authority to explain matters that had been left open in Homer's epics. Homer, though a great poet, never claimed the authority of being an eyewitness. In fact, he was thought to have lived some four hundred years after the war.[21] Thus how the poet derived his information was subject to perennial dispute. Part of Homer's account was putatively obtained from divine revelation (for instance, the catalogue of ships in the *Iliad*, book 2). Yet the bulk of the information was traditional material sung by poets across many generations. Dictys, by contrast, required neither the Muses nor human traditions to compose his work. He had seen most of the events themselves, a "fact" that lent him great authority.

Dictys presents himself as so sober a historian that Homer is made to look unreliable by comparison. The Cretan suppresses the mention of divine agents. There is no scheming of the gods behind the scenes and no climactic battle of deities played out on Trojan soil (as in the *Iliad*, book 20). Homer's cyclops is turned into a prideful Sicilian potentate angry at Odysseus for abducting his daughter. Whereas Homer spiced up his epics with fantastic elements (including a talking river and weeping horses), Dictys's account is an unadorned military journal in plain prose.[22] Accordingly, Dictys's *Diary* became one of "the most authoritative accounts of what happened at Troy" up until modern times.[23]

The only problem is that, in the view of all scholars working today, Dictys did not exist. He is entirely the creation of an author who wrote the *Diary* presumably in the first century CE (a papyrus from the early second century survives). This author portrayed Dictys as an eyewitness, but Dictys himself (never mentioned in Homer) is in fact a fictional character previously unknown. Whether or not the ancients realized it, "Dictys of Crete," or rather the person who forged the *Diary of the Trojan War*, was a literary artist posing as an eyewitness to make what we would call vivid historical fiction seem like historiography.

And "Dictys" was not alone. Many other revisionist accounts of the Trojan War were forged in antiquity under the names of so-called eyewitnesses. They include "Dares of Phrygia," "Sisyphus of Cos," "Pheidalius of Corinth," "Antipatrus the Acanthian," "Corinnus of Ilium," and "Cephalus of Gergithion." All these names appear to be invented.[24] Nevertheless, the sober and clear details of their accounts, the stories about how their writings were found, and especially their eyewitness claims served to authenticate their accounts.

Damis

Another writer used the eyewitness authenticating device with more daring skill. I refer to Philostratus, famous rhetor and prolific writer of the early third century. Probably shortly after 217 CE, Philostratus published his *Life of Apollonius of Tyana*.

Philostratus was not the first person to write a biography of Apollonius. He mentions two previous attempts, one by a man called Maximus (Apollonius's Cilician countryman) and the other by Moeragenes, whom Philostratus claimed was "undeserving of attention."[25] Philostratus rejected Moeragenes because, although he wrote a four-book biography of Apollonius, he was ignorant of many things. Moeragenes was ignorant, Philostratus claimed, because he lacked the best sources.

In this way, Moeragenes's work becomes a foil for Philostratus's endeavor. Philostratus, by his own report, had a superior source—one composed by an eyewitness. This eyewitness was reputedly a close disciple of Apollonius whose name was "Damis." Damis wrote notebooks (*hypomnēmata*) in a rough style. The empress Julia Domna, who was given the notebooks, asked Philostratus to rewrite them (*metagrapsai*) to produce a literary work. This project resulted in the *Life of Apollonius*. The Damis document is thus portrayed as a key source for Philostratus's biography.

Who was this Damis? Philostratus portrays him as a man from Old Ninos (Hierapolis in ancient Syria) who became Apollonius's companion and fellow philosopher.[26] At Damis's first encounter with Apollonius, he intuited the significance of his teacher. He offered to be Apollonius's tour guide and interpreter as he traveled toward Babylon. When Apollonius informed him that he knew all languages and human thoughts, Damis addressed Apollonius as a divine being (compare John 1:49, where Nathanael on his first encounter with Jesus addresses him, "Rabbi, you are the son of God!"). From that point on, Damis traveled around with Apollonius as his constant companion.[27]

We are informed by Philostratus that Damis remembered everything he learned from Apollonius—over a fifty-year period—and exhaustively recorded what Apollonius said and did.[28] Damis is portrayed, in short, as the ideal eyewitness. He is ideal, moreover, in not leaving his memories unrecorded. Damis composed and preserved dozens, if not hundreds, of tablets (*deltai*) containing Apollonius's deeds and sayings. When Damis died, his notebooks were preserved among his kin.

Damis's notebooks secured Philostratus's supreme advantage. Previous biographers of Apollonius did not possess these writings. Thus the reliability and completeness of their accounts was called into question. Philostratus, however, claimed to have been given the notebooks by the Roman empress herself.[29] Philostratus was writing about a hundred years after Apollonius died. Nevertheless, his use of Damis's notebooks allowed him

to advertise his accuracy like no biographer before him. Philostratus suc-
ceeded, at any rate, in composing a more vivid, detailed, and history-like
account. His success may be gauged by the fact that competing biographies no longer survive.

Philostratus appealed to the eyewitness tradition of Damis about forty
times in his eight-book biography. The appeal apparently worked. Eighty
years after Philostratus wrote, the reliability of his account was said to be
guaranteed "by Damis the philosopher who lived constantly with him."[30]

The problem is that, once again, most scholars do not believe that Damis ever lived.[31] As a character in the story, he appears most frequently in
the sections concerning Apollonius's travels to Babylon and India. This
material contains fantastic elements and historical inaccuracies unlikely
for an eyewitness to attest.[32] Furthermore, Damis's interests (for instance,
artwork and natural history) suspiciously resemble those of Philostratus
himself. Finally, we know that Philostratus (or an imitator) concocted an
anonymous eyewitness in another of his works (the *Heroicus*), namely, the
vinedresser who claims to have communed with the hero Protesilaus.[33]

Most scholars conclude that Damis's notebooks were either a creation
of Philostratus himself or a previously composed document that he employed. In the latter case, Damis's notebooks may have been put together
by devotees of Apollonius.[34] In the former case, Philostratus himself invented the notebooks to validate his biography. The idea of outright invention is bold, though not impossible. Philostratus probably knew Dictys's
Diary. Philostratus could have used the same technique of creative invention to authenticate the new and vivid details of his biography.

For Philostratus to rely so heavily on the Damis source was risky, since
the nature of the material did not always inspire faith. For instance, Damis
included several miracles (including a resurrection) performed by Apollonius that skeptics could have carped at (see chapter 10). Damis also included long speeches and dialogues of Apollonius that resemble transcript
reports. How exactly these speeches were remembered and recorded is
left open. Accuracy is presumably only guaranteed if Damis recorded the
speeches from memory soon after they were given. By portraying Damis as
writing tablets along the way, Philostratus leads the reader to imagine that
Damis recorded the speeches when they were still fresh in his mind. Philostratus also made an effort to show how, even if Damis was not present at
a speech, he could reliably report it.[35]

Damis is not only Philostratus's main source, but also functions as a trusted character in the story. Although somewhat obtuse at first, Damis repeatedly proves that he is worthy to serve as Apollonius's most intimate disciple, fellow philosopher, and eventually his envoy. When Damis is used as a source, then, his accrued trustworthiness as a character serves to authenticate his written testimony.

Thus two narrating voices combine to guarantee the plausibility of the biography. The authenticating eyewitness is the star-struck yet loyal Damis. The narrator, whom we can call Philostratus, depicts himself as an elite, cosmopolitan sophisticate who knows multiple sources and exercises critical judgment as to what is best to include in the biography.[36] When combined, the eyewitness report rewritten by the erudite biographer attained maximum cogency.

Comparison

From these examples, it is evident that introducing a literary eyewitness was a known historiographical convention from at least the first to the third century CE. It was used to authenticate revisionary works that otherwise might have been questioned for their novelty in form and content. I propose that the author of John knew and used this convention to increase the credibility of his account. If he knew the Synoptic gospels (as seems likely to many scholars),[37] he may have used the eyewitness authenticating device to outperform his perceived competitors. The device was a way for him to demonstrate that his gospel was superior even though it introduced novel elements. At the end of the gospel, the Beloved Disciple's testimony confirms the entire biography (John 21:24).[38]

There are other vivid details in John that could easily be thought to go back to historical reminiscence: John the Baptist was baptized at Aenon near Salim (John 3:23); the lame man lay for thirty-eight years at the pool of Beth-zatha (5:3–5); the slave whose ear was cut off was named Malchus (18:10); Peter stood at a charcoal fire outside Annas's house during Jesus's trial (18:18). The biblical scholar Paul N. Anderson claims, "John has more archaeological, topographical, sensory-empirical, personal knowledge and first-hand information than all of the other gospels combined."[39] Such vivid presentation (what the Greeks called *enargeia*) was a known technique of historiographical discourse.[40]

Vividness may, however, having nothing to do with historical accuracy. It is simply one way that the category of "witness" is established. The witness provides graphic descriptions that seem to derive from careful observation. These descriptions "may have features that might seem hard to make up because of their specificity, perhaps, or their oddness."[41] One thinks of the blood and water flowing separately from Jesus's side in John 19:34–35. Only someone carefully observing an event from close up could attest such a detail—or so the reader is led to suppose.

As one reads and rereads the narrative, such inferences multiply. Many of the details in the story do not have eyewitness verification, such as Jesus's private conversation with the woman by the well (John 4) or the story that he raised Lazarus from the dead (and cried on the way to the tomb; John 11:35). Yet the memory of the eyewitness retrospectively leads the reader to credit their accuracy.

Philostratus explicitly mentioned that Apollonius informed Damis of his private conversations, thus enabling Damis to record them accurately. Perhaps the same point is implied in John (that Jesus told the Beloved Disciple about his private talks). Philostratus left such matters up to the intuition of the reader. He did not, that is, appeal to Damis for every detail. Nevertheless, he led the reader to believe that, since the eyewitness was virtually always present, he could always confirm the precise details. This point applies also to the reporting of fantastic events. Both the fourth evangelist and Philostratus, for instance, claim that the subjects of their biographies performed resurrections—wonders whose credibility required a credible eyewitness to be believed.[42]

Like Damis, the Beloved Disciple appears as a character in the story for which he is the source. This narrative device is a skillful means of authentication, since the character in the story establishes a rapport with the reader and gradually builds his own sense of trustworthiness. The trust of the eyewitness is built in part through characterizing his relationship with the master. Damis, for instance, is Apollonius's closest disciple who sticks by him and even suffers arrest in Rome. To Damis, Apollonius reveals the secret of his divine identity.[43] A basic similarity can be detected in John. Although Jesus loves all his disciples, the Beloved Disciple is arguably the most intimate. Unlike Jesus's other followers, the Beloved Disciple does not abandon Jesus after he is arrested. Instead, he follows Jesus into the courtyard of his enemy (John 18:15). Presumably it was even more dangerous for this disciple to stand at the foot of the cross (John 19:26).

The use of the third person, moreover, increases the sense of objectivity. The Beloved Disciple in John never actually speaks in the first person (saying "I"). His testimony, though intimate, is always put in the third person when retold by the main narrator. The same technique is used for the Damis memoirs. Damis's testimony is almost always introduced with the words "Damis says" or the like. Dictys also uses third-person discourse except at the beginning and end of his *Diary*. As is common in historiographical discourse, the testimony offered in the third person generates a distance that fosters a sense of impartiality and objectivity.

Significantly, Damis, Dictys, and the Beloved Disciple all wrote down their testimony. John 21:24 reads, "This is the disciple who is testifying to these things and has written [*grapsas*] them." Here it is made explicit that the Beloved Disciple did not transmit his information solely by word of mouth. He actually wrote down (presumably a draft of) his testimony, which was then rewritten as the final version of the gospel. Or so the reader imagines (since if the Beloved Disciple is dead, as presumably implied in John 21:23, he cannot be the voice of the main narrator). As in the case of Philostratus, it is difficult to determine whether the author of John actually had a previous document written by a supposed eyewitness or only gave the impression that he had such a document.[44]

At any rate, by representing the original testimony as a document in stable form, the perception of its accuracy was increased. The eyewitness's testimony was not lost or allowed to degrade through the vagaries of oral transmission. Of course, the original draft of the eyewitness's testimony was lost in the case of Damis and the Beloved Disciple; thus its original wording cannot be verified. Yet this may have been the intent of the authentication device. A past eyewitness is generated whose testimony is put beyond falsification.

As is the case in the *Life of Apollonius*, there is a metanarrative about the composition of John. The main narrator composes the surviving account. Yet interventions toward the end of the book lead the reader to realize retrospectively that the main narrator is in fact rewriting a story previously written by the Beloved Disciple. The two levels of narration, as in the *Life of Apollonius*, serve to authenticate the biography as a whole. The main narrator accepts the testimony of the Beloved Disciple and seeks to persuade the reader to accept the same (rewritten) testimony.

Damis and Dictys are not anonymous, but the Beloved Disciple remains unnamed. An unnamed eyewitness is not entirely unheard of in mythic historiography. Earlier we noted that the *Life of Aesop* is anonymous. In the *Heroicus*, Philostratus (or Philostratus the Younger) preserved the anonymity of his eyewitness, who was a devotee of the hero Protesilaus. Some scholars have speculated that in John the anonymity of the Beloved Disciple better enables readers to identify with him (through an act of modeling or identification, they become, as it were, the ideal disciple).[45] Alternatively, the disciple's anonymity calls the reader to return to the text and realize that the witness of the Logos is self-authenticating and sufficient.[46]

Yet there is another, more practical reason for not naming the eyewitness. The anonymity of the eyewitness is a technique to prevent invalidation. If the reader knows the name of the eyewitness, the eyewitness can be more easily exposed as a fiction. One of the reasons that scholars today doubt the existence of Damis and Dictys is because they are figures that are completely unattested elsewhere. By leaving an eyewitness without a name, however, the eyewitness is in a sense neither attested nor unattested. It is impossible to prove that an anonymous eyewitness did not exist on the grounds that his name and identity are not witnessed elsewhere.

The anonymous eyewitness could be identified with any number of disciples—and enormous intellectual energy has gone into discovering his identity. In actuality, it seems that the nameless eyewitness does not have an identity beyond the fact of being an eyewitness. One can reject the eyewitness as an eyewitness, but one has no basis to reject an individual eyewitness because his name is unattested. In short, the eyewitness in John is unverifiable—and therefore unfalsifiable as well. For an author who values religious belief, unverifiability is not a weakness but a strength, since unverifiability demands the response of faith. "Blessed are those who have not seen and yet have believed" (John 20:29).[47]

Conclusion

Despite some differences in the eyewitness appeal, there are basic similarities that the fourth gospel shares with the historiographical literature compared here. These similarities do not necessarily prove that the eye-witness in John is a fictional device. Nevertheless, the similarities invite us to reflect on why scholars even today argue for the historicity of the Be-loved Disciple and his testimony while casually discounting the historicity of similar eyewitness claims in contemporary literature.[48]

In an ancient bookshop, there was no label indicating which works were fiction and which were nonfiction. Authors of all genres used devices of authentication to validate works that included elements of both historio-graphy (a representation of what was thought to have happened) and fic-tion. In a sense, all historiography is fiction (*fictio* meaning "fashioning" or "formation"), insofar as it is a representation of what is imagined to have happened.[49] Yet one does not need to become a relativist to see that in both the past and present, historiography and fiction blend in often mysterious ways. Consequently, even texts that *read* like historiography are not neces-sarily so. Even when truth seems to be based on firsthand observation, such "observation" can still be a literary representation.

It seems that the author of John wanted his text to be read as historio-graphy. Yet there were certain obstacles he had to overcome. His depar-ture from the Synoptics was daring, and he included elements that were both fantastical and unattested elsewhere (the healing of the man born blind, the resurrection of Lazarus, the added resurrection appearance of Jesus, and so on). Sensing this vulnerability, the fourth evangelist intro-duced his—previously unheard of—star witness, the Beloved Disciple. The Beloved Disciple was, in all likelihood, a fictional device used to affirm the historicity of the fourth gospel. It was a convention that has convinced readers both ancient and modern that John's gospel is—whatever else it is—a historiographical work.[50]

The famous biblical scholar Raymond Brown argued that the Beloved Disciple as literary fiction would involve deceit, since the author of the fourth gospel "reports distress in the community over the Beloved Dis-ciple's death."[51] Upon returning to the text, however, one finds no distress recorded. The text does not even explicitly say that the Beloved Disciple died. If it is implied, nothing prevents fictional characters from dying.[52]

It may be correct that introducing a fictional eyewitness involves some form of deceit. Yet this point is not an argument that the fourth evangelist would *not* have created an eyewitness. Recent scholarship has sufficiently demonstrated that Christian authors felt little inhibition about employing deceit in the cause of what they perceived as true.[53]

We know that contemporaneous biographies readily mixed fact with fiction, especially when the fiction had some profound moral or spiritual pay-off.[54] In the case of John, the perceived benefit to the reader is long lasting and substantial: "eternal life." The character of the Beloved Disciple may be fictional, but the faith that he inspires is real. "These things are written that you may believe" (John 20:31). Presumably, this is why the Beloved Disciple was written as well.[55]

Further Reading

Ewen Bowie, "Philostratus: Writer of Fiction," in *Greek Fiction: The Greek Novel in Context,* ed. J. R. Morgan and Richard Stoneman (London: Routledge, 1994), 181–99.

Ismo Dunderberg, *The Beloved Disciple in Conflict* (Oxford: Oxford University Press, 2006).

James A. Francis, "Truthful Fiction: New Questions to Old Answers on Philostratus' 'Life of Apollonius,'" *American Journal of Philology* 119 (1998): 419–41.

William Hansen, "Strategies of Authentication in Ancient Popular Literature," in *The Ancient Novel and Beyond,* ed. Stelios Panayotakis, Maaike Zimmerman, and Wytse Keulen (Leiden: Brill, 2003), 301–16.

Christopher P. Jones, "Apollonius of Tyana's Passage to India," *Greek, Roman and Byzantine Studies* 42 (2001): 185–99.

Andrew T. Lincoln, "The Beloved Disciple as Eyewitness and the Fourth Gospel as Witness," *Journal for the Study of the New Testament* 85 (2002): 3–26.

Stefan Merkle, "Telling the True Story of the Trojan War: The Eyewitness Account of Dictys of Crete," in *The Search for the Ancient Novel,* ed. James Tatum (Baltimore: Johns Hopkins University Press, 1994), 183–96.

CONCLUSION

THE MYTH OF HISTORICITY

This scholarly bias concerning the status of the Bible as a sacred text
takes concrete form in the many claims and arguments made to support
its historical veracity. . . . "Historiography" is understood not as a genre
classification, but rather as a sort of truth claim founded upon the
assumption of equivocation between historical fact and truth.
— *Thomas M. Bolin*[1]

In this book I have argued that the many fantastic tales of the gospels
can be classified according to a category here called mythic historiography.
Historiography is a discourse about events that fall within the culturally
defined concept of "reality." It is a discourse that is naturally taken to refer
to external reality.[2] Generally speaking, if readers do not consider a story
to be "real," they do not consider it to be plausible. At the precise time
when these cultural presumptions were dominant, the evangelists were
motivated to present their stories in historiographical form.

Registers of plausibility change with time. In the preceding chapters, I
was concerned with *ancient* standards of plausibility. By these standards, the
gospels could and were meant to be read as historiographies (specifically
biographies). The evangelists, like other Greek and Roman writers of their
time, used the tropes of historiographical discourse to advance their claims
of truth.

The main tropes discussed in this work are ten: (1) objectification (describing individually experienced phenomena as if they were fully knowable and observable by others); (2) synchrony (noting well-known persons or occurrences); (3) syntopy (mentioning known places on the map); (4) straightforward, matter-of-fact presentation (which often frames the description of fantastical or anomalous events); (5) vivid presentation (which includes the addition of random and circumstantial details) and the rhetoric of accuracy (*akribeia*), which includes (6) the introduction of literary eyewitnesses (such as the Beloved Disciple); (7) staged skepticism among the eyewitnesses (as in Matt. 28:17; John 20:25); (8) alternative reports (as in Matt. 28:13); (9) stated links of causation (as in Matt. 28:15); and (10) literary traces of a past event (such as tomb tokens). Admittedly, each of the individual evangelists did not use all these tropes, and they did not use them all consistently. The evangelists were not elite court historians, but they knew enough to create works that seemed historiographical.[3]

By modern standards, however, the gospels cannot be classified as historiography. Post-Enlightenment registers of plausibility have shifted like tectonic plates over long stretches of time. The gospels can continue to inform—and in some measure create—the life-world of Christian believers. They can continue to "change the way in which people decide what is real and unreal."[4] Yet by and large, there will always be a gap between the story world of the gospels and the lived worlds of most modern people. Perceiving this gap is the first step toward realizing that the gospels can function as what modern scholars define—in various ways—as "myth."[5]

Myth in a modern scholarly sense typically designates a traditional story whose meaning shapes the identities of human communities over time.[6] In this sense, the story that Yahweh gave the land of Israel to Abraham, father of the Jews, is a myth. The story that eighteenth-century English sailors found no human inhabitants of Australia (*terra nullius*) is a myth. The story that the United States has a duty to be a model of freedom and democratic government (the "city on a hill") is a myth. There are good myths and bad ones, true myths and false ones, and by the act of interpretation, people have power to make them so.[7]

Whether a myth is considered true or false depends in large part on a community's prior investment in it. At the surface-level presentation, myths may feature what is considered to be fantastic (for instance, non-human beings acting like humans). At the same time, myths form the identities of those who uphold them. Thus when myths become implausible by normal cultural processes, a religious community does not typically dispose of them. Instead, it continually revises or re-presents its myths in order to make them culturally credible.

The case of Christian myths is no different. No matter how impossible a gospel myth might seem today, Christians invested in it try to redeem it by creative reinterpretation. Instead of rejecting biblical myths, Christians make sense of them so that they accord with modern canons of rationality. Rationality is not a universal but a culturally conditioned human capacity. Thus the strategies and outcomes of rationalization will always differ depending on the circumstances.

In the West, a major species of rationalization is historicization. Historicization means the process of making a myth look like historiography. The "historical" is another admittedly fluid category. In different ages, different events seem historically plausible. It might have been credible fifteen hundred years ago to believe that a man could stop the rotation of the sun or sail from Europe to India across the Atlantic or discover a continent engulfed by the sea. Until modern times, it seemed rather implausible that a man could walk on the moon.

Yet beliefs change on the basis of accrued knowledge. Today, someone who cannot believe in the intervention of gods may believe in the clandestine invasion of aliens. Some of these aliens act very much like ancient gods. On the scale of plausibility, are aliens any more likely than gods? To some empirically minded persons, they are very much so (given the vast size of the universe and the existence of other, Earth-like planets). The point is that stories, if they are to survive, must be updated in accordance with peoples' various belief systems.[8]

No One Is Above Myth

In saying that some gospels stories are myths, the point is not, in a kind of reverse apologetics, to make them unworthy of belief. The point is to inspire awareness that gospel narratives always require intellectual labor to become plausible. Myths are not true or false in themselves.[9] Believers will inevitably construct truth out of their myths if their myths—and their communities—are going to survive.

No one, including scholars, is "above" myth. The human condition is such that we cannot but live our own conceptions of reality and promote the myths that ground them. Nevertheless, it is healthy to recognize that our sense of reality (shared to some degree by members of our society and culture) is not the *only* version of reality. It is given to us by our cultural for-bears. The discourse of reality must be constantly refurbished and main-tained to remain credible. It is our task to modify myths when they cease to be plausible or to adequately reflect new data and modes of perception.

There is a dialectic here. One realizes that one's myths are put into his-torical form to increase their plausibility. At the same time, belief in the myth endures after hermeneutical modifications of the myth's meaning. Yet the belief is of a different sort. Viewed from the outside, myths no lon-ger convey absolute truths. Rather, they contain contingent and contex-tual truths that necessarily change generation after generation. Both kinds of truths can be categorized as "revelation" if people believe that a deity invisibly inspires the human imagination.

Understandably, believers in gospel mythology still deny that it contains "myths" in the vulgar sense of "false stories." To religious insiders, gospel myths report a sacred "history" that they experience as "gospel truth." The critical scholar is not in a position to judge what is or is not truth for the believer. At the same time, however, scholars can point out that myths are never transparent media of reality. Language itself is an imaginative creation of humans, who use it not to unveil naked reality but to achieve more practical ends of life.

It would be wrong to say that those who consciously acknowledge (and study) their mythology cannot simultaneously live it. Both the scholar and the believer can recognize that gospel stories are transformative, if for dif-ferent reasons. For the believer, the power often derives from divine inspi-ration and the salvific function of the myths. For the scholar, the power of gospel myths frequently lies in their versatility and world-making potential. The scholar and the believer can also, of course, be the same person.

The Myth of Historicity

In the novel *The Flight of Peter Fromm*, Martin Gardner tells a story that reflects a common experience in modern theological education. A pious young man goes to divinity school (or a school of theology) and loses his childhood faith. It happens slowly—almost imperceptibly—but for this reason all the more surely. Such is the "flight" of Peter Fromm ("pious" Peter), a former Bible-thumper from small-town America.

In one episode of the novel, a disillusioned Peter angrily interrogates Norman Wesley Middleton, a prominent minister in the community. Speaking of the resurrection of Jesus, Peter poses this dilemma: "So let's assume there actually was a corpse. What happened to it? There are only two possibilities. Either it was revivified, the way the Gospels tell it, or it wasn't. If it wasn't, it stayed on earth. There isn't any third possibility. What happened to the body? Did it come alive or didn't it?"[10]

The horns of this dilemma have gored the faith of some people. The meaning of Jesus's resurrection—and of Christianity itself—is widely assumed to hang on its historicity. The value of any sort of "spiritual meaning" is discounted if there is no historical and physical basis for it. As Peter says, "If the physical event didn't take place, Norman, how can it have much spiritual meaning?"[11]

Peter's questions only make sense with a peculiar set of presuppositions about what counts as reality and knowledge. Peter identifies the real with the historical (in the sense of "what happened"). Yet in the game of historical writing we *never* actually know exactly what happened. Historicity is not a cross from which the truth hangs in all its glory. It is at best a social agreement that something happened in the past. This assertion is not merely an outgrowth of postmodern philosophy; the ancients suggested something similar. The sophist Nicolaus (late fifth century CE) wrote that historical narratives are about past events acknowledged by consensus (*homologoumenōs*) to have happened.[12] I emphasize "by consensus." Historians do not have direct access to a past occurrence, though they might agree that it happened.

The current consensus regarding the "historical Jesus" is that he lived in Palestine, that he was a Jew crucified around 30 CE by Roman authorities. Needless to say, early Christians did not consider this bare-bones story a complete account of Jesus's significance. By the time the gospels were composed, many Christians worshiped Jesus as their divine savior. Most evangelists were fully committed to portraying Jesus as a superhuman being who came to save people from their sins and from evil superhuman agents. Gospel writers thus stressed elements of the story that underscored Jesus's superhuman nature: fulfilled prophecies, divine conception, miracles, transfiguration, resurrection, and ascension. Today, these fantastic elements are historically the most opaque. Yet they are also the elements that have proved most significant throughout time—hence their appearance in early creeds.[13]

Like Peter Fromm, empirically minded Christians search for a way to believe in Christ. Yet the Christ they serve is often the one protected under the sheltering wings of the goddess History. Christians take pride in the fact that their Jesus is historical. The New Testament theologian Ernst Käsemann wrote that early Christians "were agreed only in one judgment: namely, that the life history of Jesus was constitutive for faith, because the earthly and the exalted Lord are identical."[14] To be sure, there is a transcendent truth revealed in Christ, but there is also a truth verified in the pastness of Jesus. The philosopher C. Stephen Evans remarked, "in affirming the importance of the historicity of the incarnational narrative, Christians affirm . . . that it is important that the events which the narrative depicts actually occurred."[15] Christians assume, like most modern people, that "what happened," assuming we have reliable access to it, is "real."[16] To be real, then, the events in the gospels must have happened as physical events in time and space.[17]

Yet to say with William Arnal that Christians "*must* assert the fundamental historicity of th[eir] mythology" is not necessarily true.[18] For the past two thousand years, Christians have asserted the truth of their mythology in a whole variety of (symbolic and allegorical) ways. Yet historicization is certainly a popular technique for increasing plausibility, especially given the historiographical form of the gospels. Maximizing the plausibility of one's myth by representing it as "what happened" works even better after the Enlightenment.

Logically, then, many Christian defenders of the faith will continue to insist that a historical examination of their founding myths will produce data that justify their faith. To continue the quote from Arnal, "This peculiar insistence on 'sacred history' as genuinely historical thus ensures that Christianity treats its own central myth as non-mythic, as radically different from *all other* myths. It is this *theological* datum that appears to have established the parameters for what can and cannot responsibly be said about the gospels, or about the Jesus they present."[19]

One must be clear: *some* gospel stories reflect historical events, and it is vital to read the gospels in their historical context. In some environments, however, reading the gospels *in* their historical contexts is unlawfully yoked with reading the gospels *as* historical reports. Yet just because the gospels have a historiographical form does not mean that they are historical documents in the modern sense.[20] Just because Jesus once lived does not mean that the Christian representations of his life describe what happened. And what happened in the external world of the past, even if it is recoverable, is not a clear measure for what is true or real. In the words of John J. Collins, "By affirming that the event in question is an act of God, the biblical account is claiming that it had an abiding significance for the community since it provides, in effect, a revelation of God. The significance of such an event cannot be adequately appreciated by merely asking whether it happened."[21]

The "Historical Jesus"

Part of the continuing mythology of Western culture is historicity itself. Especially since the nineteenth century, historiography often counts as "fact" among popular audiences and passes for what is "true." The ambiguity between history as "real event" and "narrative reconstruction of the past" is exploited time and time again.[22] Christian apologists, by reading and writing about their sacred stories as "history," defend "gospel truth" and shore up their own cultural authority.

Today, scholars play a central role in making Jesus seem "historical" and thus believable to modern people. From the many late and varied accounts of his life, they establish a demythologized space and reconstruct several different versions of "the historical Jesus." One version exemplifies apocalyptic thinking, another rabbinic wisdom, another the Cynic lifestyle, another magical practice, and so on. They all have one thing in common: they present a human Jesus who reflects the thoughts and views of the reconstructing historian.[23]

Mine is not a critique of the "historical Jesus"—who has every right to exist in the minds of modern scholars—but an observation about the conditions that make his construction a felt need. The historical Jesus is sometimes taken to be more "real" because he is a better representation of the "earthly" Jesus of the past. Although the past is gone, it is still sometimes thought that historical representations can make Jesus present—at least to the minds of believers.

Yet historiography can only signify the past, not make it present. Ann Rigney quotes Roland Barthes in her study of modern historiographical techniques: "historical discourse does not follow the real, it signifies it."[24] The danger is that people will think that the realistic discourse of historiography is an inherently truthful mode of representation. But as Elizabeth Tonkin points out, this way of thinking is false: "all representations are effective illusions, so that there are conventions and rhetorics of fictitious realism."[25] Historical conventions and rhetorics, as I hope is clear by this point, are never true in themselves or even reliable media of truth.

The "historical" is a human construction, and what defines it, as Jens Schröter observes, are the current conditions of plausibility. The "reality" of the historical Jesus is determined by what is "plausible in light of current presuppositions of understanding."[26] By admitting this, one also admits that there is no stable reality of Jesus and that our shifting sense of what is reality in part determines the Jesus who is considered to be plausible today.[27]

Despite Jesus's being more believable to the public at large—hence his appearance on the History Channel and other documentary programming—the historical Jesus is almost never the Jesus considered ultimately "real" by Christian believers. After all, believers worship a divine Jesus, one that historians cannot—and can never—give them. Historians often construct their versions of Jesus by picking apart the pieces of the gospels, throwing away or reinterpreting the fantastical (unbelievable) elements, and resynthesizing the "historical" (or historicized) bits into a plausible narrative. These new narrative versions never present a Christian deity, the superhuman savior of humanity. Therefore what they reconstruct is always incompatible in some measure with the gospel portraits.[28]

Imagination and Reality

Both the modern and postmodern historian represent what is taken to be "real," but they understand reality in different ways. The modern historian typically assumes that the object of his or her discourse is real because it corresponds to an event in the past. (Since the past is gone, however, no historian's account can actually be verified.) The postmodern historian can also claim that his or her material corresponds to something. What it corresponds to is not some event in the past but a reality in the human imagination that has been informed by the traces of the past (both material and textual). Imagined reality has been demeaned as "fancy" in previous generations, but such mockery confuses the issue. The disciplined imagination is an important factor in human experience and regularly shapes the course of human events.

Not every happening in space and time is an event. An event becomes an event by passing through the laboratory of the human imagination. What humans remember as an event is something that has been crafted and cooked in the human mind. Hayden White remarked almost forty years ago, "How else can any 'past' which is by definition comprised of events, [and] processes . . . that are considered to be no longer perceivable, be represented in either consciousness or discourse except in an 'imaginary' way? Is it not possible that the question of narrative in any discussion of historical theory is always finally about the function of imagination in the production of a specifically human truth?"[29]

To be more concrete: the evangelists might have described Jesus's resurrection as a historical event, but their *account* of it is the product of their imagination. The Christian believer is sometimes unwilling or even unable to distinguish a fact of the communal imagination from a fact of the past. The lived experience of these same Christians indicates the power of the imagined fact to be read as "reality." If a "historical" product of the imagination is understood to be reality, effectively it becomes reality for the believer whether or not it happened in the past.[30]

As works of the imagination, historiography and mythography are never completely opposed. Insofar as historiography imagines a past according to mythic plots and templates (such as the self-sacrificing hero), historiography can become mythic. The historian might deny that he or she uses mythic templates, but that is often because the templates are invisible to the cultural insider. In another culture or time, the emperor's clothes are removed, and the mythical substructures of important historical narratives are exposed.[31]

These mythic structures preserve the meaning of human events. "What happened" is, all too often, chaotic, meaningless, and even absurd. On a

Friday afternoon outside Jerusalem in 29 CE, it seems, a man was nailed naked to a cross and left there to asphyxiate. Let us affirm that he was innocent. This state of affairs only makes his death more absurd. The brute (and brutalizing) "fact" of this violent death actually means nothing in itself. Only when the event is understood according to mythic patterns—a primordial sacrifice, a martyr's death, a victory over daimons, and so on—does it begin to mean something and become collectively important. Only when it is seen as a product of the imagination is the story itself redeemed.

I do not deny the historical basis for some gospel stories (notably the crucifixion);[32] my point is that the mythic imagination transforms historical memory, and it does so in often unpredictable ways. The historical Jesus is *always* an imaginative creation that, to some degree, fits modern needs—otherwise, no one would make the effort to remember and (re)construct him as a believable figure.

Some historians might imply that they have recovered the true historical Jesus in part because this Jesus is fundamentally different from modern forms of life. This Jesus is the suffering apocalyptic prophet who sacrificed himself to lift the curtain of the world's final epoch. But this Jesus is still useful because he continues to fulfill Christian needs. The greatest need for Christians, perhaps, is the sense that Jesus is unique. If Jesus brings in the once-for-all moment when history is fulfilled, then that sense of uniqueness is perceived to be verified.[33]

The apocalyptic Jesus also helps Christians attain a more practical, ethical end. Modern pastors have a need to criticize the materialistic lifestyles of modern people. The self-emptying apocalyptic preacher, however strange he may seem today, serves as a useful antidote to the modern gospel of girth (or prosperity gospel). He is alien to the majority Christian culture in the West and thereby becomes an important means of cultural criticism. In this way, the apocalyptic Jesus—an imaginative creation if there ever was one—preserves his relevance for modern times.

Myth and Identity

Today, we in Western societies must face our own arbitrariness, an arbitrariness rooted in the need to confirm our own identities. "Myth" and "history" are *our* cultural terms that are clumsy, ambiguous, and laced with emotion. "History," among its various meanings, tends to designate *our* story, the story that we believe, that we allow to shape our identity. "Myth," on the other hand, refers to *their* story, the story of *other* people that *our* community may consider strange, wrongheaded, or implausible. The fact that people still assume that their group or national "history" is a true account of reality shows the continuing vitality of myth.

"Myth" (in the scholarly sense) and "history" (in the popular sense) often function in similar ways. As Claude Lévi-Strauss observed, "I am not far from believing that, in our own societies, history has replaced mythology and fulfills the same function."[34] That function is to provide people with meaningful stories that mold human identity. Compare the insight of another French theorist, Michel de Certeau: "History is probably our myth. It combines what can be thought, the 'thinkable,' and the origin, in conformity with the way in which a society can understand its own working."[35]

Both historiography and mythography are important for maintaining societies. To survive, a community needs identity-making stories that community members perceive as "real" events, as *their* events, as events that found their community and justify their existence. Using historiography as the format of religious myth allows a modern community to map itself onto a perceived reality that provides it with an enduring sense of meaning and value. It establishes a "memory" that is shared by all individuals socialized in the community. It makes meaningful the experienced dimensions of many aspects of life.

Focusing specifically on Christian communities, we observe that Christians read themselves into a story ("salvation history") that had a past before Jesus, a moment of supreme culmination (Jesus's life and death), and a final resolution (the beginning of a new, heavenly world). In this constructed "sacred time," Christians have a common frame of reference for working out their activities. They feel linked with the spiritual predecessors and obligated to their successors, which offers them a sense that they have transcended human finitude.[36]

Christians, by reading their myths as historical events, perceive that they are a community that transcends time itself. Jesus's "historical" resurrection is a model for the resurrection of each individual believer. By believing in the historicity of the resurrection, Christians assure themselves of its reality. By assuring themselves of its reality, they guarantee the reception of the promise of Jesus's immortality for themselves. The gospel story guarantees that believers will never die and thus that their community (the "body of Christ") will never perish but will persist eternally—just as Christ himself.

The Metamorphosis of Myth

If there is one persistent ideological message in the gospels, it is that the Christian hero is superior to all who came before him. All previous mythology—Jewish and Greek—is made into a sign system pointing to Jesus. Indeed, Christians are still trying to say that mythology comes to an end with Jesus, whose stories are often raised to the level of sober history and absolute truth.

Despite these claims, the vast wheel of mythmaking rolls on, grinding even the gospels to powder. This powder is then mixed into the wet concrete of ever new mythologies, which explicitly and implicitly recycle and adapt gospel plots and motifs. Hollywood has colonized gospel narratives, in that self-sacrificing heroes continue to die and rise on the silver screen. Artists, poets, filmmakers, and novelists readily adapt stories of angelic visitations and breathtaking resuscitations because they still inspire the thrill of hope.

Ways of interpreting the Bible change, but in some respects there is nothing new under the sun. Prior to the Enlightenment, Christian scholars looked for the spiritual kernel in biblical stories using the complex methods of allegory. After the Enlightenment, Christian scholars began looking for the historical kernel in the Bible using the methods of historical criticism. In the twentieth century, the theologian Rudolf Bultmann looked for what might be called the existential kernel: how the stories address the question of human existence. But this, too, is a form of allegory, in that allegorical readings tend to bypass the "content plane" of the biblical stories themselves. The Holy Grail, as it were, is something "in, with, and under" the stories, not the stories themselves.[37]

One might claim that reading the gospels as myths is a more "natural" way to read them. History must be panned from the Bible with sweat and painstaking research; myths lie on its surface, crying out to be read and compared with other Greco-Roman stories that are already classed as myths. New Testament scholars are often trained as historians and literary scholars but are rarely given proper instruction in classical and comparative mythology. Perhaps it is time to redirect some of the energy that goes into examining the "historical Jesus" into studying Jesus as one of Western culture's historicized myths.

Looking Ahead

What is the future of gospel studies? There is little doubt that gospel myths will continue to be of collective importance across the globe. Since many of them belong to a large and diverse set of Christian communities, gospel stories show few signs of losing their significance. Conceivably for the next two millennia, they will continue to be recited in churches, freshly printed in Bibles, and interpreted in new and creative ways.

Nonetheless, signs of change are present. The more that the Bible drifts into the margins of Western culture, the more Jewish and Christian stories become "other" and unfamiliar to people in the West. The more foreign the stories become, the easier it will be to acknowledge them as myths in the scholarly sense (namely, as traditional tales that are important for communal identity). Making one's own mythology seem plausible takes serious intellectual labor. If there is no felt need to foster plausibility, then the stories will inevitably lose their ability to mediate "the real."

If Christian religion(s) ever fades away (or evolves into something new), its stories will still likely survive not just in cavernous library stacks but in the archives of the human imagination. University students might take courses in Christian mythology, as they do now with classical (Greek and Roman) mythology or Hindu mythology. Alternatively, Christian mythology may simply be incorporated into a course on classical mythology, ancient Middle Eastern history, or ancient literature. That is to say, if gospel myths cease to be formative for religious communities, they will continue to be of collective and historical importance.

What, then, is the end of our story? The four gospels are a profoundly significant corpus of history-like myths—and not just for religious readers. For all who treat mythology in literature courses, classes in mythology, or in Western civilization, the stories of Jesus should be studied and treasured. These stories, moreover, should be compared with other stories of collective importance throughout the globe and across the centuries. They should appear in our handbooks and journals of comparative mythology and find a place in conferences and other venues that go far beyond the confines of biblical studies. The study of the gospels has a sure place in the humanistic university if, that is, its stories are reclassified as myths—myths that in manifold ways can still become our own.

Further Reading

Dale C. Allison, *Resurrecting Jesus: The Earliest Christian Tradition and Its Interpreters* (New York: T&T Clark, 2005), 337–44.

Hal Childs, *The Myth of the Historical Jesus and the Evolution of Consciousness* (Atlanta: SBL, 2000).

John David Dawson, *Christian Figural Reading and the Fashioning of Identity* (Berkeley: University of California Press, 2002), 65–82, 114–40.

Jean Pépin, "Christian Judgments on the Analogies between Christianity and Pagan Mythology," in *Mythologies Compiled by Yves Bonnefoy*, ed. Wendy Doniger, vol. 2 (Chicago: University of Chicago, 1991), 655–65.

W. Taylor Stevenson, *History as Myth: The Import for Contemporary Theology* (New York: Seabury, 1969), 9–32.

Paul Veyne, *Writing History: Essay on Epistemology*, trans. Mina Moore-Rinvolucri (Middletown, CT: Wesleyan University Press, 1984), 12.

Hayden White, *Tropics of Discourse: Essays in Cultural Criticism* (Baltimore: Johns Hopkins University Press, 1978).

NOTES

All translations in this book, unless otherwise noted, are my own.

Introduction. The Gospels, Mythography, and Historiography

1. Sextus Empiricus, *Outlines of Pyrrhonism* 1.147 (μυθικὴ δὲ πίστις ἐστὶ πραγμάτων ἀγενήτων τε καὶ πεπλασμένων παραδοχή . . . ταῦτα γὰρ πολλοὺς εἰς πίστιν ἄγει.).

2. Hereafter the "gospels" refers to the four documents later canonized and incorporated into the New Testament. The "evangelists" refers to the authors of these documents.

3. Note the warnings of Claude Calame about importing Enlightenment understandings of myth back into antiquity (*Myth and History in Ancient Greece: The Symbolic Creation of a Colony*, trans. Daniel W. Berman [Princeton, NJ: Princeton University Press, 2003], 9–11; *Greek Mythology: Poetics, Pragmatics and Fiction*, trans. Janet Lloyd [Cambridge: Cambridge University Press, 2009), 3–8).

4. In what follows, I use "plausibility" as a synonym for believability or credibility. What is plausible can also connote what is probable in the sense of what commends itself as worthy of trust. Cicero defined the probable (*probabile*) as "that which customarily happens for the most part [*id quod fere solet fieri*], or what is established in opinion [*quod in opinione positum est*], or what has in itself some likeness to these, whether the likeness be true or false" (*On Invention* 46).

NOTES TO PAGE 2

5. For this project, see D. F. Strauss, *Life of Jesus Critically Examined*, trans. G. Eliot (London: SCM, 1973), originally published in German in 1835. After Strauss, the application of the category "myth(us)" to the gospels had a long and varied afterlife. For a sampling, see Robert Oden, *The Bible without Theology: The Theological Tradition and Alternatives to It* (New York: Harper and Row, 1987); Susan Ackermann, "Myth," in *The Oxford Companion to the Bible*, ed. Bruce M. Metzger and Michael D. Coogan (New York: Oxford University Press, 1993), 539–41; Peter G. Bietenholz, *Historia and Fabula: Myths and Legends in Historical Thought from Antiquity to the Modern Age* (Leiden: Brill, 1994), 311–39; Richard G. Walsh, *Mapping Myths of Biblical Interpretation* (Sheffield, UK: Sheffield Academic, 2001); Burton L. Mack, *The Christian Myth: Origins, Logic, and Legacy* (New York: Continuum, 2001); Giovanni Garbini, *Myth and History in the Bible*, trans. Chiara Peri (Sheffield, UK: Sheffield Academic, 2003); Oda Wischmeyer, "Probleme des gegenwärtigen Mythosbegriffs aus neutestamentlicher Sicht," in *Von Ben Sira zu Paulus. Gesammelte Aufsätze zu Texten, Theologie und Hermeneutik*, ed. E.-M. Becker (Tübingen: Mohr Siebeck, 2004), 361–88; Roland Boer, *Political Myth: On the Use and Abuse of Biblical Themes* (Durham, NC: Duke University Press, 2009); Northrop Frye, *Words with Power: Being a Second Study of "The Bible and Literature,"* ed. Michael Dolzani (Toronto: University of Toronto Press, 2008); Justin Meggitt, "Popular Mythology in the Early Empire and the Multiplicity of Jesus Traditions," in *Sources of the Jesus Tradition: Separating History from Myth*, ed. R. Joseph Hoffmann (Amherst, NY: Prometheus, 2010), 55–80, 269–75; Emanuel Pfoh, "Jesus and the Mythic Mind: An Epistemological Problem," in *"Is This Not the Carpenter?": The Question of the Historicity of the Figure of Jesus*, ed. Thomas L. Thompson and Thomas S. Verenna (Durham, UK: Acumen, 2012), 79–94; Dexter Callender Jr., "Mythology and Biblical Interpretation," in *The Oxford Encyclopedia of Biblical Interpretation*, ed. Steven L. McKenzie, 2 vols. (Oxford: Oxford University Press, 2013), 2:26–35; Dexter Callender, *Myth and Scripture: Contemporary Perspectives on Religion, Language, and Imagination* (Atlanta: SBL, 2014).

6. Robert A. Kaster writes that entry into the grammarian's school (or primary education) offered the children of the well-to-do the "one thing that approached a common experience" (*Guardians of Language: The Grammarian and Society in Late Antiquity* [Berkeley: University of California Press, 1997], 11).

7. Asclepiades in Sextus Empiricus, *Against the Grammarians* 1.263; cf. Cicero, *On Invention* 1.27; Ps.-Cicero, *Rhetoric to Herennius* 1.8.13; Alfred Hilgard, ed., *Scholia in Dionysii Thracis artem grammaticam* (Leipzig: Teubner, 1901), 449.23–27 (μῦθος δὲ ξένων πραγμάτων ἀπηρχαιωμένων διήγησις, ἢ ἀδυνάτων πραγμάτων παρεισαγωγή). See further Hubert Cancik, *Mythische und historische Wahrheit: Interpretationen zu Texten der hethitischen, biblischen und griechischen Historiographie* (Stuttgart: Katholisches Bibelwerk, 1970), 30–32; William J. Slater, "Asklepiades and *Historia*," *Greek, Roman, and Byzantine Studies* 13:3 (1972): 317–33, esp. 324–26; Roos Meijering, *Literary and Rhetorical Theories in Greek Scholia* (Groningen: Egbert Forsten, 1987), 76–79; Gioia Rispoli, *Lo spazio del verisimile: Il racconto, la storia e il mito* (Naples: M. D'Auria, 1988), 170–204; Bietenholz, *Historia and Fabula*, 59–61; G. W. Bowersock, *Fiction as History: Nero to Julian* (Berkeley: University of California Press, 1994),

10–11; D. L. Blank, *Sextus Empiricus "Against the Grammarians" (Adversus Mathematicos I)* (Oxford, UK: Clarendon, 1998), 277–81; Alan Cameron, *Greek Mythography in the Roman World* (Oxford: Oxford University Press 2004), 90–93.

8. Quintilian, *Orator's Education* 2.4.2. The word "exposition" (*expositio*) is important, because historiography is always an interpretive rendition of events that happened in the past. For postmodern reflections on this point, see Linda Hutcheon, *A Poetics of Postmodernism: History, Theory, Fiction* (London: Taylor and Francis, 1988), 87–157; Keith Jenkins, *On "What Is Historiography?" from Carr and Elton to Rorty and White* (London: Routledge, 1995), 15–42.

9. Plato, *Timaeus* 29d; cf. Plato, *Phaedo* 60b—61c.

10. George A. Kennedy, *Progymnasmata: Greek Textbooks of Prose Composition and Rhetoric* (Atlanta: SBL, 2003), 4. For the Greek text, see L. Spengel, *Rhetores Graeci*, vol. 2 (Leipzig: Teubner, 1854), 59.

11. Plutarch, *On the Fame of the Athenians* 4.348a–b.

12. Plutarch, *Theseus* 1.5.

13. Cf. the distinction of Nicolaus the Sophist (fifth century CE but dependent on earlier sources): "Mythical narratives [μυθικὰ διηγήματα] share with *mythoi* the need to be persuasive [δεῖσθαι πίστεως], but they differ because *mythoi* are agreed to be false and fictional, while mythical narratives differ from others in being told as though they had happened [ὡς γεγονότα] and being capable of having happened [καὶ τῶν ἐνδεχομένων ἐστὶ γενέσθαι] or not having happened" (*Progymnasmata* 13 [Felten], translated in Kennedy, *Progymnasmata*, 136–37). The key distinction is between pure *mythos* (which does not seem true) and "mythical narrative" (which can seem true). See further Meijering, *Literary and Rhetorical Theories*, 79–82.

14. Perhaps it is significant that Philo (about 20 BCE–45 CE) regularly referred to "mythical fictions" (μυθικοῖς πλάσμασι, *On the Creation* 1; μυθικῶν πλασμάτων, *Special Laws* 4.178) and the "fiction of myth" (πλάσμα μύθου, *Abraham* 54). The author of 2 Peter also associates μύθοι with πλάστοι λόγοι (1:16, 2:3).

15. S. C. Humphreys, "Fragments, Fetishes, and Philosophies: Towards a History of Greek Historiography after Thucydides," in *Collecting Fragments*, ed. G. Most (Göttingen: Vandenhoeck & Ruprecht, 1997), 218. Humphreys goes on to write that historians gave "a more secure footing by rationalizing interpretations that stripped legends of their less plausible details without entirely discarding them" (218–19).

16. "A *mythos* that is made up" can still "carry conviction" (σχῇ πίστιν) (*Alexander Romance* 2.15.5). Lucian reported that some *mythoi* were taken to be so obvious and true that *not* to believe them was considered impious (*Lover of Lies* 3). On the whole question of myth and belief, see Paul Veyne, *Did the Greeks Believe in Their Myths? An Essay on the Constitutive Imagination*, trans. Paula Wissing (Chicago: University of Chicago Press, 1988).

17. Elizabeth Rawson writes that "myth and marvels became an almost essential ornament even to basically serious [historiographic] works and, like rhetorical elaboration of more recent events in order to bring out pathos and drama, and to give vividness, they often ran riot. In a society in which there was a limited amount of prose fiction . . . some

historiography probably presented the best light reading available" (*Intellectual Life in the Late Roman Republic* [London: Duckworth, 1985], 217).

18. Origen, *Against Celsus* 2.58.

19. Origen, *Against Celsus* 3.27.

20. See further C. K. Barrett, "Myth and the New Testament: The Greek Word *mythos*," *Expository Times* 68 (1957): 345–48.

21. Plato often depicted myth tellers as old women (*Gorgias* 523a5–6; *Republic* 350e2–4). Josephus, a Jewish writer contemporary with the evangelists, used a similar tactic in his *Jewish Antiquities* 1.15, 22–23 (perhaps dependent on Dionysius of Halicarnassus, *Roman Antiquities* 2.18); cf. Josephus, *Against Apion* 2.236–56 (dependent on Platonic theology); Philo, *On the Creation* 1–2; *Epistle of Aristeas* 168. See further René Bloch, *Moses und der Mythos: Die Auseinandersetzung mit der griechischen Mythologie bei jüdisch-hellenistischen Autoren* (Leiden: Brill, 2011), 23–50, 89–104, 173–90.

22. I emphasize this point in contradistinction to Dennis R. MacDonald, who recently claims that "Mark and Luke knew that they were writing fictions" (*Mythologizing Jesus: From Jewish Teacher to Epic Hero* [Lanham, MD: Rowman and Littlefield, 2015]), 142, cf. 1–2. MacDonald's point of view is represented in the work of his student Richard C. Miller, who claims that the translation (or resurrection) stories of the gospels were taken as "fables"—as if the evangelists themselves did not believe that they actually happened (*Resurrection and Reception in Early Christianity* [London: Routledge, 2015]). In Miller's language, "the earliest Christians comprehended the resurrection narratives of the New Testament as instances within a larger conventional rubric commonly recognized as fictive in modality" (181). For helpful correctives of this position, see Sylvie Honigman, *The Septuagint and Homeric Scholarship in Alexandria: A Study in the Narrative of the Letter of Aristeas* (London: Taylor and Francis, 2003), 65–91.

23. Celsus in Origen, *Against Celsus* 4.51.

24. Celsus in Origen, *Against Celsus* 2.55.

25. Celsus in Origen, *Against Celsus* 6.34.

26. Celsus in Origen, *Against Celsus* 6.77, cf. 8.45. Celsus also attacked what he considered to be *mythoi* in the Jewish scriptures. The accounts of the Jewish deity making a man out of clay and taking a woman from the man's side Celsus considered to be *mythoi* (*Against Celsus* 4.36). The same is true for the story of the serpent in Gen. 3 (*Against Celsus* 4.39). According to Celsus, the Greeks regard as a *mythos* the story of Yahweh writing down the law with his own finger (*Against Celsus* 1.4, referring to Exod. 31:18). In general, Celsus supposed that the "stories [ἱστορίας] and laws of Moses" to be "empty *mythoi* [μῦθοι κενοί]" (*Against Celsus* 1.20). Although Origen shared some stories with the Jews, he himself thought that the "doctrines of the Jews living now are *mythoi* and trash [μύθους καὶ λήρους]." Origen also reported that the Marcionite Christian Apelles considered the Jewish scriptures to be *mythos* (*Against Celsus* 5.54).

27. Aristotle, *Poetics* 9.1, 1451b5.

28. Asclepiades as reported by Sextus Empiricus, *Against the Grammarians* 1.263.

29. Cicero, *On Invention* 1.27. Cf. Quintilian, *Orator's Education* 2.4.2; Isidore of Seville, *Etymologies* 1.41.1, 1.44.5. See further A. J. Woodman, *Rhetoric in Classical Historiography: Four Studies* (London: Croom Helm, 1988), 114n141; T. P. Wiseman, "Lying Historians: Seven Types of Mendacity," in *Lies and Fiction in the Ancient World*, ed. Christopher Gill and T. P. Wiseman (Exeter: University of Exeter Press, 1993), 130; Blank, *Sextus Empiricus*, 277–81. This ancient conception of historiography has been carried over to modern history writing as well. Hayden White, discussing common conceptions of historiography, writes, "The content of historical stories is real events, events that really happened, rather than imaginary events, events invented by the narrator" ("The Question of Narrative in Contemporary Historical Theory," *History and Theory* 23:1 [1984]: 2).

30. Andreas Mehl, *Roman Historiography: An Introduction to Its Basic Aspects and Development*, trans. Hans-Friedrich Mueller (Malden, MA: Blackwell, 2014), 26, emphasis original.

31. Cicero, *On the Orator* 2.62–63. Cf. Polybius, *Histories* 2.56.11–12. See further A. J. Woodman, "Cicero and the Writing of Historiography," in *Oxford Readings in Classical Studies: Greek and Roman Historiography*, ed. John Marincola (Oxford: Oxford University Press, 2011), 241–90.

32. Polybius, *Histories* 34.4.2 (τῆς μὲν οὖν ἱστορίας ἀλήθειαν εἶναι τέλος), cf. 12.4d.1–2.

33. Cicero, *On the Orator* 2.36 (*lux veritatis*).

34. Diodorus, *Library of History* 1.2.2 (τὴν προφῆτιν τῆς ἀληθείας ἱστορίαν).

35. Dionysius, *Roman Antiquities* 1.1.2. Cf. Josephus, *Jewish War* 1.16: "when it comes to history, one must speak the truth and may only assemble the facts through much exertion" (πρὸς δὲ τὴν ἱστορίαν, ἔνθα χρὴ τάληθῆ λέγειν καὶ μετὰ πολλοῦ πόνου τὰ πράγματα συλλέγειν).

36. Pliny the Younger, *Epistles* 7.33.10 (*nec historia debet egredi veritatem*).

37. Lucian, *How to Write History* 7. Cf. §8, where he claims that *mythos* is an adornment of poetry that cannot be brought into history. Lucian is exaggerating, but his exaggeration indicates that the ancients could conceive of an ideal type of history without *mythoi*.

38. Tacitus, *Annals* 1.1 (*sine ira et studio*).

39. See T. J. Luce, "Ancient Views on the Causes of Bias in Historical Writing," in *Greek and Roman Historiography*, ed. John Marincola (Oxford: Oxford University Press, 2011), 291–313. See also T. P. Wiseman, *Clio's Cosmetics: Three Studies in Greco-Roman Literature* (Totowa, NJ: Rowman and Littlefield, 1979), 32–40.

40. Cicero, *Letter to Brutus* 42.

41. Cicero, *Letters to Friends* 5.12.3 (*leges historiae negligas*).

42. Miller, *Resurrection and Reception*, 133. Miller concludes that "the ecclesiastical distinction endeavored by Irenaeus of Lyons *et alii* to segregate and signify some such works as canonical, reliable histories appears wholly political and arbitrary" (133). Miller wrongfully conflates the "canonical" and "historical." Viewing the gospels (and Acts) as works of ancient historiography is not arbitrary, as is shown by key recent monographs: Gregory E. Sterling, *Historiography and Self-Definition: Josephos, Luke-Acts, and Apologetic Historiography* (Leiden: Brill, 1992); Clare K. Rothschild, *Luke-Acts and the Rhetoric of History: An Investigation*

of Early Christian Historiography (Tübingen: Mohr Siebeck, 2004); and Eve-Marie Becker, *The Birth of Christian History: Memory and Time from Mark to Luke-Acts* (New Haven, CT: Yale University Press, 2017).

43. Although the evangelists did not cite sources, they certainly used them and, in the case of Luke, gave the impression that they used eyewitness reports (Luke 1:2).

44. Cicero, *Laws* 1.5. Aristotle had earlier called Herodotus ὁ μυθολόγος, the "myth teller" (*Generation of Animals* 3.5, 756b6–7). Plutarch accused Herodotus of telling "lies and fictions" (ψεύσματα καὶ πλάσματα) (*Malice of Herodotus* 1.854f).

45. Thucydides, *History of the Peloponnesian War* 1.22.4, cf. 5.20.2, 5.26.5, 5.68.2, 6.54–55.

46. Cicero, *On the Orator* 2.55–56.

47. Lucian, *How to Write History* 42 (νομοθέτης τῆς ἱστοριογραφίας). Note also the comparisons in Quintilian, *Orator's Education* 10.1.73. See further Bietenholz, *Historia and Fabula*, 21–46; Thomas F. Scanlon, "'The Clear Truth' in Thucydides 1.22.4," *Historia* 51 (2002): 131–48; Tim Whitmarsh, *Beyond the Second Sophistic: Adventures in Postclassicism* (Berkeley: University of California Press, 2013), 20–23; Roberto Nicolai, "*Ktēma es aei*: Aspects of the Reception of Thucydides in the Ancient World," in *Thucydides*, ed. Jeffrey S. Rusten (Oxford: Oxford University Press, 2009), 382–404.

48. Seneca, *Natural Questions* 7.16.1–2. See further Wiseman, "Lying Historians," 122–23, 142–43; Rothschild, *Luke-Acts and the Rhetoric of History*, 71–76.

49. Ephorus reported by Diodorus, *Library of History* 9.3.11. As a genre, mythography arose contemporaneously with historiography and shared some of its methods and characteristics. See Robert Fowler, "How to Tell a Myth: Genealogy, Mythology, Mythography," *Kernos* 19 (2006): 35–46.

50. On history as a branch of rhetoric, see Woodman, *Rhetoric in Classical Historiography* (entire); Wiseman, *Clio's Cosmetics* (entire); Gill and Wiseman, *Lies and Fiction;* Michael Grant, *Greek and Roman Historians: Information and Misinformation* (London: Routledge, 1995), 61–99.

51. Lucian, *How to Write History*, preface.

52. For further examples, see John Miller and A. J. Woodman, eds., *Latin Historiography and Poetry in the Early Empire: Generic Interactions* (Leiden: Brill, 2010); D. S. Levene and D. P. Nelis, eds., *Clio and the Poets: Augustan Poetry and the Traditions of Ancient Historiography* (Leiden: Brill, 2014).

53. Vergil, *Aeneid* 6.285–95.

54. Lucian played on this basic assumption by calling his two-volume spoof on historiography *True Stories*.

55. Jens Schröter, "The Gospels as Eyewitness Testimony? A Critical Examination of Richard Bauckham's *Jesus and the Eyewitnesses*," *Journal for the Study of the New Testament* 31:2 (2008): 195–209; Judith C. S. Redman, "How Accurate Are Eyewitnesses? Bauckham and the Eyewitnesses in the Light of Psychological Research," *Journal of Biblical Literature* 129:1 (2010): 177–97. See also Redman's essay "Eyewitness Testimony and the Characters in the Fourth Gospel," in *Characters and Characterization in the Fourth Gospel*, ed. Christopher W. Skinner (London: Bloomsbury, 2013), 59–78.

56. See further Harold W. Attridge, "Genre Bending in the Fourth Gospel," *Journal of Biblical Literature* 121 (2002): 3–21; Attridge, "Genre Matters," in *The Gospel of John as a Genre Mosaic*, ed. Kasper Bro Larsen (Göttingen: Vandenhoeck & Ruprecht, 2015), 27–46.

57. The phrase is taken from Roland Barthes, *The Rustle of Language*, trans. Richard Howard (Oxford, UK: Blackwell, 1986), 139–48.

58. See further Greta Hawes, ed., *Myths on the Map: The Storied Landscapes of Ancient Greece* (Oxford: Oxford University Press, 2017).

59. Diodorus, *Library of History* 4.8.4–5. See further Charles E. Muntz, *Diodorus Siculus and the World of the Late Roman Republic* (Oxford: Oxford University Press, 2017), 89–132.

60. Dionysius of Halicarnassus, *Roman Antiquities* 2.61.3.

61. Strabo, *Geography* 1.2.35. Compare the "mythic history" (*historia fabularis*) mentioned by Suetonius, *Tiberius* 70.2–3. The author of the *Historia Augusta* also used the words *mythistoria* and *mythistoricus* (Ronald Syme, *Fictional Historiography Old and New: Hadrian; A James Bryce Memorial Lecture Delivered in the Wolfson Hall, Somerville College on 10 May 1984* [Oxford, UK: Somerville College, 1986], 24).

62. The Jewish historian Josephus proudly upheld this *mythos* as part of his own local history (*Jewish War* 3.420).

63. Livy, for his part, admitted that the material he dealt with regarding the oldest of the city's traditions was more fitting for poetic fables (*poetics fabulis*) than the "uncontaminated record of events" (*incorruptis rerum gestarum monumentis*) (*From the Foundation*, preface §6). Lucian mentions that historians too, along with poets and philosophers, composed things that were "marvelous and fantastical" (τεράστια καὶ μυθώδη) (*True Histories* 1.2).

64. Josephus, *Against Apion* 1.25.

65. Cf. the category of "mythistory" proposed by Joseph Mali, *Mythistory: The Making of a Modern Historiography* (Chicago: University of Chicago Press, 2003), 1–35; William H. McNeill, *Mythistory and Other Essays* (Chicago: University of Chicago Press, 1986), 1–22. Cf. also the concept of "intentional history" as developed by Hans-Joachim Gehrke, "Representations of the Past in Greek Culture," in *Intentional History: Spinning Time in Ancient Greece*, ed. Lin Foxhall, Hans-Joachim Gehrke, and Nino Luraghi (Stuttgart: Franz Steiner, 2010), 15–34.

66. Thomas M. Bolin, following Arnaldo Momigliano (*Studies in Historiography* [New York: Harper Torchbooks, 1966], 1–39), draws a distinction between antiquarian writing and historiography ("History, Historiography, and the Use of the Past in the Hebrew Bible," in *The Limits of Historiography: Genre and Narrative in Ancient Historical Texts*, ed. Christina Shuttleworth Kraus [Leiden: Brill, 1999], 124–40). The former is based on written, not oral, sources and focuses in part on the "ephemeral details of the distant past rather than on the immediately political or national history of the author" (137). One might argue that my category of "mythic historiography" is a form of antiquarian writing, as opposed to historiography. Yet this opposition, I think, cannot be maintained. Antiquarian writing was considered to be a form of historiography, and the writers of contemporary history could include the fantastical (τὸ μυθῶδες) in their works. Plutarch and Philostratus mixed

in antiquarian concerns and mythical elements when they spoke of (nearly) contemporary figures, and they had Xenophon and Herodotus as worthy models in this regard. In the same volume in which Bolin's essay appeared, John Marincola urged against "the relegation of certain types of information to the category of 'antiquarianism.' . . . The whole notion of 'antiquarian' literature has recently been seen as problematic [mostly due to anachronism]. . . . Attempts, therefore, to distinguish 'annalists' from 'historians' by pointing to subject matter fail because they try to establish an artificial dividing line between what could and could not be included in a history" ("Genre, Convention, and Innovation in Greco-Roman Historiography," in Kraus, *Limits of Historiography*, 307–8).

67. The Roman writer Aulus Gellius (about 130–80 CE) purchased and eagerly read several paradoxographical works in the port city of Brundisium (modern Brindisi) on the eastern coast of Italy (*Attic Nights* 9.4.1–4). This passage is discussed at length by Guido Schepens and Kris Delcroix, "Ancient Paradoxography: Origin, Evolution, Production and Reception," in *La letteratura di consumo nel mondo greco-latino: Atti di convegno internazionale, Cassino (Settembre 14–17, 1994)*, ed. Oronzo Pecere and Antonio Stramaglia (Cassino, Italy: Università degli Studi, 1996), 373–460. Phlegon of Tralles, freedman of the emperor Hadrian (ruled 117–37 CE) wrote a sixteen-book account of marvels (*Mirabilia*). In the *Suda*, Phlegon is classified as a "historian" (ἱστορικός).

68. Palaephatus, preface to *On Unbelievable Tales*. On this preface, see Richard Hunter, "'Palaephatus,' Strabo and the Boundaries of Myth,' *Classical Philology* 111 (2016): 245–61.

69. Strabo, *Geography* 1.2.19.

70. Pausanias, *Description of Greece* 8.2.7.

71. Lucian, *Passing of Peregrinus* 38–40. For the context of this work, see C. P. Jones, *Culture and Society in Lucian* (Cambridge, MA: Harvard University Press, 1986), 117–32.

72. Plutarch once complained, "Already patently false and fabricated accounts about new and recent events have gained credibility" (*Banquet of the Seven Sages* 146b). For mythicizing the recent past, see E. L. Bowie, "Ancestors of Historiography in Early Greek Elegiac and Iambic Poetry," in *The Historian's Craft in the Age of Herodotus*, ed. Nino Luraghi (Oxford: Oxford University Press, 2001), 45–66; D. Boedeker, "Heroic Historiography: Simonides and Herodotus on Plataea," *Arethusa* 29 (1996): 223–42; Boedeker, "Epic Heritage and Mythical Patterns in Herodotus," in *Brill's Companion to Herodotus*, ed. E. J. Bakker, I. J. F. de Jong, and H. van Wees (Leiden: Brill, 2002), 97–116; M. Flashar, "Die Sieger von Marathon Zwischen Mythisierung und Vorbildlichkeit," in *Retrospektive: Konzepte von Vergangenheit in der griechisch-römischen Antike*, ed. H. Flashar, H.-J. Gehrke, and E. Heinrich (Munich: Biering and Brinkmann, 1996), 63–86.

73. See, for instance, Herodotus, *Histories* 2.113–20; Thucydides, *History of the Peloponnesian War* 1.3.1–3; Polybius, *Histories* 34.2.9–11; Strabo, *Geography* 1.2.9. See further A. E. Wardman, "Myth in Greek Historiography," *Historia* 9 (1960): 401–13; Anna Maria Biraschi, "Strabo and Homer: A Chapter in Cultural History," in *Strabo's Cultural Geography*, ed. Daniela Dueck, Hugh Lindsay, and Sarah Pothecary (Cambridge: Cambridge University

Press, 2005), 73–85; Lawrence Kim, *Homer between History and Fiction in Imperial Greek Literature* (Cambridge: Cambridge University Press, 2010).

74. Dennis Feeney, *Caesar's Calendar: Ancient Time and the Beginnings of History* (Berkeley: University of California Press, 2007), 19. The date stems from Eratosthenes, who wrote in the late third century BCE. It has been adjusted to the modern dating system.

75. Origen, *Against Celsus* 1.42.

76. Hellanicus, frag. 28, in Robert L. Fowler, *Early Greek Mythography I* (Oxford: Oxford University Press, 2000), 167. See further Fowler's *Early Greek Mythography II: Commentary* (Oxford: Oxford University Press, 2013), 688.

77. Lucian, *How to Write History* 40. For the context of this work, see Jones, *Culture and Society*, 59–68.

78. For the phrase, see Dionysius of Halicarnassus, *Roman Antiquities* 1.41.1; Strabo, *Geography* 1.2.35.

79. On Palaephatus, see J. Stern, "Rationalizing Myth: Methods and Motives in Palaephatus," in *From Myth to Reason? Studies in the Development of Greek Thought*, ed. Richard Buxton (Oxford: Oxford University Press, 1999), 215–22; Kai Brodersen, "'Das aber ist eine Lüge!'—Zur rationalistischen Mythenkritik des Palaiphatos," in *Griechische Mythologie und frühes Christentum*, ed. Raban von Haehling (Darmstadt: Wissenschaftliche Buchgesellschaft, 2005), 44–57; Alexandra Trachsel, "L'explication mythologique de Palaïphatos: Une stratégie particulière," *Maia* 57:3 (2005): 543–56; Greta Hawes, *Rationalizing Myth in Antiquity* (Oxford: Oxford University Press, 2014), 27–94; Hawes, "Story Time at the Library: Palaephatus and the Emergence of Highly Literate Mythology," in *Between Orality and Literacy: Communication and Adaptation in Antiquity*, ed. Ruth Scodel (Leiden: Brill, 2014), 125–47. The classic discussion of historicization is Wilhelm Nestle, *Vom Mythos zum Logos: Die Selbstentfaltung des griechischen Denkens von Homer bis auf die Sophistik und Socrates*, 2d ed. (Stuttgart: Alfred Kröner, 1942), 131–52. Nestle viewed historicization as a sign of decay, but in fact it is a sign of the continued vitality of ancient *mythoi*. Note also Cancik, *Mythische und historische*, 35–45.

80. Polybius, *Histories* 3.91.7, accepts the story that the gods struggled for the plain of Capua because it is reasonable (εἰκός) that they would fight for so fertile and beautiful a land. Gary Forsythe concludes that "Livy appears to have been a theist who believed that the gods could and did influence the outcome of human events, but that they did so impersonally without transgressing nature's laws" (*Livy and Early Rome: A Study in Historical Method and Judgment* [Stuttgart: Franz Steiner, 1999], 93).

81. Quoted in Charles William Fornara, *The Nature of History in Ancient Greece and Rome* (Berkeley: University of California Press, 1983), 81.

82. Palaephatus, *On Unbelievable Tales* §14 (ed. Stern).

83. This very historicization is repeated in a writer closer to the period of the evangelists, namely, Heraclitus the Paradoxographer. See J. Stern, "Heraclitus the Paradoxographer," *Transactions of the American Philological Association* 133 (2003): 51–97. Stern dates Heraclitus to the first or second century CE (53).

84. Dionysius, *Roman Antiquities* 1.39.1.

85. Dionysius, *Roman Antiquities* 1.41.1.

86. Dionysius, *Roman Antiquities* 1.39–42. Dionysius's "mythical" account can be compared with Vergil, *Aeneid* 8.193–272; and his historical account can be compared with Livy, *From the Foundation* 1.7.4–14.

87. Plutarch, *Romulus* 4.3 (compare Livy, *From the Foundation* 1.4.7); Plutarch, *Theseus* 16.1. Plutarch feminizes myth, making her submit to historiography as to a husband. Myth is a young virgin wife who needs to be compressed into historiography, tamed in her habits, controlled by the rational spouse. But like many Greek wives, presumably, some myths refused to be tamed. When myths proved stubborn, Plutarch could only, like a sheepish husband, beg indulgence. See further Frank J. Frost, "Plutarch and Theseus," *Classical Bulletin* 60:4 (1984): 67, with key references on 71; Christopher Pelling, *Plutarch and History: Eighteen Studies* (Swansea, UK: Classical Press of Wales, 2002), 143–70; Craig Cooper, "Making Irrational Myth Plausible History: Polybian Intertextuality in Plutarch's 'Theseus,'" *Phoenix* 61 (2007): 212–33; Hawes, *Rationalizing Myth*, 149–95.

Chapter One. Jesus Myth Theory

1. John P. Meier, *A Marginal Jew: Rethinking the Historical Jesus*, vol. 1, *The Roots of the Problem and the Person* (New York: Doubleday, 1991), 26.

2. Maurice Casey, *Jesus: Evidence and Argument or Mythicist Myths?* (London: Bloomsbury, 2014).

3. Quoted in Bruno Bauer, *Trumpet of the Last Judgment against Hegel, the Atheist and Antichrist: An Ultimatum*, trans. Lawrence Stepelevich (Lewiston, NY: Edwin Mellen, 1989), 109, emphasis original.

4. Bruno Bauer, *Kritik der evangelischen Geschichte der Synoptiker*, 3 vols. (Leipzig: Otto Wigand, 1841; repr., Hlidescheim: Georg Olms, 1974), 1:391–416. Page numbers refer to the 1974 edition.

5. Bruno Bauer, *Kritik der evangelischen Geschichte der Synoptiker und des Johannes* (Braunschweig: Friedrich Otto, 1842; repr., Hildesheim: Georg Olms, 1974), 14 (*In der Weissagung, wie in der Erfüllung war der Messias nur ein ideales Product des religiösen Bewusstseyns, als sinnlich gegebenes Individuum hat er nicht existiert*). Page numbers refer to the 1974 edition.

6. Bauer, *Kritik der evangelischen Geschichte der Synoptiker und des Johannes*, 314–15.

7. Bauer, *Kritik der evangelischen Geschichte der Synoptiker*, 3.308 (*Die Frage, mit der sich unsere Zeit so viel beschäftigt hat, ob nämlich Dieser, ob Jesus der historische Christus sei, haben wir damit beantwortet, dass wir zeigten, dass Alles, was der historische Christus ist, was von ihm gesagt wird, was wir von ihm wissen, der Welt der Vorstellung und zwar der christlichen Vorstellung angehört, also auch mit einem Menschen, der der wirklichen Welt angehört, Nichts zu tun hat. Die Frage ist damit beantwortet, dass sie für alle Zukunft gestrichen ist*).

8. Quoted in Zvi Rosen, *Bruno Bauer and Karl Marx: The Influence of Bruno Bauer on Marx's Thought* (The Hague: Martinus Nijhoff, 1977), 60n61.

9. Rosen, *Bruno Bauer*, 60.

10. Lawrence Stepelevich, "Translator's Introduction," in Bauer, *Trumpet*, 30–31.

11. Bruno Bauer, *Christ and the Caesars: The Origin of Christianity from Greek Culture in Its Roman Form* (1877; repr., Frankfurt am Main: Minerva Verlag, 1981).

12. Quoted in Stepelevich, "Translator's Introduction," in Bauer, *Trumpet*, 45.

13. A classic treatment of Bauer in English can be found in Albert Schweitzer, *The Quest for the Historical Jesus*, trans. W. Montgomery (Mineola, NY: Dover, 2005), 137–60.

14. Bernard Treacy, "From the Editor's Desk: Official Dominican Response to a Controversial Book," *Doctrine and Life* 64:5 (2014): 3.

15. Thomas L. Brodie, *Beyond the Quest for the Historical Jesus: Memoir of a Discovery* (Sheffield, UK: Sheffield Phoenix, 2012), 35.

16. Brodie, *Beyond the Quest*, 211.

17. Brodie, *Beyond the Quest*, 196.

18. Brodie, *Beyond the Quest*, 123.

19. Brodie, *Beyond the Quest*, 125.

20. Brodie, *Beyond the Quest*, 115–20.

21. Brodie, *Beyond the Quest*, 160–68.

22. Brodie, *Beyond the Quest*, 213.

23. Brodie, *Beyond the Quest*, 60–65.

24. Brodie, *Beyond the Quest*, 133–34.

25. Brodie, *Beyond the Quest*, 85–86.

26. See further Jeremy Corley, "Review Article," *Irish Theological Quarterly* 79:2 (2014): 177–94; and the reviews in *Doctrine and Life* 63:6 (2013): 2–31.

27. Richard Carrier, "From Taoist to Infidel" (2001), infidels.org, accessed October 19, 2016, http://infidels.org/library/modern/testimonials/carrier.html.

28. Richard Carrier, "The Spiritual Body of Christ and the Legend of the Empty Tomb," in *The Empty Tomb: Jesus beyond the Grave*, ed. Robert M. Price and Jeffery Jay Lowder (Amherst, NY: Prometheus, 2005), 185.

29. Carrier, "Spiritual Body," 185.

30. Carrier, "Spiritual Body," 185.

31. Carrier, "From Taoist to Infidel."

32. Two things tend to distinguish Carrier from scholars working in the academy: his rigidly rationalist epistemology (seemingly unaffected by postmodern thought and the linguistic turn) and his cavalier, brazen—essentially polemical—rhetoric.

33. Carrier, "From Taoist to Infidel."

34. Carrier, "From Taoist to Infidel."

35. Carrier, "From Taoist to Infidel."

36. Alan Dundes, *In Quest of the Hero* (Princeton, NJ: Princeton University Press, 1990), 138.

37. Richard Carrier, *On the Historicity of Jesus: Why We Have Reason to Doubt* (Sheffield, UK: Sheffield Phoenix, 2014), 233. In general, Carrier tweaks Raglan's pattern so that it better fits Jesus. For instance, although Raglan said that the hero's father is a king, Carrier says

that the father can be an *heir* of a king in order to fit the fact that Joseph, Jesus's "father," was only a distant descendant of King David. The same sort of fudging appears in Robert M. Price, *Deconstructing Jesus* (Amherst, NY: Prometheus, 2000), 259–60.

38. See further Daniel N. Gullotta, "On Richard Carrier's Doubts: A Response to Richard Carrier's *On the Historicity of Jesus: Why We Might Have Reason for Doubt*," *Journal for the Study of the Historical Jesus* 15 (2017): 342–43.

39. For the argument, see Carrier, *Historicity*, 37–48. For his argument, Carrier is almost entirely dependent on Earl Doherty, *Jesus: Neither God nor Man: The Case for a Mythical Jesus* (Ottawa: Age of Reason, 2009), 119–26.

40. See further Gullotta, "On Richard Carrier's Doubts," 331–34.

41. Carrier, *Historicity*, 47–48.

42. Enrico Norelli, ed., *Ascensio Isaiae: Commentarius*, Corpus Christianorum Series Apocryphorum 8 (Turnhout, Belgium: Brepols, 1995), 535–38.

43. *Ascension of Isaiah* 9:12–14. The angels supposing Christ to be flesh occurs in the Ethiopic version.

44. Carrier, *Historicity*, 168–73.

45. Carrier, *Historicity*, 36–37, 47, 169–70.

46. Sophocles, *Women of Trachis* 1191–93; Diodorus, *Library of History* 4.38.

47. Diodorus, *Library of History* 3.62.6, 5.75.4, compare 3.62.8.

48. Jaime Alvar, *Romanising Oriental Gods: Myth, Salvation and Ethics in the Cults of Cybele, Isis and Mithras*, trans. Richard Gordon (Leiden: Brill, 2008), 133.

49. Arnobius, *Against the Nations* 5.7.

50. Giulia Sfameni Gasparro, *Soteriology and Mystic Aspects in the Cult of Cybele and Attis* (Leiden: Brill, 1985), xvi, 50, 125.

51. Carrier, *Historicity*, 172.

52. Carrier, *Historicity*, 237.

53. M. L. West, "The Invention of Homer," *Classical Quarterly* 49:2 (1999): 379.

54. Gullotta, "On Richard Carrier's Doubts," 327–28, with further sources on 327n56.

55. Casey, *Jesus*, 203.

Chapter Two. A Theory of Comparison

1. Jonathan Z. Smith, "Prologue: In Comparison a Magic Dwells," in *A Magic Still Dwells: Comparative Religion in the Postmodern Age*, ed. Kimberley C. Patton and Benjamin C. Ray (Berkeley: University of California Press, 2000), 26.

2. For MacDonald's more sophisticated comparisons, see his *The Homeric Epics and the Gospel of Mark* (New Haven, CT: Yale University Press, 2000); and *Does the New Testament Imitate Homer? Four Cases from the Acts of the Apostles* (New Haven, CT: Yale University Press, 2003).

3. MacDonald, *Does the New Testament Imitate Homer?*, 4–7; MacDonald, *Homeric Epics*, 8–9.

4. Margaret M. Mitchell, "Homer in the New Testament?," *Journal of Religion* 83 (2003): 244–58; Karl Olav Sandnes, "*Imitatio Homeri?* An Appraisal of Dennis R. MacDonald's 'Mimesis Criticism,'" *Journal of Biblical Literature* 124 (2005): 715–32. MacDonald responded to their criticisms in "My Turn: A Critique of Critics of 'Mimesis Criticism,'" *Institute for Antiquity and Christianity Occasional Papers* 53 (2009): 1–18. In my judgment, MacDonald's response does not adequately address the concerns raised by Mitchell and Sandnes.

5. Mitchell, "Homer in the New Testament?," 252.

6. This tendency is documented also by Mitchell, "Homer in the New Testament?," 252.

7. Dennis R. MacDonald, *The Gospels and Homer: Imitations of Greek Epic in Mark and Luke-Acts* (Lanham, MD: Rowman and Littlefield, 2015), 100–104; MacDonald, *Mythologizing Jesus*, 49–54.

8. MacDonald, *Gospels and Homer*, 76.

9. Unfortunately anyone who dares to suggest stricter linguistic and structural criteria for MacDonald is in danger of being accused of "philological fundamentalism" (MacDonald, *Gospels and Homer*, 10).

10. MacDonald, *Gospels and Homer*, 206.

11. Umberto Eco, *Interpretation and Overinterpretation*, ed. Stefan Collini (Cambridge: Cambridge University Press, 1992), 48, italics removed. He goes on: "the difference between the sane interpretation and the paranoiac interpretation lies in recognizing that this relationship [between 'while' and 'crocodile'] is minimal, and not, on the contrary, deducing from this minimal relationship the maximum possible."

12. Quoted in MacDonald, *Gospels and Homer*, 6.

13. MacDonald, *Does the New Testament Imitate Homer?*, 15.

14. For pantomime, see C. P. Jones, *Culture and Society in Lucian* (Cambridge, MA: Harvard University Press, 1986), 68–77.

15. Tertullian, *Apology* 15.4; Tertullian, *Against the Nations* 1.10.46–47.

16. 1 Clement 6.2; Tertullian, *Against the Nations* 1.10.46–47; Tertullian, *Apology* 15.4. Cf. Martial, *On the Spectacles* 6 (5): "whatever Fame sings, the arena affords you"; 9 (7): "what had been fables became punishment." See further Kathleen M. Coleman, "Fatal Charades: Roman Executions Staged as Mythological Enactments," *Journal of Roman Studies* 80 (1990): 44–73; Thomas E. J. Wiedemann, *Emperors and Gladiators* (London: Taylor and Francis, 1992), 84–89.

17. William H. Sewall, Jr., "The Concept(s) of Culture," in *Beyond the Cultural Turn: New Directions in the Study of Society and Culture*, ed. Victoria E. Bonnell and Lynn Hunt (Berkeley: University of California Press, 1999), 53–55. For important criticisms of the term *culture* and a history of its use, see Tomoko Masuzawa, "Culture," in *Critical Terms for Religious Studies*, ed. Mark C. Taylor (Chicago: University of Chicago Press, 1998), 70–93. For explorations of local culture and "glocalization," see Tim Whitmarsh, ed., *Local Knowledge and Micro-Identities in the Imperial Greek World* (Cambridge: Cambridge University Press, 2010), 1–10.

18. Horace, *Epistles*, in *The Satires, Epistles, and Art of Poetry of Horace*, trans. John Conington (London: Bell, 1902), 2.1.156–57. For the pervasiveness of Greek myth in the early Roman

Empire, see Alan Cameron, *Greek Mythography in the Roman World* (Oxford: Oxford University Press 2004), 217–52; he notes that "Greek mythology was the cultural currency of even the remotest corners of the Roman world" (221).

19. Tacitus, *Annals* 1.9. See further G. W. Bowersock, *Fiction as History: Nero to Julian* (Berkeley: University of California Press, 1994), 29–32.

20. See further Robert A. Kaster, *Guardians of Language: The Grammarian and Society in Late Antiquity* (Berkeley: University of California Press, 1997); Liv Mariah Yarrow, *Historiography at the End of the Republic: Provincial Perspectives on Roman Rule* (Oxford: Oxford University Press 2007), 1–17.

21. Josephus, *Against Apion* 2.121–23. See further René Bloch, *Moses und der Mythos: Die Auseinandersetzung mit der griechischen Mythologie bei jüdisch-hellenistischen Autoren* (Leiden: Brill, 2011), 71–88.

22. See further Joan E. Grusec and Paul D. Hastings, introduction to *Handbook of Socialization: Theory and Research*, ed. Joan E. Grusec and Paul D. Hastings (New York: Guilford, 2006), 1–9. For a classic discussion of the topic, see Peter L. Berger and Thomas Luckmann, *The Social Construction of Reality: A Treatise in the Sociology of Knowledge* (New York: Doubleday, 1966), 119–59.

23. See further John Marincola, "Genre, Convention, and Innovation in Greco-Roman Historiography," in *The Limits of Historiography: Genre and Narrative in Ancient Historical Texts*, ed. Christina Shuttleworth Kraus (Leiden: Brill, 1999), 281–324; and Christopher Pelling, epilogue to Kraus, *Limits of Historiography*, 325–60; Christina Shuttleworth Kraus, "Historiography and Biography," in *A Companion to Latin Literature*, ed. Stephen Harrison (Malden, MA: Blackwell, 2005), 252–56.

24. The work of Richard A. Burridge (*What Are the Gospels? A Comparison with Graeco-Roman Biography* [Cambridge: Cambridge University Press, 1992]) has proved influential in this regard. See also David Aune, *The New Testament in Its Literary Environment* (Philadelphia: Westminster, 1987), 46–76; Dirk Frickenschmidt, *Evangelium als Biographie: Die vier Evangelien im Rahmen antiker Erzählkunst* (Tübingen: Francke, 1997); Aage Pilgaard, "The Classical Biography as Model for the Gospels," in *Beyond Reception: Mutual Influences between Antique Religion, Judaism, and Early Christianity*, ed. David Brakke, Anders-Christian Jacobsen, and Jörg Ulrich (Frankfurt am Main: Peter Lang, 2006), 209–26; Tomas Hägg, *The Art of Biography in Antiquity* (Cambridge: Cambridge University Press, 2012),148–86. For further sources, see David Aune, "Biography," in *The Westminster Dictionary of New Testament and Early Christian Literature and Rhetoric* (Louisville, KY: Westminster John Knox, 2003), 78–81. Some scholars prefer to define the first gospel as a kind of historiography or historical monograph (Adela Yarbro Collins, *Mark: A Commentary* [Minneapolis: Fortress, 2009], 42–44; Eve-Marie Becker, *Das Markus-Evangelium im Rahmen antiker Historiographie* [Tübingen: Mohr Siebeck, 2006]). The differences between classifying the gospels as histories or biographies (which I understand as a subgenre of historiography) do not much matter for my purposes. These genres were fluid, a point noted by Craig Cooper, "'The Appearance of History': Making Some Sense of Plutarch," in *Daimonopylai: Essays in Classics and the Classical Tradition Presented*

to Edmund G. Berry, ed. R. B. Egan and M. A. Joyal (Winnipeg: University of Manitoba, 2004), 33–55.

25. Just as in historiography, the rules of ancient biography (or *bios* literature) are different from those of modern biography (which generally requires, for instance, a discussion of the entire life and the citation of sources).

26. Plutarch, *Alexander* 1.1–3. See further Eve-Marie Becker, *Birth of Christian History: Memory and Time from Mark to Luke-Acts* (New Haven, CT: Yale University Press, 2017), 65–66.

27. Becker, *Birth of Christian History* 46–47.

28. Pliny the Younger, *Letters* 5.8.4.

29. Cicero, *On the Orator* 2.64.

30. Lucian, *How to Write History* 44.

31. Plutarch, *Pythian Oracle* 24 (*Moralia* 406e).

32. Southern Syria or Galilee are also options. See further John R. Donahue, "The Quest for the Community of Mark's Gospel," in *The Four Gospels 1992: Festschrift Frans Neirynck,* ed. F. Van Segbroeck, C. M. Tuckett, G. van Belle, and J. Verheyden, 2 vols. (Leuven: Leuven University Press, 1992), 2:823–28, 832–35. See also Collins, *Mark,* 7–10, 96–102; Joel Marcus, *Mark 1–8: A New Translation with Introduction and Commentary,* Anchor Bible Commentary (New York: Doubleday, 2000), 33–37.

33. Clare K. Rothschild, *Luke-Acts and the Rhetoric of History: An Investigation of Early Christian Historiography* (Tübingen: Mohr Siebeck, 2004), 93–95.

34. My selection of authors is based on their frequency of mention in the comparisons that follow. Thus Tacitus, only mentioned in chapter 10, for instance, is not treated.

35. See further on Diodorus, Kenneth S. Sacks, *Diodorus Siculus and the First Century* (Princeton, NJ: Princeton University Press, 1990); Iris Sulimani, *Diodorus' Mythistory and the Pagan Mission: Historiography and Culture-Heroes in the First Pentad of the Bibliotheke* (Leiden: Brill, 2014).

36. See further C. P. Jones, "Towards a Chronology of Plutarch's Works," *Journal of Roman Studies* 56 (1966): 60–74.

37. This discussion of Plutarch is adapted from Burridge, *What Are the Gospels?,* 156; and Frickenschmidt, *Evangelium,* 167–69. See further Tim Duff, *Plutarch's Lives: Exploring Virtue and Vice* (Oxford: Oxford University Press, 1999); Hägg, *Art of Biography,* 239–81.

38. On Suetonius, see further Barry Baldwin, *Suetonius* (Amsterdam: Hakkert, 1983); Andrew Wallace-Hadrill, *Suetonius* (Bristol, UK: Bristol Classics, 1995); Hägg, *Art of Biography,* 214–31.

39. See further Hägg, *Art of Biography,* 318–51.

40. See further Hägg, *Art of Biography,* 352–67.

41. This is a point oft repeated by J. Z. Smith, for instance, in *Drudgery Divine* (Chicago: University of Chicago Press, 1990), 53.

42. For comparing stories and settings, see the model comparisons of Smith, *Drudgery,* 85–143.

Chapter Three. Incarnation

1. Wolfhart Panneberg, *Basic Questions in Theology*, vol. 3 (London: SCM, 1973), 71–72.

2. John Hick, ed., *The Myth of God Incarnate* (London: SCM, 1977). See also Michael Goulder, ed., *Incarnation and Myth: The Debate Continued* (London: SCM, 1979).

3. Homer, *Iliad* 21.407, 14.285.

4. SH 24 in M. David Litwa, *Hermetica II: The Excerpts of Stobaeus, Papyrus Fragments, and Ancient Testimonies in an English Translation with Notes and Introductions* (Cambridge: Cambridge University Press, 2018), 132–33.

5. Philo, *Life of Moses* 1.27.

6. Justice appears in Hesiod's *Works and Days* weeping by the abodes of wicked people. When she is wronged, she sits beside her father, Zeus, and reports the evil deed (lines 220–24, 256–61) According to the poet Aratus, Justice lived with men of the Golden Age, put up with the Silver race, and finally left earth at the start of the Bronze Age (*Phaenomena* 96–136; cf. Vergil, *Eclogues* 4.6; Ovid, *Met.* 1.149–50; Ps-Eratosthenes, *Catasterisms* 9; Hyginus, *Astron.* 2.25). In her present state, she is often said to sit by Zeus, keeping a record of human wrongdoing (Sophocles, *Oedipus at Colonus* 1381–82). Plutarch writes that the eye of Justice watches over all that happens at sea (*Banquet of the Seven Sages* 18 [*Mor.* 161 e]). For Justice in Jewish mythology, cf. Wisd. 9:4; Philo, *On the Confusion of Tongues* 118; Philo, *Joseph* 48; 4 Macc. 18:22. See further Hugh Lloyd-Jones, *The Justice of Zeus* (Berkeley: University of California Press, 1971), 35–36, 86–87, 99–101; Lynn Allan Kauppi, *Foreign but Familiar Gods: Greco-Romans Read Religion in Acts* (London: T&T Clark, 2006), 110–12.

7. Aristotle, *Rhetoric* 2.24, 1401 a12; cf. *Suda* s.v. κοινὸς Ἑρμῆς: "Hermes possesses the common logos and created everything through it."

8. D. L. Page, *Greek Literary Papyri*, 2 vols. (Cambridge, MA: Harvard University Press, 1942), 1:547–49 (no. 136).

9. SH 23.30 in Litwa, *Hermetica II*, 115.

10. Homer, *Iliad* 24.325–48; compare also Horace, *Odes* 1.2.

11. Horace, *Odes* 1.2.41–52.

12. Cicero advised his brother on how to govern the Greeks, describing the Greek response: "they will look up on you, a living man, like someone from the history books or even suppose that you are a divine person [*divinum hominem*] sent down from heaven" (*Letters to Quintus* 1.1.7).

13. Philo complains that a later emperor, Gaius Caligula, though he dressed up like Mercury, did not bring peace (*Embassy to Gaius* 100–102).

14. For the contexts of their biographies, see Gillian Clark, "Philosophic Lives and the Philosophic Life: Porphyry and Iamblichus," in *Greek Biography and Panegyric in Late Antiquity*, ed. Tomas Hägg and Philip Rousseau (Berkeley: University of California Press, 2000), 29–51.

15. Their contents and sources are discussed by Kurt von Fritz, *Pythagorean Politics in Southern Italy: An Analysis of the Sources* (New York: Columbia University Press, 1940), 3–32. On Aristoxenus, see also Tomas Hägg, *The Art of Biography in Antiquity* (Cambridge: Cambridge University Press, 2012), 69–73.

16. Diogenes, *Lives of Philosophers* 8.46. The disciples are named in Iamblichus, *Pythagorean Way of Life* 248–51.

17. Cicero, *Letters to Atticus* 6.2.3. See further W. W. Fortenbaugh and E. Schütrumpf, eds., *Dicaearchus of Messana: Text, Translations, and Discussion* (New Brunswick, NJ: Transactions, 2001), 1–142.

18. H. B. Gottschalk, *Heraclides of Pontus* (Oxford, UK: Clarendon, 1980), 116.

19. Some of this material is preserved in Apollonius, *Incredible Tales* 4, 6.

20. Aristotle, frag. 171 (Gigon), from Aelian, *Historical Miscellany* 2.26 (Pythagoras as Apollo); and Apollonius, *Incredible Tales* 6 (golden thigh).

21. Diogenes, *Lives of Philosophers* 8.11.

22. Iamblichus, *Pythagorean Way of Life* 133.

23. Iamblichus, *Pythagorean Way of Life* 30.

24. Iamblichus, *Pythagorean Way of Life* 30, cf. 10, 16. Earlier, Iamblichus mentioned the daimonic interpretation of Pythagoras (*Pythagorean Way of Life* 10). The same interpretation appears again when Pythagoras sails to Egypt in §16. In Platonic mythology, souls preexist their sojourn in bodies. The souls of the wise follow in the train of particular deities (Plato, *Phaedrus* 246e–47a). The soul of Pythagoras was in the retinue of Apollo and intimately linked with him (Iamblichus, *Pythagorean Way of Life* 8) before being incarnated on earth.

25. Iamblichus, *Pythagorean Way of Life* 31 (printed as Aristotle, frag. 156 [Gigon]). Aristotle represented this remark as one of the most secret teachings of the Pythagoreans (ἐν τοῖς πάνυ ἀπορρήτοις). Cf. Iamblichus, *Pythagorean Way of Life* 144.

26. Cf. Plato, *Symposium* 202d–e.

27. Iamblichus, *Pythagorean Way of Life* 140. Walter Burkert traced this material back to Aristotle (*Lore and Science in Ancient Pythagoreanism*, trans. Edwin L. Minar [Cambridge, MA: Harvard University Press, 1972], 168).

28. Pindar, *Pythian Odes* 10.29–30.

29. Herodotus, *Histories* 4.13.

30. Pindar, *Pythian Odes* 10.40–43; Alcaeus, frag. 1.1–14, quoted in James S. Romm, *The Edges of the Earth in Ancient Thought: Geography, Exploration, and Fiction* (Princeton, NJ: Princeton University Press, 1992), 63–64.

31. Strabo, *Geography* 1.3.22, cf. 11.6.2 (Hyperboreans live beyond the Black Sea and the Danube River).

32. Hellanicus, as reported by Clement of Alexandria, *Stromata* 1.72.2. See further Timothy P. Bridgman, *Hyperboreans: Myth and History in Celtic-Hellenic Contacts* (London: Routledge, 2011).

33. Porphyry, *Life of Pythagoras* 28.

34. Herodotus, *Histories* 4.36.

35. Heraclides of Pontus, frag. 24A (Schütrumpf).

36. Porphyry, *Life of Pythagoras* 29.

37. Iamblichus, *Pythagorean Way of Life* 90–91.

38. In another account, Abaris concludes that Pythagoras is a god from the power of his teachings (Iamblichus, *Pythagorean Way of Life* 216).

39. By means of this arrow, it was later thought, Pythagoras traveled to and from far-away places on the same day (Porphyry, *Life of Pythagoras* 28). See chapter 13.

40. On the golden thigh, see further Stephan Scharinger, *Die Wunder des Pythagoras: Überlieferungen im Vergleich* (Wiesbaden: Harrassowitz, 2017), 163–66.

41. Iamblichus, *Pythagorean Way of Life* 93, cf. 140–41. It is unknown how far back this story goes. Aristotle may or may not be the source (Isidore Lévy, *Recherches sur les sources de la légende de Pythagore* [New York: Garland, 1987], 14–18). P. Corssen ("Der Abaris des Heraklides Ponticus," *Rheinische Museum* 67 [1912]: 38) argues that Hermippus of Smyrna (third century BCE) is the source. Burkert concluded, "Probably his meeting with Pythagoras had been recounted even before Aristotle's time" (*Lore and Science*, 150). For Abaris, see further J. D. P. Bolton, *Aristeas of Proconnesus* (Oxford, UK: Clarendon, 1962), 157–59.

42. Iamblichus, *Pythagorean Way of Life* 35.

43. Iamblichus, *Pythagorean Way of Life* 140; Apollonius, *Incredible Tales* 6; Aelian, *Historical Miscellany* 2.26, 4.17.

44. Plutarch, *Life of Numa* 8.

45. W. Schmithals, "Der Markusschluss, die Verklärungsgeschichte und die Aussendung der Zwölf," *Zeitschrift für Theologie und Kirche* 69 (1972): 395–97; R. H. Stine, "Is the Transfiguration (Mark 9:2–8) a Misplaced Resurrection Account?," *Journal of Biblical Literature* 95 (1976): 88–89.

46. For the tropes of epiphany, see M. David Litwa, *Iesus Deus: The Early Christian Depiction of Jesus as a Mediterranean God* (Minneapolis: Fortress, 2014), 125–40. Epiphanies were an appropriate topic for historiography. A third-century BCE historian, Syriscus son of Heracleidas, wrote a history called *Epiphanies of the Maiden*, referring to Persephone (*FGrH* 807 T1). For epiphanies in the New Testament, see Margaret Mitchell, "Epiphanic Evolutions in Earliest Christianity," *Illinois Classical Studies* 29 (2004): 183–204.

47. Litwa, *Iesus Deus*, 123–25.

48. See further Jerome H. Neyrey, "The Apologetic Use of the Transfiguration in 2 Peter 1:16–21," *Catholic Biblical Quarterly* 42:4 (1980): 504–19.

49. Jonathan Potter, *Representing Reality: Discourse, Rhetoric and Social Construction* (London: Sage, 1996), 161.

50. F. F. Bruce, "The Trial of Jesus in the Fourth Gospel," in *Gospel Perspectives*, ed. R. T. France and David Wenham, 2 vols. (Sheffield, UK: JSOT, 1980), 1:18. C. S. Lewis adapts this idea in his essay "Myth Became Fact," in *God in the Dock: Essays on Theology and Ethics*, ed. Walter Hooper (Grand Rapids, MI: Eerdmans, 1970), 63–67.

Chapter Four. Genealogy

1. Diodorus, *Library of History* 4.1.1

2. See further M. L. West, *Hesiod: Theogony* (Oxford, UK: Clarendon, 1966); West, *The Hesiodic Catalogue of Women* (Oxford, UK: Clarendon, 1985), 1–30.

3. Famous examples include the genealogy of Glaucus (*Iliad* 6.145–211) and Aeneas (*Iliad* 21.188–90).

4. See the genealogies, e.g., in Gen. 5, 10, 36.

5. Plato, *Theaetetus* 174e–75b.

6. Polybius, *Histories* 9.1.4.

7. Plato, *Greater Hippias* 285d.

8. See further R. Scott Smith and Stephen Trzaskoma, *Apollodorus' "Library" and Hyginus' "Fabulae": Two Handbooks of Greek Mythology* (Indianapolis: Hackett, 2007), xxxii–xxxv, xliii–xliv.

9. See the genealogies of famous heroes in Plutarch, *Theseus* 3; Plutarch, *Pyrrhus* 1; Plutarch, *Lycurgus* 1; Philostratus, *Life of Apollonius* 1.4; Diogenes Laertius, *Lives of Philosophers* 3.1 (Plato).

10. This kind of phenomenon is common in ancient genealogies. Famous distant ancestors were commonly agreed on, but lesser-known intervening ancestors were often disputed, telescoped, or omitted.

11. Charles William Fornara, *The Nature of Historiography in Ancient Greece and Rome* (Berkeley: University of California Press, 1983), 6.

12. Josephus, *Against Apion* 1.16.

13. "History" (ἱστόρια) in the grammatical sense refers to any subject matter in literature including historical, geographical, mythological, or scientific information (Alan Cameron, *Greek Mythography in the Roman World* [Oxford: Oxford University Press 2004], 90). According to D. L. Blank, by "genealogy" Asclepiades meant "the fantastic stories of births and metamorphoses characteristic of mythology" (*Sextus Empiricus "Against the Grammarians" (Adversus Mathematicos I)* [Oxford, UK: Clarendon, 1998], 269). Compare Philo's use of τὸ γενεαλογικόν to describe the stories of the patriarchs in Genesis (*Life of Moses* 2.47).

14. Compare how closely Polybius also associates "genealogies and myths" (γενεαλογίας καὶ μύθους) in his *Histories* 9.2.1.

15. The ability of a genealogy to express male (productive) power is highlighted by the presence of a penis with testicles etched onto a genealogical inscription found at Dodona (in western Greece). In this inscription, a certain Agathon of Zacynthus recorded the link of proxeny between himself and the community of Molossians on Epirus through the mythic ancestress Cassandra, the Trojan prophetess. See further P. M. Fraser, "Agathon and Kassandra (*IG* IX.1² 4.1750)," *Journal of Hellenic Studies* 123 (2003): 26–40.

16. Herodotus, *Histories*, 7.204, 8.131.

17. Livy, *From the Founding* 1.3. Castor of Rhodes (first century BCE) wrote a *Chronicle* in six books with royal lineages from Assyria, Argus, Alba, and Rome. Though Castor may have invented the names and their relations, his chronicle was used as a standard historical source by Varro, Josephus, Plutarch, and later Christian authors.

18. Herodotus, *Histories* 2.143.1. See further Robert L. Fowler, *Early Greek Mythography II: Commentary* (Oxford: Oxford University Press, 2013), 661–66.

19. Herodotus, *Histories* 2.53.1–3.

20. Aristophanes, *Acharnians* 47–54.

21. Namely, kings Ahaziah, Jehoash, Amaziah, and Jehoiakim.

22. Homer, *Iliad* 20.104–9, 206–17.

23. Suetonius, *Deified Julius* 6.1.

24. Cicero, *Brutus* 62.

25. Livy, *From the Foundation* 8.40.4–5. Plutarch, dependent on Clodius, also opined that genealogies "were forged to flatter the pride of some men by inserting their names among the first families and the most illustrious houses" (*Numa* 1.2).

26. Suetonius, *Galba* 2.

27. Suetonius, *Deified Vespasian* 12.

28. Manuscripts of the A and C versions are entitled βίος Ἀλεξάνδρου (*Life of Alexander*). Marius Reiser, "Der Alexanderroman und das Markusevangelium," in *Markus-Philologie: Historische literaturgeschichtliche und stilistische Untersuchungen zum zweiten Evangelium* (Tübingen: Mohr Siebeck, 1984), 158. In this article, Reiser presents mostly stylistic and formal parallels linking the *Alexander Romance* and the gospel of Mark. See also Tomas Hägg, *The Art of Biography in Antiquity* (Cambridge: Cambridge University Press, 2012), 117–33.

29. Grammatiki A. Karla opines that the Nectanebo narrative is "based on Egyptian popular traditions and possibly translates or adapts an earlier Egyptian folktale" ("Fictional Biography vis-à-vis Romance: Affinity and Differentiations," in *Fiction on the Fringe: Novelistic Writing in the Post-Classical Age* [Leiden: Brill, 2009], 25). For further discussion, see Reinhold Merkelbach, *Die Quellen des griechischen Alexander-romans*, 2d ed. (Munich: Beck'sche 1977), 77–83.

30. Plutarch, *Alexander* 2–3. Cf. the case of Theseus, son of Aegeus, reputed son of Poseidon (Plutarch, *Theseus* 2, 6, 36); and Apollonius, in Philostratus, *Life of Apollonius* 1.4, 6.

31. Likewise, Pythagoras was genetically son of Apollo, but in terms of human reckoning, he was son of Mnesarchus of Samos (Apollonius, cited by Porphyry, *Life of Pythagoras* 2). For further examples, see Cyrus Gordon, "Paternity at Two Levels," *Journal of Biblical Literature* 96 (1977): 101; Andrew T. Lincoln, "Luke and Jesus' Conception: A Case of Double Paternity?," *Journal of Biblical Literature* 132:3 (2013): 653–56.

Chapter Five. Divine Conception

1. Paul Veyne, *Did the Greeks Believe in Their Myths? An Essay on the Constitutive Imagination*, trans. Paula Wissing (Chicago: University of Chicago Press, 1988), 66.

2. Origen, *Against Celsus* 1.67. The *Catalogue of Women* attributed to Hesiod is organized by a list of women who had sex with deities.

3. Origen, *Against Celsus* 1.39; compare Justin, *Dialogue with Trypho* 67. See further Joseph Verheyden, "Talking Miracles—Celsus and Origen in Dispute: The Evidence of *Contra Celsum I*," in *Credible, Incredible: The Miraculous in the Ancient Mediterranean*, ed. Tobias Nicklas and Janet E. Spittler (Tübingen: Mohr Siebeck, 2013), 260–67.

4. Even striking phrases such as when Yahweh says to the Israelite king, "today I have begotten you" (Ps. 2:7) and "from the womb before the morning star I begot you" (Ps. 109:3, LXX), have not broken this consensus.

5. Philo, for instance, considered stories of divine marriage (θεογάμια) and divine births (θεογόνια) to be the "inventions of myths" (μύθων πλάσματα) (*Decalogue* 156).

6. Origen, *Against Celsus* 1.39.

7. Dionysius of Halicarnassus, *Thucydides* 6; cf. his *Roman Antiquities* 1.39–40, 41–44.2.

8. Justin, *1 Apology* 21.1, 33.4 (δύναμις θεοῦ ἐπελθοῦσα τῇ παρθένῳ ἐπεσκίασεν αὐτῆν).

9. Plutarch, *Table Talk* 8.1 (*Moralia* 717e–18b). This work was composed between 99 and 116 CE. The historical setting of the *Table Talk*, however, is earlier—going as far back as the 60s CE.

10. It was common for authors to reject the idea that a hero was the product of divine-human sex, even if they wanted to retain the idea that the hero was in some sense a child of the deity. See Cicero, *Republic* 2.2.4 (regarding Romulus); Plutarch, *Theseus* 6; Iamblichus, *Pythagorean Way of Life* 5–8.

11. Plutarch, *Table Talk* 8.1.717e–f.

12. Plato, *Republic* 2.380d–81e.

13. Plutarch, *Table Talk* 8.1.718a.

14. Compare Aristotle, *History of Animals* 541a27, 560b14; Vergil, *Georgics* 3.274–75; Pliny, *Natural History* 2.116, 10.102, 166; Aelian, *Nature of Animals* 17.15. The idea is scoffed at in Lucian, *Toxaris* 38; Lucian, *True History* 1.22.

15. Plutarch, *Numa* 4.1–3. Thus Numa could serve as a moral exemplar.

16. Diogenes Laertius indicates that the myth was supported by Plato's nephew Speusippus (*Lives of Philosophers* 3.2).

17. Plutarch, *Numa* 4.4; Plutarch, *Table Talk* 8.1.718a.

18. Aristotle, *Generation of Animals* 736a–b39.

19. Aristotle, *Generation of Animals* 736a28.

20. According to Aeschylus, the family of the Danaids—and specifically Epaphus, son of Ino—was generated "from the contact and in-breathing [ἐπιπνοίας] of Zeus" (*Suppliant Maidens* 16–18, 41–45). In this play, the whole land rejoices at Epaphus's birth with the cry, "This is indeed the son of life-begetting Zeus!" (581–85). Compare Aeschylus, *Prometheus Bound* 849–51, where Zeus, touching Io by his "unterrifying hand" and "only touching her," causes her to give birth to "Epaphus" (meaning the "touched one").

21. For Plutarch's status and education, see C. P. Jones, *Plutarch and Rome* (Oxford, UK: Clarendon, 1971), 8–10, 39–47. Luke's social status is more difficult to determine. From the text of *Luke-Acts* itself, Joseph Fitzmyer remarks that the author "is obviously a rather well educated person, a writer of no little merit, acquainted with both O[ld] T[estament] literary traditions . . . and Hellenistic literary techniques" (*The Gospel According to Luke: Introduction, Translation and Notes*, 2 vols., Anchor Bible 28 [Garden City, NJ: Doubleday, 1981–85], 1.35). According to François Bovon, "The cultivated language [of Luke] indicates that the author's roots are in one of the higher strata of society, and that the author had a good education encompassing Greek rhetoric as well as Jewish methods of exegesis" (*Luke 1: A Commentary on the Gospel of Luke 1:1–9:50*, trans. Christine M. Thomas, ed. Helmut Koester [Minneapolis: Fortress, 2002], 8).

22. The *Testament of Reuben* makes clear that the "sons of god" (here called "Watchers") "were transformed into human males" and appeared to women who were already married (5:5–6).

23. Plutarch, *Theseus* 1.3.

24. Plutarch, *Isis and Osiris* 12.355d, 20.358e.

25. Plutarch, *Daimonion of Socrates* 21.589f–90a.

26. Plutarch, *Amatorius* 762a.

27. Plutarch, *Isis and Osiris* 58.374e.

Chapter Six. Dream Visions and Prophecies

1. Northrop Frye, *Words with Power: Being a Second Study of "The Bible and Literature,"* ed. Michael Dolzani (Toronto: University of Toronto Press, 2008), 45.

2. See the edition of Daniel E. Harris-McCoy, *Artemidorus' "Oneirocritica": Text, Translation, and Commentary* (Oxford: Oxford University Press, 2012), and the discussion of G. W. Bowersock, *Fiction as History: Nero to Julian* (Berkeley: University of California Press, 1994), 77–98.

3. Cicero, *On Divination* 1.55.

4. Livy, *From the Founding* 2.36; Valerius Maximus, *Memorable Deeds and Sayings* 1.7.4; Augustine, *City of God* 4.26.

5. Plutarch also characterized people by how they responded to dreams. See Eugénie Fournel, "Dream Narratives in Plutarch's *Lives:* The Place of Fiction in Biography," in *The Art of History: Literary Perspectives on Greek and Roman Historiography,* ed. Vasileios Liotsakis and Scott Farrington (Berlin: de Gruyter, 2016), 214. See further Christopher Pelling, "Tragical Dreamer: Some Dreams in the Roman Historians," *Greece & Rome* 44 (1997): 197–213.

6. Plutarch, *Alexander* 2.2–3.

7. Dio Cassius, *Roman History* 45.1.3.

8. Conon, *Narratives* 33, in Malcolm Kenneth Brown, *The Narratives of Konon* (Munich: K. G. Sauer, 2002), 230–31. The story is also attested in Varro (quoted in Brown, *Narratives,* 234).

9. Statius, *Thebaid* 3.478–79, with further sources in Brown, *Narratives,* 234–35.

10. Plutarch, *Table Talk* 8.1.717e.

11. Plutarch, *Alexander* 2.3.

12. Compare *Protoevangelium of James* 19:3–20:3.

13. Josephus, *Jewish Antiquities* 2.215–16. In a variant account, Amram's daughter Miriam sees a dream and tells the vision to her parents. Moses will work signs, deliver the chosen people, and "exercise leadership always" (Pseudo-Philo, *Biblical Antiquities* 9.10, in *Old Testament Pseudepigrapha,* ed. James H. Charlesworth, 2 vols. [New York: Doubleday, 1983], 2.316).

14. Hesiod, *Shield* 27–29.

15. For Alcides, see Pseudo-Apollodorus, *Library* 2.4.12.

16. Iamblichus, *Pythagorean Way of Life* 5.

17. Cicero, *Against Vatinius* 14.

18. Lucan, *Civil War* 1.639–73.

19. Jerome, *Chronicle* 156H.

20. See Livy, *From the Foundation* 2.3–4 (Lucius Junius Brutus authorizes the execution of his own sons).

21. Suetonius, *Deified Augustus* 94.5.

22. Clare K. Rothschild points out that Simeon's prophecies are fulfilled later in the narrative, a historiographical trope that serves the purposes of verification (*Luke-Acts and the Rhetoric of History: An Investigation of Early Christian Historiography* (Tübingen: Mohr Siebeck, 2004), 180).

23. Pindar, *Nemean Odes* 1.59–74.

24. Theocritus, *Idyll* 24.68–69.

25. Plutarch, *Alexander* 3, reporting the tradition of Eratosthenes (276–195 BCE). Eratosthenes was a famous Greek polymath, known for his research into mathematics, astronomy, geography, and history. Around 235 BCE, Eratosthenes became director of the famous library at Alexandria.

26. The common tradition was that Zeus had sex with Olympias in the form of a snake (Plutarch, *Alexander* 3.1). Plutarch had a rationalizing explanation for how snakes got into Olympias's bedsheets (2.5–6).

Chapter Seven. Magi and the Star

1. Adrienne Mayor, *The Poison King: The Life and Legend of Mithridates, Rome's Deadliest Enemy* (Princeton, NJ: Princeton University Press, 2010), 32–33.

2. Num. 23:7, 24:17; Philo, *Life of Moses* 1.276 (Balaam as *magos*).

3. Mary Boyce and Franz Grenet, *A History of Zoroastrianism*, vol. 3 (Leiden: Brill, 1991), 368.

4. Diogenes Laertius, *Lives of Philosophers*, prologue §§6–9. See further Boyce and Grenet, *History of Zoroastrianism*, 3:511–39.

5. Joseph Bidez and Franz Cumont, *Les Mages Hellénisés: Zoroastre, Ostanès et Hystaspe d'après la tradition grecque*, 2 vols. (Paris: Belles Lettres, 1938), 1:52–53, 2:128n4; Mary Boyce, *A History of Zoroastrianism*, vol. 1 (Leiden: Brill, 1975), 282; Boyce and Grenet, *History of Zoroastrianism*, 3:397.

6. Boyce, *History of Zoroastrianism*, 1:293.

7. For the following, see Herodotus, *Histories* 1.107–30; cf. Valerius Maximus, *Memorable Deeds and Sayings* 1.7 ext. 5.

8. Cf. the dream reported by Ctesias in Jan P. Stronk, *Ctesias' Persian History Part I: Introduction, Text and Translation* (Düsseldorf: Wellem, 2010), 293 (from Nicolaus of Damascus).

9. Josephus, *Jewish War* 1.660; Josephus, *Jewish Antiquities* 17.174–78.

10. Plutarch, *Alexander* 3.4. Cicero (*On Divination* 1.47) indicates that this particular story was widely known. Compare the brief reference in Quintus Curtius, *History of Alexander*, summary of the lost book 1 (see the *Summaries* in the Loeb Classical Library edition, vol. 368, page 4); Cicero, *Nature of the Gods* 2.27.69.

11. Quintus Curtius, *History of Alexander* 5.19–22. On Curtius, see further Elizabeth Baynham, *Alexander the Great: The Unique History of Quintus Curtius* (Ann Arbor: University of Michigan Press, 1998).

12. Interestingly, some Greek authors said that the Jews descended from the Magi, possibly because Abraham, the father of the Jews, was originally a Chaldean and associated with astrology (Diogenes Laertius, *Lives of Philosophers* 1.9). Diogenes himself (writing in the early third century CE) preserves the distinction between the Chaldeans and the Magi (*Lives of Philosophers* 1.6).

13. Herodotus, *Histories* 7.37.

14. Cicero, *On Divination* 1.46. Chaldean astrologers were active in the late first century CE, when the gospels were written. They predicted that Vitellius would one day become emperor (Dio Cassius, *Roman History* 64.4). Domitian was wrongly skeptical of a Chaldean prophecy that proved true (Suetonius, *Domitian* 15). Chaldean astrologers were expelled by Tiberius, Claudius, Vitellius, and Vespasian (Tacitus, *Annals* 2.32, 12.52; Tacitus, *Histories* 2.62; Dio, *Roman History* 66.9). These expulsions indicate that the astrologers' influence was known and feared by certain members of the Roman political elite. Astrologers are also said to have predicted the reigns of Augustus (Suetonius, *Deified Augustus* 94), Tiberius (Tacitus, *Annals* 6.21; Suetonius, *Tiberius* 14), Galba (Tacitus, *Annals* 6.20), and Otho (Suetonius, *Otho* 4). The data presented here is taken from Richmond Lattimore, "Portents and Prophecies in Connection with the Emperor Vespasian," *Classical Journal* 29:6 (1934): 444–45.

15. See, for instance, Suetonius, *Nero* 36; Tacitus, *Annals* 14.22.

16. Justin, *Epitome of Pompeius Trogus* 37.2.1–3.

17. Ignatius, *Letter to the Ephesians* 19.2.

18. SH 6.16, in M. David Litwa, *Hermetica II: The Excerpts of Stobaeus, Papyrus Fragments, and Ancient Testimonies in an English Translation with Notes and Introductions* (Cambridge: Cambridge University Press, 2018), 57–58.

19. Origen, *Against Celsus* 1.58–59. Livy described several comet portents. At Setia, a comet (*facem stellae*) was seen stretching from east to west. The next year at Anagnia, scattered fires appeared in the skies and then an enormous torch (*From the Founding* 29.14.3, 30.2.11). Cf. Livy, *From the Founding* 41.21.13 (three suns burn during the day, and at night flaming comets fall from the sky).

20. Josephus, *Jewish War* 6.289.

21. Diodorus of Sicily, *Library of History* 16.66.1, 3.

22. Plutarch, *Timoleon* 8.3–6. Compare the star torch that is said to have dashed from east to west and to have encouraged Roman soldiers under Aulus Plautius to invade and conquer Britain in 43 CE (Dio Cassius, *Roman History* 60.19.4).

23. Varro, reported by Servius, *Commentary on Aeneid* 1.382. Perhaps it is significant that Christians could identify the planet Venus as a symbol of Jesus himself, "the scion and offspring of David, the bright morning star" (ὁ ἀστὴρ ὁ λαμπρὸς ὁ πρωϊνός; Rev. 22:16).

24. Servius, *Commentary on Aeneid* 1.382.

Chapter Eight. Child in Danger, Child of Wonder

1. Horace, *Art of Poetry* 338–39.

2. We know that fictional trips to Egypt were part of the Greek biographical tradition. See Mary R. Lefkowitz, "Visits to Egypt in the Biographical Tradition," in *Die griechische Biographie in hellenistischer Zeit: Akten des internationalen Kongresses vom 26.–29. Juli 2006 in Würzburg*, ed. Michael Erler and Stefan Schorn (Berlin: de Gruyter, 2007), 101–14.

3. Pseudo-Apollodorus, *Library* 2.4.1.

4. Suetonius, *Deified Augustus* 79.2.

5. Suetonius, *Deified Augustus* 94.3.

6. Plutarch, *Life of Romulus* 3–6. Compare the story of Romulus in Ovid, *Fasti* 3.11–76.

7. Josephus, *Jewish Antiquities* 2.205–6.

8. Diodorus, *Library of History* 1.73.4.

9. b. *Sanhedrin* 101b; *Pirqe de-Rabbi Eliezer* 48.

10. Raymond Brown, *The Birth of the Messiah: A Commentary on the Infancy Narratives in the Gospels of Matthew and Luke* (Garden City, NY: Doubleday, 1977), 225.

11. Brown, *Birth of the Messiah*, 227.

12. Brown, *Birth of the Messiah*, 228.

13. Josephus, *Jewish War* 1.660; Josephus, *Jewish Antiquities* 17.174–78.

14. Josephus, *Jewish Antiquities* 12.387.

15. Xenophon, *Cyropaedia* 1.3.1, 1.3.4–1.4.3. Compare Cambyses in Herodotus, *Histories* 3.3.

16. Yet as Cicero observed, Xenophon's portrait of Cyrus was beneficial not because it was written according to historical truth but because it shows the image of a just ruler (*Cyrus ille a Xenophonte non ad historiae fidem scriptus est, sed ad effigiem iusti imperii*) (*Letters to His Brother Quintus* 1.1.23). See further Tomas Hägg, *The Art of Biography in Antiquity* (Cambridge: Cambridge University Press, 2012), 51–66.

17. Plutarch, *Alexander* 5.1; compare Plutarch, *Fortune of Alexander* 342b–c. See further Philostratus, *Life of Apollonius* 1.7; Epicurus, in Diogenes Laertius, *Lives of Philosophers* 10.14; Solon, in Plutarch, *Solon* 2; Themistocles, in Plutarch, *Themistocles* 2.1; and Theseus, in Plutarch, *Theseus* 6.4.

18. Suetonius, *Deified Augustus* 8.1.

19. Quintilian mentions it as a well-known example in the late first century (*Orator's Education* 12.6.1).

20. Nicolaus of Damascus, *Life of Augustus* 3. Nicolaus for most of his life was a close adviser of Herod the Great in Judea. Nicolaus composed his biography of Augustus around 20 BCE. See further Hägg, *Art of Biography*, 197–203.

21. Nicolaus of Damascus, *Life of Augustus* 5–6.

22. Josephus, *Jewish Antiquities* 5.348. Compare *Jubilees* 11.18–24 (of Abraham) and Susannah 45–50 (of Daniel).

23. Philo, *Life of Moses* 1.20–21.

24. Josephus, *Jewish Antiquities* 2.230.

25. Josephus, *Life* 9.

Chapter Nine. The Righteous Lawgiver

1. Quintilian, *Orator's Education* 10.1.31 (*historia . . . est enim proxima poetis et quodam modo carmen solutum est*).

2. See further Aristotle, *Politics* 2.12, 1273b27–74b27.

3. Timaeus, in Cicero, *Laws* 2.6.15.

4. Diodorus, *Library of History* 1.94.1–2; Josephus, *Against Apion* 2.162–63.

5. Nicolaus, frag. 26, in *Paradoxographorum graecorum*, ed. Alexander Giannini (Milan: Italian Editorial Institute, 1967), 157.

6. Herodotus, *Histories* 1.65; compare Plutarch, *Lycurgus* 5.3; Diodorus, *Library of History* 7.12; Pausanias, *Description of Greece* 3.16.6. For the cult of the god Lycurgus in the imperial age, see A. Hupfloher, *Kulte im kaiserzeitlichen Sparta: Eine Rekonstruktion anhand der Priesterämter* (Berlin: Akademie, 2000), 178–82.

7. Herodotus, *Histories* 4.95–96; cf. Strabo, *Geography* 16.2.39–40.

8. Josephus tells the story of Moses in books 3–4 of his *Jewish Antiquities*. See also Philo, *Life of Moses*, in two volumes.

9. Plutarch, *Numa* 8.4–10, 14.1–6, 22.2–4. Plutarch admits, however, that chronologically Numa could not have been influenced by Pythagoras (*Numa* 1.2–4).

10. They are opposed by Dionysius of Halicarnassus, *Roman Antiquities* 2.59; Livy, *From the Founding* 1.18.1; Cicero, *Republic* 2.15; Cicero, *On the Orator* 2.154; Cicero, *Tusculan Disputations* 4.1.

11. Plutarch, *Aemilius Paulus* 2.1.

12. Plutarch, *Numa* 8.20; Pliny, *Natural History* 34.12.26.

13. Horace, *Epistles* 2.1.50–53; Tertullian, *On the Soul* 33.8.

14. Georges Dumézil, *Archaic Roman Religion*, 2 vols. (Chicago: University of Chicago Press, 1970), 2:524.

15. Philo, *Life of Moses* 1.20–29; Plutarch, *Numa* 1, 3, 8.

16. Artapanus, frag. 3, in *Old Testament Pseudepigrapha*, ed. James H. Charlesworth, 2 vols. [New York: Doubleday, 1983], 2.898–99, partially rendered by Hermetic Testimony (TH) 1, in M. David Litwa, *Hermetica II: The Excerpts of Stobaeus, Papyrus Fragments, and Ancient Testimonies in an English Translation with Notes and Introductions* (Cambridge: Cambridge University Press, 2018), 259–60

17. Iamblichus, *Pythagorean Way of Life* 45–59.

18. Philo, *Flight and Finding* 184–85.

19. Plato, *Laws* 745d.

20. The Christian theologian Origen was familiar with this story shortly before 250 CE (*Against Celsus* 8.35).

21. Philo had already spent significant hermeneutical effort in arguing for the φιλανθρωπία (humanity, kindness) of Mosaic law. The second-century Christian Ptolemy later

argued that the eye-for-eye rule is "interwoven with injustice" (Bentley Layton, *The Gnostic Scriptures* [New York: Doubleday, 1987], 311).

Chapter Ten. Miracles

1. Augustine, *City of God* 21.8 (*Portentum ergo fit non contra naturam, sed contra quam est nota natura*). Cf. Isidore of Seville, *Etymologies* 11.3.

2. Aristotle, *Poetics* 1460a13–14.

3. Valerius Maximus, *Memorable Deeds and Sayings* 1.8.1. Strabo was willing to define the wondrous more broadly as the unusual or uncommon (*Geography* 1.3.16); cf. Pliny the Elder, *Natural History* 2.239.

4. Stefan Alkier, "'For Nothing Will Be Impossible with God' [Luke 1:37]: The Reality of 'The Feeding the Five Thousand' [Luke 9:10–17] in the Universe of Discourse of Luke's Gospel," in *Miracles Revisited: New Testament Miracle Stories and Their Concepts of Reality*, ed. Stefan Alkier and Annette Weisenrieder (Berlin: de Gruyter, 2013), 8.

5. *Brill's New Jacoby* 124 F 31 Callisthenes, from Eustathius, *Commentary on the Iliad* 13.29. Homer had written of Poseidon that sea creatures recognized their lord and that the sea parted before him (*Iliad* 13.27–29).

6. Josephus, *Jewish Antiquities* 2.347–48.

7. Arrian, *Anabasis* 1.26.1–2. Arrian, however, presents the event as a wind miracle. The wind was a natural phenomenon, even if it was "not without the divine" (οὐκ ἄνευ τοῦ θείου); Strabo (*Geography* 14.9) does not present the event as a miracle at all, although he notes that Alexander's men had to pass through water that reached to their navels. The miracle is ridiculed by Menander (died around 290 BCE) in frag. 924 (Kock): "Now this is Alexandrine! If I seek someone, he automatically appears. Even if one must cross some sea-swept region, it becomes my highway" (ὡς Ἀλεξανδρῶδες ἤδη τοῦτο· κἂν ζητῶ τινα, αὐτόματος οὗτος παρέσται· κἂν διελθεῖν δηλαδὴ διὰ θαλάττης δέη τόπον τιν,' οὗτος ἔσται μοι βατός).

8. Josephus, *Jewish Antiquities* 2.348. Josephus was exaggerating. See the previous note.

9. Diodorus, *Library of History* 4.8.2–3.

10. Pausanias, *Description of Greece* 8.2.4.

11. See further Sarah Iles Johnston, "The Greek Mythic Story World," *Arethusa* 48:3 (2015): 288–92.

12. Homer, *Odyssey*, trans. A. T. Murray, Loeb Classical Library (Cambridge, MA: Harvard University Press, 1924), 5.44–45, 50–54.

13. Ovid, *Metamorphoses* 10.654–55 (Atalanta); Vergil, *Aeneid* 7.807–11 (Camilla).

14. Apollonius Rhodius, *Argonautica* 1.179–84; compare Hyginus, *Fables* 14. An ancient gloss indicates that Euphemus went across the sea without trouble as on dry land (διαπορεύεσθαι ὡς διὰ γῆς; scholium to Pindar, *Pythian Odes* 4.61). The authority for this scholium is Asclepiades, probably the fourth-century BCE mythographer from Tragilus (Brian D. McPhee, "Walk, Don't Run: Jesus's Water Walking Is Unparalleled in Greco-Roman Mythology," *Journal of Biblical Literature* 135 [2016]: 772n30).

15. ἐπὶ τῶν κυμάτων πορεύεσθαι καθάπερ ἐπὶ τῆς γῆς, from Pseudo-Eratosthenes, *Catasterism* 32 = Hesiod, frag. 244 (Glen Most); cf. Pseudo-Apollodorus, *Library* 1.4.3 (διαβαίνειν τὴν θάλασσαν).

16. Thus I take exception to McPhee's claim that Greek and Roman mythology "contains no unambiguous reference to *walking* on the sea as Jesus does" ("Walk, Don't Run," 765, emphasis original). In fact his assertion that "water walking is not represented by any extant mythological tradition" (775) is simply false given the data he presents (771–73). For further examples of superhuman water travel, see 765–73.

17. Lucian, *Lover of Lies* 13. Pace McPhee ("Walk, Don't Run," 774), there is no evidence that Abaris walking on water is "Lucian's own creation." It is more likely that Lucian parodied a known tradition. It was known, for instance, that Abaris could travel over land and sea on his arrow. Possibly this tradition had been rationalized so that Abaris walked on water.

18. According to the *Epistula Apostolorum* 11.1–8, a daimonic ghost's feet do not touch the ground. Cf. Ps. 76:20 LXX, where the footprints of God "will not be known" in the waters. McPhee emphasizes that Jesus's deed is a "levitation miracle" ("Walk, Don't Run," 769). See further Jason Robert Combs, "A Ghost on the Water? Understanding an Absurdity in Mark 6:49–50," *Journal of Biblical Literature* 127:2 (2008): 345–58.

19. Similar indications of time before an epiphany occur in Luke 1:8, 26; 2:8; 24:1, 36; Matt. 28:1; Mark 16:2; John 20:1, 19, 26; 21:4; Acts 1:10. These references are taken from John Paul Heil, *Jesus Walking on the Sea: Meaning and Gospel Functions of Matt. 14:22–33; Mark 6:45–52 and John 6:15b–21* (Rome: Biblical Institute, 1981), 10.

20. Prince Yam is a major character in the Ugaritic Baal cycle. See the English translation in Mark S. Smith and Simon B. Parker, eds., *Ugaritic Narrative Poetry* (Atlanta: Scholars, 1997), 81–180.

21. Thus there is no need to rationalize the water-walking episode along the lines of Bruce Malina, who argues that the episode is an instance of the disciples' (collective) altered state of consciousness ("Assessing the Historicity of Jesus' Walking on the Sea: Insights from Cross-Culture Social Psychology," in *Authenticating the Activities of Jesus*, ed. Bruce Chilton and Craig Evans [Leiden: Brill, 2002], 351–72).

22. The author of Luke, interestingly, simply omitted the water-walking episode. His reasoning is unknown, but perhaps the story seemed too fantastical to conform to his conception of historiography. We know that Plutarch, among others, sometimes omitted a myth that he could not convincingly historicize.

23. The date of Seneca's play is difficult to determine. John G. Fitch observes that "passages from *Hercules* are echoed in *Apocolocyntosis*, a satire by Seneca on Claudius' official deification." This "suggests that the play may have been written shortly before 54 [CE]" (*Seneca: Hercules, Trojan Women, Phoenician Women, Medea, Phaedra*, Loeb Classical Library [Cambridge, MA: Harvard University Press, 2002], 12).

24. Pseudo-Apollodorus, *Library* 2.5.10; Athenaeus, *Learned Banqueters* 11.469d—470d. See further Timothy Gantz, *Early Greek Myth: A Guide to Literary and Artistic Sources* (Baltimore: Johns Hopkins University Press, 1993), 404–6.

NOTES TO PAGES 141-144

25. Diodorus of Sicily, *Library of History* 4.18.2.

26. Servius, *Commentary on Vergil's Aeneid* 7.662.

27. Seneca, *Hercules* 319–24. Compare Julian, *Oration* 7.219d (Heracles walked over the sea as if it were dry land [βαδίσαι δὲ αὐτὸν ὡς ἐπὶ ξηρᾶς τῆς θαλάττης]). The problem is not that this passage "does not pass on a genuine tradition of Heracles walking on the sea" (pace McPhee, "Walk, Don't Run," 774) but that its evidence is too late (fourth century CE). There is nothing ingenuine about Julian's interpretation, even if it is his own.

28. This is the supposition of McPhee, "Walk, Don't Run," 771. McPhee's supposition that Heracles would have enjoyed far too much "ease" by traveling on water is not supported by the text. Also unsupported is his suggestion that his land journey to the Libyan interior (Apollonius of Rhodes, *Argonautica* 4.1477–80) refers back to the Syrtes episode reported by Seneca ("Walk, Don't Run" 771nn21–22).

29. Lucan, *Civil War* 9.308 (*aequora fracta vadis, abruptaque terra profundo*). Cf. Apollonius Rhodius, *Argonautica* 4.1235–1304.

30. Lucian, *True History* 2.4. As McPhee ("Walk, Don't Run," 774n38) notes, they could also go at walking pace (ἐβάδιζον). Compare Lucian, *How to Write History* 8; Lucian, *Lover of Lies* 13.

31. Walking on water was traditionally represented as an impossible task (Homer, *Odyssey* 1.173, 11.158–59, 14.190).

32. Seneca, *Hercules* 317–24.

33. I am aware that Seneca's *Hercules Furens* is a play, not a work of historiography. Still, the play emphasizes an episode that brings out the humanity of Heracles: his temporary bout of madness and the guilt he feels after killing his own family. It is a profound meditation on the meaning of a hero who is both human and divine, who lives in the "real" human world of pain and grief.

34. Odysseus and Aeneas also slept in the stern of the boat (Homer, *Odyssey* 13.73–80; Vergil, *Aeneid* 4.553). They are different than Jonah, who slept in the ship's hold (Jon. 1:5). Rudely awoken by the frantic captain, Jonah makes the sea calm by being tossed into it. Jesus, the greater Jonah, has only to rebuke the wind and the waves for them to become placid. Sleep in ancient Near Eastern mythology was the prerogative of the highest deities. Yahweh rests after his creation as a symbol of his rule (Gen. 2:2). See further Bernard F. Batto, "The Sleeping God: An Ancient Near Eastern Motif of Divine Sovereignty," *Biblica* 68 (1987): 153–77.

35. *Homeric Hymn to the Dioscuri* 33.6–19. Compare Euripides, *Electra* 1241–42; Theocritus, *Idyll* 22.8–22.

36. Diodorus, *Library of History* 4.43.1–2. Plutarch recounts that the Dioscuri shone like stars on the rudder of the Spartan general Lysander's ship at Aegospotami in 405 BCE (Plutarch, *Lysander* 12.1).

37. Philostratus, *Imagines* 2.15.1.

38. Horace, *Odyssey* 1.12.9–10.

39. Valerius Flaccus, *Argonautica* 8.351.

40. Porphyry, *Life of Pythagoras* 29; Iamblichus, *Pythagorean Way of Life* 135 –36. Cf. Philostratus, *Life of Apollonius* 4.13, 15.

41. The rebuke likens Jesus to Yahweh, who rebuked the Red Sea (Pss. 18:15, 104:7, 106:9; Isa. 50:2; Job 26:11 –12).

42. In Mark 1:16 –20 and Matt. 4:18 –22, the call of the disciples occurs without a fishing miracle.

43. Porphyry, *Life of Pythagoras* 23 –25.

44. Iamblichus, *Pythagorean Way of Life* 36. References in Plutarch and Apuleius show that the miracle was known at least by the early second century CE. See Plutarch, *Table Talk* 729e; Plutarch, *How to Profit by One's Enemies* 9.91 c; Apuleius, *Apology* 31. The miracle story may have already been known to Aristoxenus in the fourth century BCE or to Apollonius in the first century CE.

45. Iamblichus, *Pythagorean Way of Life* 108, cf. 168.

46. Plutarch, *Table Talk* 8.3.729e.

47. Plutarch, *How to Profit by One's Enemies* 9.91 c–d. For examples of Pythagoras's ability to commune and communicate with animals, see Iamblichus, *Pythagorean Way of Life* 60 – 62.

48. Philostratus, *Life of Apollonius* 3.38, 4.20.

49. Josephus, *Jewish Antiquities* 8.46 –48; compare Josephus, *Jewish War* 7.185; and the *Testament of Solomon*, in *Old Testament Pseudepigrapha*, ed. James H. Charlesworth, 2 vols. (New York: Doubleday, 1983), 1:935 –88.

50. Depending on how one interprets Josephus's verb ἱστόρησα (inquire, examine, observe) in his *Jewish Antiquities* 8.46.

51. Philostratus, *Life of Apollonius* 4.20.

52. Tacitus, *Histories*, 4.81; Suetonius, *Deified Vespasian* 7.2 –3; Dio Cassius, *Roman History* 65.8.1 –2.

53. Compare Plutarch, *Life of Pyrrhus* 3.4. Pliny the Elder recommended saliva as a remedy for certain kinds of blindness (*Natural History* 28.7).

54. The famous cult statue of Serapis by Bryaxis shows the god with his right foot extended. For iconographic depictions of Serapis's stand-alone right foot, see Sterling Dow and Frieda S. Upson, "The Foot of Sarapis," *Hesperia* 13:1 (1944): 58 –77.

55. *P. Fouad* 8, quoted in Brian W. Jones, ed., *Suetonius: Vespasian* (Bristol, UK: Bristol Classics, 2000), 56, originally taken from M. McCrum and A. G. Woodhead, *Select Documents of the Principates of the Flavian Emperors: Including the Year of Revolution A.D. 68–96* (Cambridge: Cambridge University Press, 1966), 41.

56. Albert Henrichs, "Vespasian's Visit to Alexandria," *Zeitschrift für Papyrologie und Epigraphik* 3 (1968): 66. Henrichs shows how Vespasian was portrayed as the new Serapis (70 –71).

57. Kenneth Scott, *The Imperial Cult under the Flavians* (Stuttgart-Berlin: Kohlhammer, 1936), 10 –11. Cf. Richmond Lattimore, "Portents and Prophecies in Connection with the Emperor Vespasian," *Classical Journal* 29:6 (1934): 446: "the miracles of Alexandria . . . might even be construed as an effort to work up something resembling a Vespasian myth; and the healing of the afflicted, arguing, as it would, superhuman power in the healer,

might well have been staged for the benefit of the Alexandrian citizens and soldiers and the world at large."

58. Compare Mark 7:33 (Jesus spits and touches a deaf man's tongue).

59. Dio Cassius, *Roman History* 65.8.2.

60. Philostratus's biography of Apollonius would seem to indicate that Apollonius was born about 3 BCE and died in 97 CE. If so, Apollonius would be a contemporary of Jesus. Yet Philostratus elsewhere makes Apollonius a contemporary of Dio Chrysostom (thus born about 40 CE), in *Lives of the Sophists* 1.7. Dio Cassius (*Roman History* 78.18.4) indicates that Apollonius flourished under the emperor Domitian (ruled 81–96 CE).

61. Philostratus, *Life of Apollonius* 4.45. Compare the similar myth in Iamblichus, *Babyloniaka*, summarized by Photius, *Library*, codex 94 (74b42), and translated by Susan A. Stephens and John J. Winkler, in *Ancient Greek Novels, the Fragments: Introduction, Text, Translation, and Commentary* (Princeton, NJ: Princeton University Press, 2014), 192.

62. Pascal Boyer, *Religion Explained: The Evolutionary Origins of Religious Thought* (New York: Basic Books, 2001), 62–75.

Chapter Eleven. The *Pharmakos*

1. πλαστὸς ἀεὶ μῦθος, ἐὰν σχῇ πίστιν, ἐκστῆναι πεποίηκε τοὺς ἀκούοντας. Text in W. Kroll, *Historia Alexandri Magni*, vol. 1 (Berlin: Weidman, 1926).

2. For the mythic historiography of Codrus, see Robert L. Fowler, *Early Greek Mythography I* (Oxford: Oxford University Press, 2000), 200–201 (Hellanicus, frag. 125); Lycurgus, *Against Leocrates* 84–87; Justin, *Epitome of Pompeius Trogus* 2.6.16–21.

3. Here I follow the version of Statius, *Thebaid*, trans. D. R. Shackleton Bailey, Loeb Classical Library (Cambridge, MA: Harvard University Press, 2003), 10,610, 665, 667–68, 676, 684–85, 762–64, 782, 798–820; 11.283–84; 12.76–79. For an earlier version, see Euripides, *Phoenician Women* 905–1018, 1090–92.

4. See further Tomas Hägg, *The Art of Biography in Antiquity* (Cambridge: Cambridge University Press, 2012), 101–16.

5. At least one modern scholar has defended Aesop's historicity (M. J. Luzzatto, "Plutarco, Socrate e l'Esopo di Delfi," *Illinois Classical Studies* 13 [1988]: 429–35).

6. Grammatiki A. Karla defines the *Life of Aesop* as a "novelistic biography" ("Fictional Biography vis-à-vis Romance: Affinity and Differentiations," in *Fiction on the Fringe: Novelistic Writing in the Post-Classical Age* [Leiden: Brill, 2009], 28). On the *Life of Aesop*'s portrayal of slaves, see Keith Hopkins, "Novel Evidence for Roman Slavery," *Past & Present* 138 (1993): 3–27.

7. Herodotus, *Histories* 2.134–35.

8. Leslie Kurke, *Aesopic Conversations: Popular Tradition, Cultural Dialogue, and the Invention of Greek Prose* (Princeton, NJ: Princeton University Press, 2011), 43.

9. Ben Edwin Perry, *Aesopica: A Series of Texts Relating to Aesop or Ascribed to Him or Closely Connected with the Literary Tradition That Bears His Name* (Urbana: University of Illinois, 1952), ix.

10. *Life of Aesop* 125.

11. *Life of Aesop* 140.

12. *Life of Aesop* 133.

13. *Life of Aesop* 127.3–4.

14. Todd M. Compton, *Victim of the Muses: Poet as Scapegoat, Warrior and Hero in Greco-Roman and Indo-European Myth and History* (Washington, DC: Center for Hellenic Studies, 2006), 30, which translates *P.Oxy* 1800 (Perry, *Aesopica*, 221, testimony 25).

15. Leslie Kurke, "Aesop and the Contestation of Delphic Authority," in *The Cultures within Ancient Greek Culture: Contact, Conflict, Collaboration,* ed. Carol Dougherty and Leslie Kurke (Cambridge: Cambridge University Press, 2003), 80. Further texts regarding Aesop and priestly corruption can be found in Anton Wiecher, *Aesop in Delphi* (Meisenheim: Anton Hain, 1961), 16–17.

16. This story resurrects an old mythic plot that appears in Hebrew mythology as well, namely, the story of Benjamin, Genesis 44:1–17.

17. *Life of Aesop* 124–32.

18. *Life of Aesop* 55.

19. *Life of Aesop* 128.11.

20. Plato, *Apology* 39c.

21. Homer, *Iliad,* trans. Stephen Mitchell (New York: Free Press, 2011), 16.851–54.

22. Homer, *Iliad* 22.358–60. These scenes are imitated in Vergil, *Aeneid* 10.739–43.

23. *Life of Aesop* 133.

24. There was a famous story of a certain Mary, for instance, who was both noble and rich. While trapped in Jerusalem, she was ruthlessly robbed of her food supplies. To stay alive, she slew her infant son, roasted him, and gobbled down half the meat in one sitting. She showed the other half to the battle-hardened guards, who took to their heels in horror (Josephus, *Jewish War* 6.200–212).

25. Compton, *Victim,* 14–18.

26. Perry, *Aesopica,* 226, testimony 45.

27. Perry, *Aesopica,* 226, testimony 47.

28. Translation taken from Compton, *Victim,* 36, from Zenobius 1.47 (testimony 27 in Perry, *Aesopica,* 222).

29. For other resurrection stories in the era of the gospels, see G. W. Bowersock, *Fiction as History: Nero to Julian* (Berkeley: University of California Press, 1994), 99–120; Proclus, as translated by William Hansen, *Phlegon of Tralles' Book of Marvels* (Exeter: University of Exeter Press, 1996), 199–200.

Chapter Twelve. Empty Tombs and Translation

1. C. S. Lewis, "Myth Became Fact," in *God in the Dock: Essays on Theology and Ethics,* ed. Walter Hooper (Grand Rapids, MI: Eerdmans, 1970), 65, 66–67.

2. For mysterious figures dressed in white, see Livy, *From the Founding* 21.62.5, 10; 24.10.10–11 (an altar seen in the sky surrounded by men in white garments). White clothing typically suggested purity, good fortune, and joy. Since white clothing is also charac-

teristic of angels, Adela Yarbro Collins understands the young man to be an angel. Angels were customarily spoken of as "men" or "young men" in Second Temple Jewish texts (*Mark: A Commentary* [Minneapolis: Fortress, 2009], 795–96).

3. See esp. Daniel A. Smith, *Revisiting the Empty Tomb: The Early History of Easter* (Minneapolis: Fortress, 2010).

4. Homer, *Odyssey*, trans. Stephen Mitchell (New York: Atria, 2013), 4.512–18.

5. Richard C. Miller, *Resurrection and Reception in Early Christianity* (London: Routledge, 2015). I prefer not to use Miller's term "fable" since it gives the impression that *mythoi* of translation were not widely believed or taken to be historical. "Fables—the very word acknowledges their falsity" (Macrobius, *Commentary on the Dream of Scipio* 1.2.7).

6. Philostratus, *Life of Apollonius* 8.30.3.

7. Pindar, *Isthmian Odes* 8.56–59.

8. Quintus Smyrnaeus, *Fall of Troy*, trans. Arthur S. Way, Loeb Classical Library (Cambridge, MA: Harvard University Press, 1962), 3.770–80.

9. This report derives from Proclus's summary of the epic *Aithiopis* translated by Martin L. West, *Greek Epic Fragments from the Seventh to the Fifth Centuries BC*, Loeb Classical Library (Cambridge, MA: Harvard University Press, 2003), 113.

10. Compare Pindar, *Olympian Odes* 2.79–80 (which places Achilles on the Isle of the Blessed) with his *Nemean Odes* 4.49–50 (a reference to Achilles on White Island). The two islands are identified by Pliny, *Natural History* 4.93.

11. Arrian, *Voyage Round the Euxine* 21.1; Euripides, *Iphigeneia among the Taurians* 435–38; cf. Strabo, *Geography* 7.3.16; Conon, *Narratives* 18.7–8, in Malcolm Kenneth Brown, *The Narratives of Konon* (Munich: K. G. Sauer, 2002).

12. Maximus of Tyre, *Orations* 9.7.

13. Arrian, *Voyage Round the Euxine* 23.

14. Philostratus, *Heroicus* 56.

15. Pausanias, *Description of Greece* 3.19.11–13. The temple tradition is confirmed by Arrian, *Voyage Round the Euxine* 21.

16. Cicero, *Nature of the Gods* 3.45; Pausanias, *Description of Greece* 3.20.8; Lycophron, *Alexandra* 856.

17. E. Belin de Ballu, *Olbia, cité antique du littoral nord de la Mer Noire* (Leiden: Brill, 1972), 77–82.

18. Hildebrecht Hommel, *Der Gott Achilleus* (Heidelberg: Carl Winter, 1980), 8–9, 16.

19. One author, Cassius Hemina, proposed a rationalizing solution for the preservation (Pliny, *Natural History* 13.27.84–85).

20. Plutarch emphasizes that no piece or remnant of the body could be found (μέρος οὐδὲν οὐδὲ λείψανον . . . τοῦ σώματος; *Numa* 22.4–5); Livy apparently believed that the process of decay could dissolve the bones (*per tabem tot annorum omnibus absumptis*). But his explanation conflicts with the pristine preservation of Numa's books (*From the Founding* 40.29.3–14). Compare also Pliny, *Natural History* 13.84–87; Varro, in Augustine, *City of God* 7.34.

21. For additional testimonies about Numa's empty coffin, see G. Garbarino, *Roma e la filosofia greca dalle origini alla fine del II secolo a. C.*, 2 vols. (Turin: Paravia, 1973), 1:64–69. See further Andreas Willi, "Numa's Dangerous Books: The Exegetic History of a Roman Forgery," *Museum Helveticum* 55 (1998): 139–72.

22. Livy, *From the Foundation* 1.16; compare Dionysius Halicarnassus, *Roman Antiquities* 2.56.2. For a more fantastical account, see Ovid, *Metamorphoses* 14.805–51; Ovid, *Fasti* 2.481–509.

23. Appian, *Civil War* 2.114; Dionysius Halicarnassus, *Roman Antiquities* 2.56.3.

24. Admittedly, alternative reports are not a persistent feature in the gospels, in part because they adhere to the tropes of Hebrew historiography, which pursues a single narrative thread (David Aune, *New Testament in Its Literary Environment* [Philadelphia: Westminster, 1987], 110).

25. Livy, *From the Founding* 1.16.4. See further David Levene, *Religion in Livy* (Leiden: Brill, 1993), 132–34. Violent death at the hands of senators does not, of course, disqualify one for deification, as seen in the case of Julius Caesar.

26. Plutarch, *Romulus* 28.6.

27. Plutarch, *Daimon of Socrates* 5.577e–f. Compare Diodorus, *Library of History* 4.58.6; Pausanias, *Description of Greece* 9.16.7; Antoninus Liberalis, *Metamorphoses* 33 (reporting Pherecydes). For another empty tomb mythos, see the story of Aspalis in Antoninus Liberalis, *Metamorphoses* 13.

Chapter Thirteen. Disappearance and Recognition

1. Plutarch, *Banquet of the Seven Sages* 146b.

2. Ovid, *Metamorphoses* 8.611–78.

3. Silius Italicus, *Punica* 7.162–211.

4. Homer, *Odyssey* 10.573–74.

5. Homer, *Odyssey* 16.161.

6. Homer, *Iliad* 3.396–97.

7. Homer, *Iliad* 1.199–200.

8. Homer, *Odyssey* 10.274–83.

9. Homeric *Hymn to Hermes* 145–46 (prior to the seventh century BCE).

10. Euripides, *Bacchae* 643–54, in *Euripides*, vol. 4, ed. and trans. David Kovacs (Cambridge, MA: Harvard University Press, 2002) (translation modified). For the resurrected Jesus walking through locked doors, see John 20:19.

11. Compare the story of the Thessalian who asserted that the deified Julius Caesar had met him on a lonely road and told him to inform Augustus that the latter would be victorious at Philippi (Suetonius, *Deified Augustus* 96.1).

12. On the disappearance theme, see Arthur Stanley Pease, "Aspects of Invisibility," *Harvard Studies in Classical Philology* 53 (1942): 1–36.

13. This epic poem was in circulation in the early sixth century BCE (Walter Burkert, *Lore and Science in Ancient Pythagoreanism*, trans. Edwin L. Minar [Cambridge, MA: Harvard University Press, 1972], 147–48).

14. Herodotus, *Histories* 4.13–16. Cf. Plutarch, *Romulus* 28.4; Origen, *Against Celsus* 3.26; Theopompus, in Athenaeus, *Learned Banqueters* 13, 605c. According to Apollonius, *History of Miracles* 2, the very day Aristeas died he appeared teaching literature in Sicily.

15. Compare the vanishing act of the daimon identified with the (apparently resurrected) Alexander the Great in Dio Cassius, *Roman History* 80.18.

16. Iamblichus, *Pythagorean Way of Life* 138.

17. Aelian, *Historical Miscellany* 2.26, 4.17; Apollonius, *History of Miracles* 6.

18. Iamblichus, *Pythagorean Way of Life* 134.

19. Apollonius, *History of Miracles* 6.

20. Philostratus, *Life of Apollonius* 4.10, 8.10.

21. Philostratus, *Life of Apollonius* 8.12.1.

22. Phlegon of Tralles, *Mirabilia* 1, in *Paradoxographorum graecorum*, ed. Alexander Giannini (Milan: Italian Editorial Institute, 1967), 170–78. A translation is printed with comments by Daniel Ogden, *Magic, Witchcraft, and Ghosts in the Greek and Roman Worlds: A Sourcebook* (Oxford: Oxford University Press, 2002), 159–61. See also the commentary of William Hansen, *Phlegon of Tralles' Book of Marvels* (Exeter: University of Exeter Press, 1996), 65–85, with his two earlier essays cited on xii. The story of Philinnion is presented in the form of a letter written by a public official who stands ready to have the facts of his account checked and reported to a "king." From the later résumé of Proclus, we learn that the king is probably Philip II, father of Alexander the Great. See further J. R. Morgan, "Love from Beyond the Grave: The Epistolary Ghost-Story in Phlegon of Tralles," in *Epistolary Narratives in Ancient Greek Literature*, ed. Owen Hodkinson, Patricia A. Rosenmeyer, and Evelien Bracke (Leiden: Brill, 2013), 293–321.

23. Herodotus, *Histories* 6.69.

24. On Jesus penetrated, see Dale B. Martin, *Biblical Truths: The Meaning of Scripture in the Twenty-First Century* (New Haven, CT: Yale University Press, 2017), 284.

25. Aeschylus, *Eumenides* 103. Compare Ovid, *Metamorphoses* 10.48–49 (the snake-bite wound of the dead Eurydice); Vergil, *Aeneid* 2.272–73, 277–79 (the wounds of Hector). These examples are taken from Gregory J. Riley, *Resurrection Reconsidered: Thomas and John in Controversy* (Minneapolis: Fortress, 1995), 50–51. See further Jan Bremmer, "The Soul, Death and the Afterlife in Early and Classical Greece," in *Hidden Futures: Death and Immortality in Ancient Egypt, Anatolia, the Classical, Biblical and Arabic-Islamic World*, ed. Jan Bremmer (Amsterdam: Amsterdam University Press, 1994), 100.

26. Philostratus, *Heroes* 2.9 (resurrection), 12.4 (scar), 11.2 (kiss). On the believability of the *Heroicus*, see Tim Whitmarsh, *Beyond the Second Sophistic: Adventures in Postclassicism* (Berkeley: University of California Press, 2013), 101–22.

Chapter Fourteen. Ascent

1. Aristotle, *Poetics* 1460a27–28.

2. Justin, *Apology* 1.21.

3. M. David Litwa, *Iesus Deus: The Early Christian Depiction of Jesus as a Mediterranean God* (Minneapolis: Fortress, 2014), 173–74.

4. Yet even the author of Luke left in his text hints of the earlier viewpoint. Immediate ascent to heaven is assumed in Jesus's words to the thief on the cross: "Today you will be with me in paradise" (Luke 23:43).

5. Pseudo-Apollodorus, *Library* 2.7.7.

6. 2 Enoch 3.1 (J text); compare 1 Enoch 14:8.

7. Josephus, *Jewish Antiquities* 4.326; cf. Dosiadas, in A. S. F. Gow, *Bucolici Graeci* (Oxford, UK: Clarendon, 1985), 182–83.

8. Tertullian, *Apology* 21.23.

9. Livy, *From the Founding* 1.16.

10. Cicero, *Republic* 2.10, cf. 6.21.

11. Cicero, *Republic* 2.10.18.

12. Varro, in Censorinus, *Birthday Book* 21.1; Augustine, *City of God* 18.8. The ancients recognized no absolute break between a mythical and historical age. The ages melted into each other, with no changes in the laws of nature.

13. Varro, in Plutarch, *Romulus* 12.3–6.

14. Cicero, *Republic* 2.10.18–20.

15. Plutarch, *Romulus* 28.7–8.

16. Josephus, *Jewish Antiquities* 4.326.

17. Philo, *On Virtues* 76.

18. Philo, *Life of Moses* 2.288.

19. See further M. David Litwa, "The Deification of Moses in Philo of Alexandria," *Studia Philonica Annual* 26 (2014): 1–27.

20. Livy, *From the Founding* 1.16.8; Plutarch, *Romulus* 28.4–5.

21. βλεπόντων, ἀτενίζοντες, [ἐμ]βλέποντες, ἐθεάσασθε.

22. Pindar, *Pythian Odes* 10.49–50.

23. Arrian, *Anabasis* 5.1.2.

24. Philo, *Questions and Answers on Genesis,* trans. Ralph Marcus, Loeb Classical Library (Cambridge, MA: Harvard University Press, 1953), 1.32.

25. Plutarch, *Coriolanus* 38.3. Other authors, such as Valerius Maximus, *Memorable Deeds and Sayings* 1.8.4, did not find it difficult to believe that the statue had talked. Cf. Dionysius, *Roman Antiquities* 8.56.2–4.

26. The idea that all things are possible for God is an idea that regularly crops up in Philo (e.g., *Virtues* 26; *Special Laws* 1.282, 4.127).

27. Iamblichus, *Pythagorean Way of Life,* trans. John Dillon and Jackson P. Hershbell (Atlanta: Scholars, 1991), 139 (translation modified). Cf. 148: "It was from his piety that Pythagoras's belief in the gods also arose; for he always commanded that one should dis-

believe nothing marvelous [θαυμαστόν] about the gods, or about divine teachings, since the gods are able to do all things."

Chapter Fifteen. Eyewitnesses

1. Cicero, *Laws* 1.5.

2. In the words of Jonathan Potter, "Detail may be organized into an internally focalized narrative, to present events from the point of view of a participant and thereby to build a special category of entitlement of the speaker as a witness" (*Representing Reality: Discourse, Rhetoric and Social Construction* [London: Sage, 1996], 175).

3. Homer, *Odyssey* 8.487–91.

4. Cited by Polybius, *Histories* 12.27.

5. Quoted by Lucian, *How to Write History* 29. See further Dionysus of Halicarnassus, *Roman Antiquities* 1.68–69.

6. Polybius, *Histories* 12.24.5–6.

7. Polybius, *Histories* 12.27.

8. Lucian, *How to Write History*, in *Lucian: Selected Dialogues*, trans. Desmond Costa (Oxford: Oxford University Press, 2009), 47 (translation modified).

9. Thucydides, *History of the Peloponnesian War* 5.26.5

10. Josephus, *Against Apion* 1.55–56. On the value of personal autopsy, see further John Marincola, *Authority and Tradition in Ancient Historiography* (Cambridge: Cambridge University Press, 1999), 82.

11. On the eyewitness literary device in gospel literature, see Loveday Alexander, *The Preface to Luke's Gospel: Literary Convention and Social Context in Luke 1.1–4 and Acts 1.1* (Cambridge: Cambridge University Press, 1993), 32–41, 120–23; Clare K. Rothschild, *Luke-Acts and the Rhetoric of History: An Investigation of Early Christian Historiography* (Tübingen: Mohr Siebeck, 2004), 220–90; Samuel Byrskog, *Story as History—History as Story: The Gospel Tradition in the Context of Ancient Oral History* (Tübingen: Mohr Siebeck, 2000), 48–91.

12. Origen interpreted the flow of blood and water in John 19:34–35 to be a miracle (*Against Celsus* 2.36).

13. Lucian, *How to Write History* 29.

14. Lucian, *True History* 1.3. Compare Photius, *Library* codex 72 (49b39–50a4): "Ctesias, writing as a fabulist, says that he writes the plainest truth, adding that he writes what he himself saw [αὐτὸς ἰδὼν γράφει] and learned from those who saw." See further Niklas Holzberg, "Novel-Like Works of Extended Prose Fiction II," in *The Novel in the Ancient World*, ed. G. L. Schmeling (Leiden: Brill, 1996), 629–33.

15. [Dictys], *Diary* 1.13.

16. Thucydides, *History of the Peloponnesian War* 1.22.

17. Thucydides, *History of the Peloponnesian War* 1.22.3.

18. [Dictys], *Diary* 5.17.

19. [Dictys], *Diary* 2.32; 3.14 ("our commander"), 2.37 ("our men"), 2.38 ("our commanders").

20. Both Malalas and Cedrenus are cited in Howard Jeffrey Marblestone, "Dictys Cretensis: A Study of the Ephemeris Belli Troiani as a Cretan Pseudepigraphon" (Ph.D. diss., Brandeis University, 1969), 387.

21. Dio Chrysostom, *Oration* 11.92; Philostratus, *Heroicus* 43.7.

22. But note that in Suetonius's biography of the *Deified Julius* 81.8, he also included weeping horses.

23. Peter Gainsford, "Diktys of Crete," *Cambridge Classical Journal* 58 (2012): 58–87.

24. Marblestone, "Dictys," 377. For Cephalus, see Athenaeus, *Learned Banqueters* 9, 393d. Dio Chrysostom also provided a revisionist account of the Trojan War in his eleventh oration (from "Egyptian" sources). Compare Philostratus, *Heroicus* (entire).

25. Philostratus, *Life of Apollonius* 1.3.1–2.

26. Philostratus, *Life of Apollonius* 1.3.1.

27. Philostratus, *Life of Apollonius* 1.19.2, cf. 3.43.

28. Philostratus, *Life of Apollonius* 1.19.3.

29. Philostratus, *Life of Apollonius* 1.3.1.

30. Hierocles, in Eusebius, *Against Hierocles* 2.24–32.

31. Eduard Meyer attacked the historicity of Damis in a lengthy article ("Apollonios von Tyana und die Biographie des Philostratos," *Hermes* 52 [1917]: 371–424). His views were advanced by Maria Dzielska, *Apollonius of Tyana in Legend and History* (Rome: L'erma, 1986), 19; Ewen Bowie, "Philostratus: Writer of Fiction," in *Greek Fiction: The Greek Novel in Context*, ed. J. R. Morgan and Richard Stoneman (London: Routledge, 1994), 181–99. Graham Anderson's qualified defense of Damis's historicity (*Philostratus: Biography and Belles-Lettres in the Third Century A.D.* [London: Routledge, 1986], 165) was refuted by Mark Edwards, "Damis the Epicurean," *Classical Quarterly* 41 (1991): 563–66.

32. C. P. Jones, "Apollonius of Tyana's Passage to India," *Greek Roman and Byzantine Studies* 42 (2001): 185–99.

33. See the essays edited by Ellen Bradshaw Aitken and Jennifer K. Berenson Maclean, in *Philostratus's "Heroikos": Religion and Cultural Identity in the Third Century C.E.* (Atlanta: SBL, 2004), esp. Jeffrey Rusten, "Living the Past: Allusive Narratives and Elusive Authorities in the World of the *Heroikos*," 143–47. Note also Christopher P. Jones, "Philostratus' *Heroikos* and Its Setting in Reality," *Journal of Hellenic Studies* 121 (2001): 141–49; Tim Whitmarsh, *Beyond the Second Sophistic: Adventures in Postclassicism* (Berkeley: University of California Press, 2013), 101–22.

34. W. Speyer, "Zur Bild des Apollonius von Tyana bei Heiden und Christen," *Jahrbuch für Antikes Christentum* 17 (1974): 50; Jaap-Jan Flintermann, *Power, Paideia, and Pythagoreanism: Greek Identity, Conceptions of the Relationship between Philosophers and Monarchs, and Political Ideas in Philostratus' "Life of Apollonius"* (Amsterdam: J. C. Gieben, 1995), 81.

35. Philostratus, *Life of Apollonius* 3.27.1. See further Graham Anderson, "Philostratus on Apollonius of Tyana: The Unpredictable on the Unfathomable," in *The Novel in the Ancient World*, ed. G. L. Schmeling (Leiden: Brill, 1996), 615–16.

36. Tim Whitmarsh, "Philostratus," in *Narrators, Narratees, and Narratives in Ancient Greek Literature: Studies in Ancient Greek Narrative*, vol. 1, ed. Irene de Jong, René Nünlist and Angus

Bowie (Leiden: Brill, 2004), 428. See further Wannes Gyselinck and Kristoffel Demoen, "Fiction and Metafiction in Philostratus' *Vita Apollonii*," in *Theios Sophistes: Essays on Flavius Philostratus' "Vita Apollonii,"* ed. Kristoffel Demoen and Danny Praet, Mnemosyne Supplements 305 (Leiden: Brill, 2009), 101–5.

37. Dwight Moody Smith, *John among the Gospels: The Relationship in Twentieth-Century Research* (Minneapolis: Fortress, 1992); Michael Labahn and Manfred Lang, "Johannes und die Synoptiker: Positionen und Impulse seit 1990," in *Kontexte des Johannesevangeliums: Das vierte Evangelium in religions-und traditionsgeschichtlicher Perspektive*, ed. Jörg Frey and Udo Schnelle, WUNT 175 (Tübingen: Mohr Siebeck, 2004), 443–515; Wendy E. S. North, "Points and Stars: John and the Synoptics," in *John, Jesus, and History*, vol. 3, *Glimpses of Jesus through the Johannine Lens*, ed. Paul N. Anderson, Felix Just, and Tom Thatcher (Atlanta: SBL, 2016), 119–32.

38. If the Beloved Disciple is identified with the anonymous disciple in John 1:35–40, then his discipleship status "from the beginning" (ἀπ' ἀρχῆς; John 15:27) is confirmed.

39. Paul N. Anderson, *The Fourth Gospel and the Quest for Jesus: Modern Foundations Reconsidered* (London: T&T Clark, 2006), 4–5. This is not an indication of historicity. As Nicholas Horsfall notes, "the more varied, complex and specific the details of the text and its survival, the more they proclaim their falsity" ("Dictys's Ephemeris and the Parody of Scholarship," *Illinois Classical Studies* 33–34 [2008–9]: 45). Richard Bauckham (*The Testimony of the Beloved Disciple: Narrative, History, and Theology in the Gospel of John* [Grand Rapids, MI: Baker, 2007], 93–112) and James H. Charlesworth ("The Historical Jesus in the Fourth Gospel: A Paradigm Shift?," *Journal for the Study of the Historical Jesus* 8 [2010]: 3–46) seem unaware of this point.

40. Homer's vivid description of towns and battles, for instance, lent his speech an air of veracity. Cf. Polybius, *Histories* 34 4 3 (τῆς δὲ διαθέσεως ἐνάργειαν εἶναι τὸ τέλος).

41. Potter, *Representing Reality*, 165.

42. Cf. Josephus, *Jewish War* 6.297–98: "there appeared a daimonic apparition, passing belief [μεῖζον πίστεως]. What I will relate, I think, would be deemed a fairy tale were it not reported by eyewitnesses [παρὰ τοῖς θεασαμένοις]. . . . Before sunset, throughout the whole country, chariots appeared in the air as well as armed battalions hurtling through the clouds and surrounding the cities."

43. Philostratus, *Life of Apollonius* 8.13.2.

44. See further Matthew D. C. Larsen, "Accidental Publication, Unfinished Texts and the Traditional Goals of New Testament Textual Criticism," *Journal for the Study of the New Testament* 39:4 (2017): 362–87.

45. See, e.g., Andrew T. Lincoln, "The Beloved Disciple as Eyewitness and the Fourth Gospel as Witness," *Journal for the Study of the New Testament* 85 (2002): 23; David R. Beck, *The Discipleship Paradigm: Readers and Anonymous Characters in the Fourth Gospel* (Leiden: Brill, 1997), 131–36. Further sources in Richard Bauckham, *Jesus and the Eyewitnesses: The Gospels as Eyewitness Testimony* (Grand Rapids, MI: Eerdmans, 2006), 394n16.

46. In short, cognitive immersion in the text disarms the reader's normal epistemological demand for human witnesses. See further Harold W. Attridge, "The Restless Quest for the

Beloved Disciple," in *Early Christian Voices: In Texts, Traditions, and Symbols. Essays in Honor of François Bovon*, ed. David H. Warren, Ann Graham Brock, and David W. Pao (Leiden: Brill, 2003), 71–80. On the cognitive changes that occur when the reader is transported into a narrative world, see M. David Litwa, *Desiring Divinity: Self-Deification in Early Jewish and Christian Mythmaking* (Oxford: Oxford University Press), 87–90.

47. For further reflections on anonymity, see Adele Reinhartz, *Why Ask My Name? Anonymity and Identity in Biblical Narrative* (New York: Oxford University Press, 1998), esp. 188.

48. For instance, Bauckham, *Jesus and the Eyewitnesses*, 409. For other arguments that the Beloved Disciple is a fictional device, see Joachim Kügler, *Der Jünger, den Jesus liebte: Literarische, theologische und historischen Untersuchungen zu einer Schlüsselgestalt johanneischer Theologie und Geschichte. Mit einem Exkurs über die Brotrede in Joh 6* (Stuttgart: Katholisches Bibelwerk, 1988), 478–88; Lincoln, "Beloved Disciple," 3–26, esp. 18–19. See further James H. Charlesworth, *The Beloved Disciple: Whose Witness Validates the Gospel of John?* (Valley Forge, PA: Trinity, 1995), 134–38.

49. Nancy F. Partner distinguishes between two kinds of fiction: (1) "the creation of form in language" and (2) "the invention or imaginary description of events and persons." I speak of fiction in the first sense. Regarding this sense, Partner observes, "The primary or formal fictions which create intelligible events and narrative structure are necessary to all depictions of event; without these artifacts historiography is not conceivable" ("Historicity in an Age of Reality-Fictions," in *A New Philosophy of History*, ed. Frank Ankersmit and Hans Kellner [Chicago: University of Chicago Press, 1995], 33).

50. Whether it is historical, in whole or in part, must be decided on other grounds.

51. Raymond Brown, *The Community of the Beloved Disciple* (New York: Paulist, 1979), 31.

52. Ismo Dunderberg, *The Beloved Disciple in Conflict* (Oxford: Oxford University Press, 2006), 124.

53. Bart D. Ehrman, *Forgery and Counterforgery: The Use of Literary Deceit in Early Christian Polemics* (Oxford: Oxford University Press, 2012), esp. 529–48. Though Armin D. Baum criticizes Ehrman, he agrees with Ehrman on this point ("Content and Form: Authorship Attribution and Pseudonymity in Ancient Speeches, Letters, Lectures, and Translations— a Rejoinder to Bart Ehrman," *Journal of Biblical Literature* 136:2 [2017]: 381–82). Bauckham claims that readers "would not have deliberately colluded in such rhetorical fabrication" (*Testimony*, 20), but he gives no reason why. As the apocryphal Acts show, Christians regularly used fiction in the cause of truth. Although Bauckham often appeals to historiographical conventions, he seems unaware of the scholarship on mendacity in all forms of ancient historiography. See for instance A. J. Woodman, *Rhetoric in Classical Historiography: Four Studies* (London: Croom Helm, 1988); T. P. Wiseman, *Clio's Cosmetics: Three Studies in Greco-Roman Literature* (Totowa, NJ: Rowman and Littlefield, 1979); Michael Grant, *Greek and Roman Historians: Information and Misinformation* (London: Routledge, 1995), 61–99; and esp. the essays in Christopher Gill and T. P. Wiseman, ed., *Lies and Fiction in the Ancient World* (Exeter: University of Exeter Press, 1993).

54. Diodorus asked, "For if the mythology [μυθολογία] about Hades, though in substance fictitious, greatly profits humans in piety and justice, how much more must we con-

sider history, the prophetess of truth, as it were the mother-city of all philosophy, better able to fashion characters for nobility?" (*Library of History* 1.2.2). Mythology for pedagogical purposes is discussed by Strabo, *Geography* 1.2.8–9. See further James A. Francis, "Truthful Fiction: New Questions to Old Answers on Philostratus' 'Life of Apollonius,'" *American Journal of Philology* 119 (1998): 419–41; Jean-Marie Schaeffer, "Fictional vs. Factual Narration," in *Handbook of Narratology*, ed. Peter Hühn, John Pier, Wolf Schmid, and Jörg Schönert (Berlin: de Gruyter, 2009), 98–114.

55. See further Kelli S. O'Brien, "Written That You May Believe: John 20 and Narrative Rhetoric," *Catholic Biblical Quarterly* 67 (2005): 284–302.

Conclusion. The Myth of Historicity

1. Thomas M. Bolin, "History, Historiography, and the Use of the Past in the Hebrew Bible," in *The Limits of Historiography: Genre and Narrative in Ancient Historical Texts*, ed. Christina Shuttleworth Kraus (Leiden: Brill, 1999), 116, 123.

2. Roland Barthes, "Historical Discourse," in *Introduction to Structuralism*, ed. Michael Lane (New York: Basic Books, 1970), 153.

3. Clare K. Rothschild discusses four other rhetorical conventions used in Lukan historiography: patterns of recurrence, the use of prophecies as authentications, divine-necessity discourse, and the use of hyperbole (by multiplying witnesses and using summaries to give the impression of greater knowledge) (*Luke-Acts and the Rhetoric of History: An Investigation of Early Christian Historiography* [Tübingen: Mohr Siebeck, 2004], 99–289).

4. Sarah Iles Johnston, "Narrating Myths: Story and Belief in Ancient Greece," *Arethusa* 48:2 (2015): 192.

5. For a model study, see Wendy Doniger, *Other Peoples' Myths: The Cave of Echoes* (New York: Macmillan, 1988).

6. A commonly accepted scholarly definition of myth is provided by Walter Burkert: "myth is a traditional tale with secondary, partial reference to something of collective importance" (*Structure and History in Greek Mythology and Ritual* [Berkeley: University of California Press, 1979], 23). For further scholarly definitions of myth, see William Doty, *Mythography: The Study of Myths and Rituals*, 2d ed. (Tuscaloosa: University of Alabama Press, 2000).

7. On true and false myths, see Dale B. Martin, *Biblical Truths: The Meaning of Scripture in the Twenty-First Century* (New Haven, CT: Yale University Press, 2017), 60–61, 152, 160, 198.

8. See further Lynn Schofield Clark, *From Angels to Aliens: Teenagers, the Media, and the Supernatural* (Oxford: Oxford University Press, 2003).

9. Doniger, *Other Peoples' Myths*, 25.

10. Martin Gardner, *The Flight of Peter Fromm* (Los Altos, CA: William Kaufmann, 1973), 240.

11. Gardner, *Flight*, 237. See note 16 below.

12. Nicolaus, *Progymnasmata* 12.19–22 (Felten). "Scientific" and "objective" historiography must wait until the nineteenth century to be invented. The current theory of "critical

realism" attempts to distinguish "experiences that advert to reality" (called "data") from reality itself (Jonathan Bernier, *The Quest for the Historical Jesus after the Demise of Authenticity: Toward a Critical Realist Philosophy of Historiography in Jesus Studies* [London: Bloomsbury, 2016], 25). But how the data can actually be measured against reality—since reality is never seen apart from human representation—is left undisclosed. The question is not whether reality as constructed can correspond to what is real (it can) but how we *know* it does, given that the experience of past reality is unrecoverable.

13. Today, creeds serve as "micromyths" relating the key points of Jesus's transcendent significance. For micromyths, see Wendy Doniger, *The Implied Spider: Politics and Theology in Myth* (New York: Columbia University Press, 2011), 88.

14. Ernst Käsemann, "The Problem of the Historical Jesus," in *Essays on New Testament Themes* (London: SCM, 1964), 25.

15. C. Stephen Evans, *The Historical Christ and the Jesus of Faith: The Incarnational Narrative as History* (Oxford: Oxford University Press, 1996), 12.

16. John P. Meier distinguished the "historical" from the "real" Jesus (*A Marginal Jew: Rethinking the Historical Jesus*, vol. 1, *The Roots of the Problem and the Person* [New York: Doubleday, 1991], 25–31). But the "real" Jesus is the Jesus who lived in history, so that for Meier the past event (unfortunately inaccessible) is still equated with the "real." C. Stephen Evans writes, "I believe that it is crucial for Christian faith to maintain not merely the possibility of the historicity of the incarnational narrative, but its actuality. . . . The Church is committed to the historical truth of the Gospel narratives, and cannot abandon history without abandoning the faith of the apostles and Church fathers" (*Historical Christ*, 67–68). The sentiment is common among theological conservatives: "an authentic link between Jesus of Nazareth and the exalted Christ is in fact *theologically indispensable* for Christianity. If there are no reasonable grounds for a personal continuity between 'crucified under Pontius Pilate' and 'seated at the right hand of God,' . . . then Christian faith would indeed be a travesty" (Markus Bockmuehl, *This Jesus: Martyr, Lord, Messiah* [Edinburgh: T&T Clark, 1994], 167, italics original). "For some items, the confidence of our theological claim, the veracity of the text's function as divine speech, depends on elements of historicity. . . . Saying that an event is unhistorical does in fact weaken the foundation of a belief" (Christopher M. Hays, "Theological Hermeneutics and the Historical Jesus," in *The Quest for the Real Jesus: Radboud Prestige Lectures by Professor Dr. Michael Wolter*, ed. Jan van der Watt [Leiden: Brill, 2014], 142, 144). "The absence of the historical Jesus from the story . . . empties the Christian Gospel of its content, and undermines any possibility of . . . discovering something of the truth about him and his claims. . . . Christianity is in essence an historical religion and that is why the on-going debate about history and its meaning is such a necessary *theological* demand" (Seán Freyne, "Closing the Door Too Early," *Doctrine and Life* 63:6 [2013]: 5).

17. Theologians who argue that faith does not depend on historical events still paradoxically concede that historical research can falsify the gospel portraits of Jesus. In the words of Graham Stanton, "it [the gospel] falls if the main lines of the early church's portrait of Jesus of Nazareth were to be falsified by historical research" (*Jesus of Nazareth in New Testa-*

ment Preaching [Cambridge: Cambridge University Press, 1974], 189). Hans Frei conceded, "Because it [the resurrection] is more nearly factlike than not, reliable historical evidence *against* the resurrection would be decisive" (*The Identity of Jesus Christ: The Hermeneutical Basis of Dogmatic Theology* [Philadelphia: Fortress, 1975], 152, emphasis original). In the paradox of C. F. D. Moule, the resurrection "transcends history; but, for all that, it is rooted in history" (*The Phenomenon of the New Testament* [London: SCM, 1967], 20).

18. William E. Arnal, "A Parting of the Ways? Scholarly Identities and a Peculiar Species of Ancient Mediterranean Religion," in *Identity and Interaction in the Ancient Mediterranean: Jews, Christians, and Others; Essays in Honour of Stephen G. Wilson*, ed. Zeba A. Crook and Philip A. Harland (Sheffield, UK: Sheffield Phoenix, 2007), 264, emphasis original.

19. Arnal, "Parting," 264, emphasis original.

20. Pace C. Stephen Evans, who writes, "One reason that it is vital to see the narrative as historical [evidently in the modern sense] is precisely that it purports to be the story of what God has done in human history" (*Historical Christ*, 57). Other ancient myths abound that purport to describe the actions of gods as past events.

21. John J. Collins, "The 'Historical Character' of the Old Testament in Recent Biblical Theology," *Catholic Biblical Quarterly* 41:2 (1979): 197.

22. Note, e.g., the use of "history" in Samuel Byrskog, *Story as History—History as Story: The Gospel Tradition in the Context of Ancient Oral History* (Tübingen: Mohr Siebeck, 2000), 292, and the even more problematic "bare history" in Byrskog, "The Historicity of Jesus: How Do We Know That Jesus Existed?," in *Handbook for the Study of the Historical Jesus*, ed. Tom Holmén and Stanley Porter, 4 vols. (Leiden: Brill, 2014), 3:2183.

23. Albert Schweitzer, *The Quest for the Historical Jesus*, trans. W. Montgomery (Mineola, NY: Dover, 2005), 4. See further Helen K. Bond's updated history of research and her "critique of the quest" in "The Quest for the Historical Jesus: An Appraisal," in *The Blackwell Companion to Jesus*, ed. Delbert Burkett (Malden, MA: Blackwell, 2011), 337–53; Chris Keith and Anthony Le Donne, eds., *Jesus, Criteria, and the Demise of Authenticity* (London: Bloomsbury, 2012), entire; and the incisive critiques of Burton L. Mack, *The Christian Myth: Origins, Logic, and Legacy* (New York: Continuum, 2001), 34–40.

24. Ann Rigney, *The Rhetoric of Historical Representation: Three Narrative Histories of the French Revolution* (Cambridge: Cambridge University Press, 1990), 12.

25. Elizabeth Tonkin, "History and the Myth of Realism," in *The Myths We Live By*, ed. Raphael Samuel and Paul Thompson (London: Routledge, 1990), 28–29.

26. Jens Schröter, *Jesus von Nazaret: Jude aus Galiäa—Retter der Welt*, 6th ed. (Leipzig: Evangelische Verlagsanstalt, 2006), 30 (*Ein solches Jesusbild muss unter gegenwärtigen Erkenntnisbedingungen nachvollziehbar und an den Quellen orientiert sein . . . 'Wirklich' meint dann: angesichts der je aktuellen Verstehensvoraussetzungen plausibel, wobei die jeweilige Gegenwart im Licht der Zeugnisse der Vergangenheit als gewordene verstanden wird*; emphasis original). Cf. the final sentence of Schröter's long essay: "The result [of Jesus research] is a historical construction that makes the claim to be plausible under current conditions of knowledge" (*Das Ergebnis ist eine historische Konstruktion, die den Anspruch erhebt, unter gegenwärtigen Erkenntnisbedingungen plausibel zu sein*)

("Von der Historizität der Evangelien: Ein Beitrag zur gegenwärtigen Diskussion um den historischen Jesus," in *Der historische Jesus: Tendenzen und Perspektiven der gegenwärtigen Forschung*, ed. Jens Schröter and Ralph Brucker, BZNW 114 [Berlin: de Gruyter, 2002], 205–6). See further Schröter, "The Criteria of Authenticity in Jesus Research and Historiographical Method," in ed. Keith and Le Donne, *Jesus, Criteria*, 49–70, esp. 61–64.

27. Plausibility has become a major criterion for historicity. See Gerd Theissen and Dagmar Winter, *The Quest for Plausible Jesus*, trans. Eugene Boring (Louisville, KY: Westminster/John Knox, 2002). On the cultural meaning of the historical Jesus, see Dale C. Allison, *Constructing Jesus: Memory, Imagination, and History* (London: SPCK, 2010); Philip R. Davies, *Rethinking Biblical Scholarship*, Changing Perspectives 4 (Durham, UK: Acumen, 2014), 194–207.

28. For the Christian believer, the historical Jesus that does not support the theological Jesus is of questionable use. To quote Scot McKnight, "The historical Jesus scholar's narrative representation of Jesus is of value only insofar as it supplements or supports the grand narrative of Jesus that is found in the gospels or the creeds" ("The Parable of the Goose and the Mirror: The Historical Jesus in the Theological Discipline," in Holmén and Porter, *Handbook for the Study of the Historical Jesus*, 2:950). On the "real" Jesus as the gospel Christ, see Luke Timothy Johnson, *The Real Jesus: The Misguided Quest for the Historical Jesus and the Truth of the Traditional Gospels* (San Francisco: HarperSanFrancisco, 1996).

29. Hayden White, "The Question of Narrative in Contemporary Historical Theory," *History and Theory* 23:1 (1984): 33.

30. Practically, then, what actually happened in the past has limited import for faith, since (1) there is no experiential access to the past and (2) imaginative representations of the past will always be adjusted to fit the needs of modern faith.

31. On the use of templates or metanarratives in narrativization, see Marshall Sahlins, *Historical Metaphors and Mythical Realities: Structure in the Early History of the Sandwich Islands Kingdom* (Ann Arbor: University of Michigan Press, 1981), esp. 3–8; Anthony Le Donne, *The Historiographical Jesus: Memory, Typology, and the Son of David* (Waco, TX: Baylor University Press, 2009), 52–59, 65–92.

32. Here one might talk of "aspects of historicity," as in Paul N. Anderson, Felix Just, and Tom Thatcher, eds., *John, Jesus, and History*, vol. 2, *Aspects of Historicity in the Fourth Gospel* (Atlanta: SBL, 2009).

33. See further Barry W. Henaut, "Is the 'Historical Jesus' a Christological Construct?," in *Whose Historical Jesus? Studies in Christianity and Judaism*, ed. Michael Desjardins and William E. Arnal (Waterloo, ON: Wilfrid Laurier University Press, 1996), 241–68; William E. Arnal, "Making and Re-making the Jesus-Sign: Contemporary Markings on the Body of Christ," in Desjardins and Arnal, *Whose Historical Jesus?*, 308–19; John S. Kloppenborg, "As One Unknown, without a Name? Co-opting the Apocalyptic Jesus," in *Apocalypticism, Anti-Semitism and the Historical Jesus: Subtexts in Criticism*, ed. John S. Kloppenborg with John W. Marshall (London: T&T Clark, 2005), 1–23.

34. Claude Lévi-Strauss, *Myth and Meaning* (New York: Schocken, 1979), 40, 42–43. See further White, "Question of Narrative," 11–12.

35. Michael de Certeau, *The Writing of History*, trans. Tom Conley (New York: Columbia University Press, 1988), 21, 44–49.

36. Peter L. Berger and Thomas Luckmann, *The Social Construction of Reality: A Treatise in the Sociology of Knowledge* (New York: Doubleday, 1966), 95.

37. For Bultmann as a theologian, see David W. Congdon, *The Mission of Demythologizing: Rudolf Bultmann's Dialectical Theology* (Minneapolis: Fortress, 2014).

INDEX OF SUBJECTS

historicization, 231n79; defined, 211; examples of, 13–18; gospels and, 18–19; plausibility and, 214; principle of, 15–16; as rationalization, 211; sea-stilling miracles and, 143–44

historicizing impulse, 13–15

historiography: alternative reports and, 175 (*see also* alternative reports, historiographical technique of); ancient, 227n29 (see also *historia*); ancient vs. modern, 113; antiquarian writing and, 229–30n66; authority of, 8; biography distinguished from, 53; cultural setting and, 62; divine providence and, 81; eyewitnesses and, 197–98 (*see also* eyewitnesses); as fact, 215; factual tone of, 144; fantastical elements in, 11–12, 121; fiction and, 207; forms of, 6–9; gospels as, 227n42 (*see also* evangelists; gospels); imagining of, 44; language of, 54–55; as light reading, 225–26n17; Logos made into, 75; miracles and, 135–36, 147; myth and, 113, 232n87; mythic, 7, 11–12 (*see also* mythic historiography); mythography and, 8, 217, 219 (*see also* mythography); *mythos* and, 92 (see also *mythos*); objectivity and, 191, 263n12; plausibility and, 62 (*see also* plausibility); realism of, 185; scientific, 263n12; signifying the past, 216; star stories and, 112; temporal markers for, 144; Thucydidean tradition of, 198; tropes of, 10–11, 81; vivid details in, 203–4 (*see also* vivid presentation); as work of the human imagination, 44; writing of, 195

history: distortions of, repairing, 16; divine elements added to, 13; false, 79; grammatical sense of, 241n13; myth and, 218–19; mythic elements presented as, 181, 182; mythic templates for, 217;

mythologized, 11–12; sacred, 212, 214; as story, 2

Homer, 7, 13, 14–15, 48–49, 66, 77, 81, 160, 164, 170, 180–81, 194–95, 201; on god's bodies, 65; invention of, 42; nonexistence of, 41–42; sources for, 199

Homeridai, 42

Horace, 51, 66–67, 144

Hyginus, 78

hymns, 8

hyperbole, in Lukan historiography, 263n3

Hyperboreans, 69–70

Iamblichus, 61, 68–71, 131, 145, 146, 147, 183, 193

identity, myth and, 218–20

Inanna, myth of, 39, 40–41

incarnation: in the ancient world, 65; Hermes's, 66–67; historicity of, 65; in John's gospel, 64–65; as metaphor, 65; Pythagoras's, 67–71; as union of divinity and humanity in an individual life, 65

infinity, self-consciousness and, 25

Israel: flight of, to and from Egypt, 115–16; Jews, national history of, 77; mythic history of, Jesus's life and, 116; national myth of, 82

Ister, 160

Jeroboam, 121

Jerome, 99

Jerusalem, destruction of, 164–65

Jesus, 101; adoration of, 166; adult depiction of, 127; apocalyptic, 218; ascent of, 40, 187–88, 191; authority of, 129; Beloved Disciple and, 196–97, 203–6; binary thinking about, 22, 32–33; *bios* of, 8; birth of, 57, 58, 86, 93, 103; in Caesarea Philippi with the disciples, 71–72; calling of, 132; casting daimons into pigs, 146; childhood precocity of,

INDEX OF MODERN AUTHORS

INDEX OF ANCIENT SOURCES